THE
JAPANESE MONARCHY

THE
JAPANESE MONARCHY

Ambassador Joseph Grew and the Making of the
'Symbol Emperor System,' 1931-1991

NAKAMURA MASANORI

**Translated by
Herbert P. Bix
Jonathan Baker-Bates and
Derek Bowen**

An East Gate Book

M.E. Sharpe Inc.

**Armonk, New York
London, England**

An East Gate Book

SHŌCHŌ TENNŌSEI ENO MICHI (The Japanese Monarchy 1931–1991:
Ambassador Joseph Grew and the Making of the "Symbol Emperor System")
Copyright © 1989 by Nakamura Masanori
Originally published in Japanese by Iwanami Shoten, Publishers, Tokyo, 1989

Library of Congress Cataloging-in-Publication Data

Nakamura, Masanori, d. 1935–   [Shōchō tennōsei e no michi. English]
The Japanese monarchy, 1931–1991:
ambassador Joseph Grew and the making of the "Symbol emperor system" /
by Masanori Nakamura :
translated by Herbert P. Bix, Jonathan Baker-Bates and Derek Bowen.
p.   cm.—(Asia and the Pacific)
"An East gate book."
Includes bibliographical references and index.
ISBN 1-56324-102-1. —ISBN 1-56324-109-9 (pbk.)
1. Japan—Politics and government—1912–1945.
2. Grew, Joseph C. (Joseph Clark), 1880–1965.
3. Japan—Foreign relations—United States.
4. United States—Foreign relations—Japan.
I. Title. II. Series: Asia and the Pacific (Armonk, N.Y.)
DS888.5..N34513   1992
952.03′3—dc20
92-14157
CIP

Printed in the United States of America

BB   10   9   8   7   6   5   4   3   2   1

Contents

Preface

The author of this book, Nakamura Masanori, was ten years old when he heard Emperor Hirohito announce the end of World War II. Growing up in wartime Tokyo, he was evacuated to the countryside to escape American bombing and later witnessed Japan's defeat and occupation by American armed forces. By the time Nakamura entered university in 1957, Japan's rise from the ashes of war was well underway; and when he published his first major work of history in 1972, Japan had catapulted into the front rank of economic powers and was reaping the benefits of uninterrupted economic growth.

Over the next ten years, however, as Japan continued its extraordinary economic growth, the political and economic milieu that had once been so congenial steadily eroded, while trade "frictions" and misunderstandings with the United States signaled the return of an increasingly conflictual international environment. At the same time, a more assertive Japanese nationalist sentiment began to manifest itself. Drawing strength mainly from the triumphs of the Japanese economy, the new nationalism also took delight in Japan's long history and in the imperial institution, whose postwar form was that of a "symbol" emperor system, which lent itself to diverse interpretations. The Shōwa Emperor reinforced this sense of pride in continuity with the past by his own persistent denial that defeat in war and constitutional revision had brought about any sharp break in the position of the monarchy under the new constitution.

In these circumstances, Nakamura began to reflect on the Japanese view of the emperor and the public debate about continuity and change in postwar history. Turning to the study of the Japanese–U.S. relationship during the watershed decades of the 1930s and 1940s, he sought to understand where the confusion in the constitutional specification of the emperor originated. While in residence at Harvard University in 1979 and 1980, he read the unpublished memoirs of Thomas A. Bisson, a leading Far East specialist who, during the 1930s and 1940s, had pioneered a radical critique of America's Asian policy. Shortly afterward he began studying the papers of Joseph C. Grew, the distinguished American ambassador to Japan during the decade 1932 to 1942. Skillfully using these and other contrasting English language sources, and querying scholars and witnesses in the United States and Britain, he proceeded to build his own image of Grew and to use him to scrutinize the role and position of the Japanese monarchy in the remaking of the Japanese–U.S. relationship after 1945.

The book that resulted from his research was published in 1989 under the title of *Shōchō tennōsei e no michi: Beikoku taishi Guruu to sono shūhen* (The road to the symbol emperor system: American Ambassador Grew and his contemporaries). In nine cogently argued chapters, Nakamura analyzes Grew's writings to learn how he viewed wartime Japan, its emperor and imperial institution, and what role Grew envisioned for the monarchy in a postsurrender state. Having returned to Washington in August 1942, nearly nine months after Pearl Harbor, Grew became in succession special adviser to the secretary of state, the director of the Office of Far Eastern Affairs, and, in 1944, under secretary of state to Cordell Hull and later Edward Stettinius and James F. Byrnes, in charge of planning for the defeat and surrender of Japan. In these important posts, he helped shape many basic decisions that still exert influence on the postwar Japanese state and on U.S.–Japanese relations.

The first notable feature of Nakamura's assessment of Grew concerns his relationship with those whom he called the "moderates" around the throne. Nakamura shows that Grew, who could neither read nor speak Japanese, subscribed to the views of people like Kabayama Aisuke, Shidehara Kijūrō, Makino Nobuaki, and Yoshida Shigeru. Grew's Japanese contacts, in other words, were limited to business magnates, cosmopolitan admirals of the imperial navy who occupied high positions in government, pro–Anglo-American diplomats in the Foreign Ministry, and members of the emperor's entourage. Grew believed that these men, whose names he always tried to conceal, were Western-style liberals, cut in the mold of the Saltonstalls, the Sedgwicks, and the Peabodys, whom he had known from his days in Boston. They served as his pipeline to the emperor and provided him with their own "pendulum theory of Japanese history." According to this view, Japanese development alternated between periods of extreme nationalism and antiforeignism and periods of international cooperation and conciliation. Grew's innate optimism and his belief that the pendulum would soon swing in America's favor may account for the overly complacent view of Japanese politics found in his reports to Washington. As Japan moved ever deeper into war, Grew failed to grasp the dynamics of Japanese politics and, in the end, failed to understand that the court had formed an alliance with the military at the start of the 1940s that made the Pacific War possible.

Nevertheless, Grew wanted power after Japan's defeat to return to these prewar elites—men of proven credentials as "moderates"—so that they might run the country in the same peaceful, constitutional manner that he imagined they had done during the 1920s. It was largely because of their connections with Grew that defenders of the status quo like Shidehara and Yoshida were able to become prime ministers after the war. Understandably, then, the first feature of Nakamura's approach is to show, at the outset, that postwar Japanese politics cannot be understood without a firm grasp of prewar and wartime political history.

A second feature of Nakamura's account is his balanced assessment of Grew's achievements. He notes how T. A. Bisson, Owen Lattimore, Edmund Wilson, and Andrew Roth, among others on the left, easily perceived the weaknesses in Grew's analysis of Japanese wartime politics. These wartime writers accused the professional diplomat of practicing "court diplomacy" while neglecting to analyze Japan's social and economic structure and its potential for mass popular movements. Above all, they recognized that Grew clung to the vision of the emperor as a peace-loving man who had consistently opposed the militarists and could by counted on to exert himself for peace in the future.

Nakamura shows the flaws in Grew's understanding of Japan and the imperial institution. But as a historian concerned primarily with discovering facts about Grew that illuminate his role in making the "symbol" emperor system, he emphasizes where Grew's instincts were sound. Grew was correct, for example, in thinking that the emperor, who straddled all the elites, was the key to Japan's unconditional surrender. He was also on firm ground in arguing that militarism could be disentangled from both the emperor system and Shinto, and that the monarchy, with its power of the imperial rescript, could be used positively for American purposes.

At the same time, Nakamura emphasizes the paternalistic class basis of Grew's monarchism. Grew viewed the Japanese people as docile children who would "disintegrate" without intelligent leadership. A traditional conservative who identified with those of similar upper-crust background, he had the same low regard for the Japanese people's capacity for democratic rule as did the Japanese "moderates." Given his distaste for those who embraced egalitarian political aspirations, it is no wonder that Grew disregarded the warning of his critics against preserving an institution designed for manipulation by elites.

An important aspect of Nakamura's account is its focus on Grew's pivotal role in preserving the Japanese monarchy. American planners for the postsurrender occupation had to decide whether to retain the institution of the throne and use the powers of the individual who occupied it, or abolish it and force the emperor to step down. Grew was the first high American official publicly to advocate retaining the monarchy as a stabilizing force in a time of cataclysmic military defeat, using its power to control the people, and working through the Japanese civil bureaucracy to effect occupation goals. He believed that Emperor Hirohito (whom he always regarded as "purely a symbol") could be made to play an indispensable role in minimizing American battle losses, avoiding political chaos, and facilitating occupation reforms. Yet even Grew never imagined that the same emperor who had led the Japanese nation through the war would be able to evade his legal and moral responsibilities and remain on the throne after the surrender.

As Nakamura shows, the scenario for Japan's surrender that Grew envisioned in 1945 actually came to pass. Hirohito used his constitutional power and charismatic authority to announce Japan's acceptance of the Potsdam Proclamation on August 15, 1945, whereupon millions of Japanese troops in all the war theaters of Asia and the Pacific obediently laid down their arms, just as Grew had predicted they would. A final battle on the Japanese home islands that Grew believed would have cost tens of thousands of American and Japanese lives was thereby avoided. A few weeks later General MacArthur arrived in Japan and threw his support to the emperor and the "moderate" politicians who in the 1930s had implanted in Grew's mind the notion that the emperor had been an opponent of General Tōjō and his group of military extremists.

Grew retired from government service after Japan's surrender. He continued to maintain an interest in General MacArthur's conduct of the occupation, however, and was no doubt surprised and disquieted when MacArthur stripped the emperor of the rights of sovereignty and all political powers. In 1948 Grew played a role, as honorary chairman of the American Council on Japan, in reversing many occupation reforms that he and other members of the American establishment, not to mention the Japanese ruling groups, regarded as "excesses." Basically, though, Grew agreed with the main lines along which postwar Japan was being reconstructed, with the monarchy given a new lease of life, with the emperor transformed by the new constitution into an icon of Japanese racial unity, and with Japan itself redefined in American strategy as a bulwark against communism.

American readers may find (as Japanese readers have) Nakamura's clarification of the origins of the keyword "symbol" in article 1 of the Constitution of Japan and his theses on "the third way" the two most original features of his analysis.

Having argued that Grew "was the first American to define the emperor as a "symbol," Nakamura shows in chapter 9 that the emperor's redefinition as a "symbol of the state and of the unity of the people" emerged from the complex interaction of three national sources. There was a British political discourse in which the writings of Walter Bagehot and the 1931 Statute of Westminster, written by Arthur Balfour, figured prominently. On the American side there were two lines of derivation of the "symbol" monarch notion, one going from Grew to Brigadier General Bonner Fellers to General MacArthur, the other deriving from the constitution drafters within General Headquarters. Finally, on the Japanese side, an indigenous discourse defined the emperor as a symbol of the nation in a sense quite different from either the American or British constructions.

What really counts for Nakamura is the long-term historical effect of this weaving of the vague word symbol into the constitution. The symbol concept in the English sense, the idea in the sense intended by the American constitution drafters in General Headquarters, and the idea of symbol monarch in the Japanese context all became intertwined. As a result, the emperor's position in postwar Japanese politics has become exceedingly ill-defined, and the question of whether he is the head of state has been left undecided. This has allowed the postwar emperors to be utilized by successive conservative party governments for political purposes, contrary to the letter and the spirit of the constitution.

In appendix 2, Nakamura introduces a second fruitful thesis, this time concerning the path that Japan failed to take in 1945. Having earlier noted that "the symbol monarchy was a product of Japanese and American bilateral cooperation," he points out that there was a third option in addition to preserving or abolishing the monarchy, namely, "to differentiate the emperor from the institution of the throne and have Emperor Hirohito abdicate, leaving behind the emperor system as a political institution." Had all progressive forces taken that path, and had they later worked together to secure the democratic rights and other provisions pertaining to peace and the emperor in the constitution, Japan would have developed differently than it did. Today this proposition, like the issue of the Shōwa emperor's war responsibility, is helping to advance debate about the political results of the monarchy's retention in the postwar period.

The first nine chapters comprise the book as Nakamura originally wrote it for a Japanese audience. For the American edition, he has added two new chapters evaluating the monarchy's role in postwar politics, plus two appendices supplementing topics alluded to in the text. Chapter 10 spells out the continuing centrality of the emperor and the imperial house in domestic politics and foreign policy both during and after the occupation period. Contrary to the conventional wisdom, the Shōwa Emperor did not stand outside the political process after Japan's defeat but was integral to it. Emperor Hirohito's 1947 message to General MacArthur recommending that the United States prolong its military occupation of the Ryukyu Islands was but one of several critical occasions in which he acted in violation of the new constitution that had stripped him of all political powers. Here readers can find more of the ingredients needed to understand a fundamental issue in postwar Japanese politics.

Finally, chapter 11 traces chronologically the fluctuations in the popularity of the emperor and the prestige of the imperial house between 1960 and 1990. At the start of this period, Japan was moving in to an era of full employment and accelerated economic growth, and the ruling conservatives began to lose the incentive to utilize the throne for purposes of social control. But by the end of 1979, when the government legalized the system of era names, many signs pointed to a new stage in the uses of monarchical ritual for purposes of furthering national integration and celebrating national power.

During the 1980s, conservative business and political leaders, such as Prime Minister Nakasone Yasuhiro, began to give expression to a more self-centered, racially conscious nationalism, which once again placed the emperor at the center of national identity. Toward the end of that decade, on September 19, 1988, the Shōwa Emperor fell ill, and three and a half months later died. His state funeral took place amid an unprecedented media campaign of "self-restraint," which lasted over half a year. The image of an open, pluralistic Japanese society suddenly gave way in this period to the older image of a closed, conformist society in which the principle of freedom of expression yielded to the ideal of all Japanese hearts beating as one for the sake of the emperor. A year later Emperor Akihito carried out his formal rituals of succession to the throne amid an opposite mood of national exaltation. But, as Nakamura notes, the enthronement of Japan's first real "symbol" emperor did not unambiguously advance the cause of democracy in Japan. For instead of being carried out on the basis of the postwar constitution, which reflected the reform of the Japanese monarchical tradition and the rejection of the notion of a state based on myth, Emperor Akihito's "Great Food Offering Ceremony" drew on rituals from the culture of Meiji era absolutism, which assumed that he was still a living deity. Thus, in affirming his support for the "peace constitution" at the very start of his reign, Akihito also reasserted the dangerous fiction that no change had occurred in the position of the emperor under the Meiji Constitution and the new constitution. In so doing, he himself restated the problem of continuity and rupture in the emperor system.

Nakamura concludes by emphasizing how profoundly antithetical to Japanese democracy has been the taboo on discussion of Emperor Hirohito's role in history. Today the Japanese media continue to underwrite the mystique of the throne by presenting it in the highest honorifics, while conservative cabinets show a disposition to exploit the emperor's authority for their own political advantage, and new grassroots conservative movements endeavor to make him the formal head of state. These tendencies may be traced back to decisions taken in

1945–46 by the governments of the United States and Japan to retain the emperor system in the form of a symbol monarchy. By his unyielding pursuit of the problem of continuity and change in the emperor system, Nakamura has made an important contribution to an ongoing political and historical debate.

Herbert P. Bix
April 26, 1992

THE
JAPANESE MONARCHY

Introduction

THE MAKING OF *TEN YEARS IN JAPAN*

AN AMERICAN career diplomat and one of the most illustrious ambassadors ever posted to Tokyo, Joseph Clark Grew (1880–1965) spent nearly ten years in Japan between 1932 and 1942, leaving his mark on U.S.-Japanese relations in many ways. During his term of office, he was able to experience at first hand the events that led to irrevocable conflict between the two countries. He closely observed the rise of Japan's military after the Manchurian Incident (1931), Japan's withdrawal from the League of Nations (March 1933), the outbreak of the Sino-Japanese War (July 1937), Japan's entry into the Tripartite Alliance with Germany and Italy (September 1940), the imposition of economic sanctions against Japan (July 1941), and finally, the Japanese attack on Pearl Harbor (December 1941).

Grew's main work, *Ten Years in Japan* (New York: Simon and Schuster), is a memoir of his experiences that was widely read when it was published in May 1944. In Japan, too, Ishikawa Kinichi's translation of the book, which appeared in 1958, attracted a considerable readership.

From March 1979 to December 1980 I was a visiting professor at the John King Fairbank Center for East Asian Research at Harvard University, working on the subject of American perceptions of Japan in the 1930s and 1940s, which naturally led me to take a keen interest in Grew. Fortunately, Harvard possesses in the world-famous Houghton Library an outstanding collection of rare books and documents, many of which pertain to Grew. These include diaries, letters, speeches, and talks, as well as numerous telegrams, newspaper and magazine clippings, personal memos, and other miscellaneous items—the amount of first-rate material is remarkable. The most valuable records, however, are Grew's diaries and letters, which best reveal his views and particular approach toward Japan.

Historian Waldo H. Heinrichs's excellent book, *American Ambassador: Joseph C. Grew and the Development of the United States Diplomatic Tradition* (1966), makes extensive use of these sources. However, while Heinrichs's balanced commentary on Grew is a valuable source of reference, I would like in this book to build up my own image of the man, basing my work on a personal reading of these documents.

I shall focus on Grew's role in the formation of U.S. postwar policy for Japan, and in particular, the part he played in the birth of what is known as the "symbol emperor system." I begin with 1942, when Grew returned to the United States after the start of the war, and carry the story forward, first to 1946–47, during which the occupation of Japan under General MacArthur was established, and then beyond to the present day.

In considering Grew's diaries and letters, several points should be noted. First, at 554 pages in length, the book *Ten Years in Japan* represents only one-tenth of the original diaries. Concerning the great volume of material that had been omitted from the published book, Grew made the following comment in his foreword.

> This book contains only a small fraction of the original diary which, for the past ten years, fills thirteen large typewritten volumes quite apart from many other volumes of my letters, speeches, records of conversations, and pertinent press clippings. Many of the items in the original possess no permanent historic value. Others overlap. Still others cannot properly be published now. And since this is an intimate off-the-record journal I have also had to keep confidential the identity of many living colleagues and other individuals who might be embarrassed or suffer some personal consequence if their names were made known.[1]

If one compares the published version with the original, one can see that Grew indeed omitted some parts for reasons of space, while purposefully concealing others. After the above statement, he commented, "The main story has, however, not been injured by these omissions," but one should be wary of taking this at face value. I will deal in more detail in chapter 5 with the question of what he published and what he decided to hide.

The second point we should pay close attention to concerns the motives behind, and timing of, the publication of *Ten Years in Japan.*

Six thousand pages of Grew's diaries cover his period in Japan alone; he used them to record almost all daily events, as well as his personal experiences, from the point of his inauguration as U.S. ambassador in 1932. Grew maintained that he did not write his diary with a view to publication; it was, rather, a personal record of his experiences intended for his own reference when considering ideas for diplomatic strategy.

While this was indeed one aspect of the diaries, Grew also clearly lamented the fact that so little was known about Japan in the United States, where all too often, historical accounts had been distorted through ignorance or prejudice. He was convinced that "accurate historical records must be based on the precise records and comments of the time," and thus it seems natural to assume that he was hoping to make future use of the diaries in this way.

As U.S.-Japanese relations deteriorated further during 1941, Grew sent the diaries to his friend and predecessor as U.S. ambassador to Japan, William R. Castle. In letters to Castle dated March 22 and May 8, 1941, Grew asked him to store the diaries away in a cellar, or some other hiding place, should they pose any problem. If the diaries had to be destroyed, they were to be burnt rather than shredded. Grew also commented that the manuscript was completely unabridged, except for a single entry that contained top-secret information regarding a matter in which he was still involved. All of this shows the importance Grew attached to the diaries, which he naturally used as his main source when he came to publish *Ten Years in Japan*. Given their contents, however, the timing and the form of their publication were matters for careful consideration, not only by Grew, but also by the U.S. State Department.

Motives Behind the Publication

Moves to publish Grew's diaries seem to have begun as soon as he returned to the United States: on October 25, 1942, Grew noted that four publishing companies had already made offers to Chester Kerr at the Office of War Information. Of these, Grew decided on Simon and Schuster, whose letter had impressed him by its concern with patriotic sentiments over commercial considerations: whereas the other companies were aiming at a sales price of $1.50 to $2.00, Simon and

Schuster's price was only $1.00, which suited Grew's main aim of reaching as many readers as possible. (The book was in fact eventually published at $3.75.) Various titles such as "The Strength of the Enemy" and "A Message to Our People" had been suggested to Kerr, but as none of these appealed to Grew, a neutral title was chosen.

Although both a publisher and a title had been found, there remained the major task of editing such a large volume of material. At the time, Grew was holding public office as an adviser to the State Department and was not permitted to publish unedited diary entries that were classified as state secrets. Furthermore, confidential telegrams sent from the U.S. Embassy in Tokyo had to be individually cleared for use in the book, by obtaining the permission of both the secretary of state and the secretary of war (see, for instance, Grew's letter to Secretary of War Henry Stimson on May 1, 1943). As one can see from his letter to Simon and Schuster of July 10, 1943, Grew went through the manuscript in minute detail, making many deletions and revisions before its eventual publication.

Despite all Grew's meticulous efforts, however, on August 12, 1943, Dr. E. Wilder Spaulding, chief of the State Department's Division of Research and Publication, advised him against using unaltered versions of official documents such as telegrams and letters, until the publication of the State Department's own white paper, "Peace and War, United States Foreign Policy 1931–1941" (published in 1943). Secretary of State Cordell Hull likewise indicated that there would be no objections to the direct quotation of government documents once the white paper had been published. Given such restrictions, Grew was unable to meet Simon and Schuster's wish to publish *Ten Years in Japan* in time for Christmas 1943. In a letter to the publisher on July 10 of that year, he even proposed delaying the date of publication until the following summer.

By early 1944, the tide of the war was turning inexorably against the Japanese. On February 1, U.S. forces landed on Kwajalein and Ruott in the Marshall Islands, and six days later, the 6,800 troops of the Japanese garrison there were effectively wiped out. On the 17th, an aerial attack on the Truk Islands inflicted huge damage on the Japanese fleet and air force. This, combined with the fact that in January the Soviet Army had embarked on a massive counteroffensive on the "Leningrad front," forcing the German army into retreat, meant that in both Europe and the Pacific, the Axis powers were being driven into a corner.

In the midst of this, the United States began in earnest to draw up its postwar plans for Germany and Japan. On January 15, 1944, it established the Office of Far Eastern Affairs within the State Department, under the directorship of Stanley Hornbeck of the "China crowd."* But after three and a half months, Hornbeck was replaced by Grew, thus strengthening the voice of the "Japan crowd," who were then able to exert a strong influence over State Department policy decisions on Japan. Grew was by now chiefly concerned with formulating surrender conditions that the Japanese government could be persuaded to accept.

From the perspective of U.S.-Japanese relations, the time was now ripe for the publication of Grew's book. As he wrote in the preface to the Japanese translation: "The motives for the U.S. publication of this book in 1944 were twofold. The first was to describe clearly the developments and trends within every area of Japanese society leading to the outbreak of war in 1941. The second was to attempt to create a more profound and educated image of Japan and the Japanese in the minds of the American public."[2]

Thus, Grew's aim was to correct the American people's views of Japan and the Japanese. He believed that it would never be possible to establish the conditions for a constructive peace between the United States and Japan without breaking down the prejudices of ordinary Americans, who believed in such wartime slogans as "The only good Jap is a dead Jap," and the mythology of "that barbaric, cunning, and cruel race." In *Ten Years in Japan*, Grew therefore repeatedly emphasized that there existed peace-loving Japanese, led by the emperor and the moderates, who had no connection with the fanatical military. He was, however, well aware that such opinions would be unpopular, and even dangerous, in the United States at that time. Indeed, while Secretary of State Hull of the China crowd (who were opposed to the emperor) indicated that his resistance to the early publication of *Ten Years in Japan* was based on concerns regarding the use of official documents, the content of the book must surely have influenced his decision.

---

*"China crowd" and "Japan crowd" (or "lobby") are terms used to describe U.S. pressure groups and bureaucratic policy currents that were supportive of either China or Japan.—Trans.

When it was finally published, *Ten Years in Japan* caused a great stir. It reached number two on the *New York Times* best-seller list for June and July, and reviews were printed in nearly all the influential regional newspapers. This was because it went beyond the scope of a personal diary, presenting themes that concerned the basis of future policy toward Japan, and in particular, the issue of the emperor.

The publication of *Ten Years in Japan* was therefore set against the complex state of affairs outlined above. Grew was promoted from director of the Office of Far Eastern Affairs to undersecretary of state in December 1944, whereupon his career became ever more intimately connected to the fate of postwar Japan. However, some of Grew's activities after his return home in August 1942 were certainly a little unexpected. What message did he have for the American people, and what was his vision for a future Japan?

1

REPORT FROM TOKYO
A Condemnation of Japanese Militarism

A Fanatical Enemy

GREW and his staff returned to the United States on August 25, 1942, having been confined to the embassy in Tokyo for over six months after the outbreak of war. Anti-Japanese feeling at home had reached a peak with the attack on Pearl Harbor, and given Grew's ten years' experience of Japan and his detailed understanding of the Japanese situation, there was great anticipation as to what he had to say. Grew was deluged with requests for speaking engagements, but in view of his public position as special adviser to the secretary of state, his speeches had to conform to official views of the war. At a meeting with Secretary Hull on September 25, 1942, Grew was instructed to confirm the content and schedule of his speeches with the head of the Office of War Information (OWI), Elmer Davis. From his return home up to the end of 1943, Grew traveled the length and breadth of the United States and gave as many as 250 lectures, following an itinerary planned in detail by the OWI.

A selection of these speeches was published as a book in 1942, under the title *Report from Tokyo—A Message to the American People*. Grew noted in a letter to his friend Fredrick Kam, on February 3, 1943, that *Report from Tokyo* had sold as many as 130,000 copies in the first few weeks of its publication.

The major distinction between this book and *Ten Years in Japan*, published later in 1944, was its open condemnation of Japan, in particular, the cruelty and violence of the Japanese military. Grew called the American people to action, quoting in his preface the following words from the diary of PFC Martin Treptow, written in 1918 just before his death on the western front in France. "I will work; I will save; I will sacrifice; I will endure; I will fight cheerfully and do my utmost; *as if the whole struggle depended on me alone.*"[1]

Grew therefore hoped that "those flaming words of his should constitute a guiding torch that every red-blooded American should take up and carry with proud determination to victory."

In his opening paragraph, Grew set out the aims behind the publication of *Report from Tokyo*.

> The purpose of this book is to overcome a fallacy in the thinking of a large proportion of my fellow countrymen about our war with Japan. That thinking, so far as I have been able to gauge it since my return from Tokyo on August 25, 1942, is clearly influenced by preconceived but unfounded assumptions as to Japan's comparative weakness and vulnerability in war. Such thinking is not only erroneous; it constitutes a grave danger to our fighting spirit, our war effort and our united will to win. If persisted in, it will be a serious obstacle to our ultimate victory.[2]

Certainly, the optimistic view prevailed among Americans that once the Nazis were out of the way, the "Japs" would be no problem. Consequently, up to the summer of 1943, Grew used his lecture tour to explain the dangers of such complacent thinking, taking as his theme the first rule of warfare: "know your enemy."

Grew's first opportunity to address the American public came just five days after his return home with a radio broadcast for CBS on August 30, 1942. In this speech, entitled "Return from Japan," Grew focused on the brutality of the Japanese authorities and the particularly aggressive nature of the Japanese military.

Grew and his staff had arrived back in New York on the trader *Gripsholm* almost nine months after Pearl Harbor, accompanied by American missionaries, teachers, journalists, and businessmen. Since the start of the Pacific War, they had all been accused of spying and had suffered barbaric torture at the hands of the Japanese authorities. During the journey home, three elderly Americans described their experience of water torture: their hands had been bound, they had been forced to lie face up, and water had been poured down their throats and noses. One elderly missionary had also suffered a broken rib after being kicked in the chest by a policeman. When he had said he was afraid that one of his ribs was broken, "One of the Japanese police asked where the broken rib was and began to feel his body. As the Japanese came to the broken bone he said, 'Is that the place?' and when the man answered, 'Yes,' the policeman hauled off with his fist and hit that broken rib as hard as he could."[3] (From the same radio broadcast.)

Relating such vivid episodes was an effective way to persuade the American people of the barbarity of the Japanese regime. Grew further emphasized the importance of this belligerent trait, which ran throughout the Japanese armed forces: "This spirit, recognized by competent military men as the most vital intangible factor in achieving victory, has been nourished and perpetuated since the foundation of the modern Japanese Army."[4] This would make the war against Japan the toughest fight of all: "When they struck, they made no provision for failure; they left no road open for retreat. They struck with all the force and power at their command. And they will continue to fight in the same manner until they are utterly crushed."[5]

In his efforts to temper the general optimism that prevailed throughout the United States, Grew often described the Japanese military with phrases such as "the all-out, do-or-die fanatical spirit of the Japanese military machine" and "The Japanese are fanatic, last-ditch, no-surrender fighters."

Having just returned from a decade in Japan, Grew drew a wide audience with his radio broadcasts for CBS, following which he went on an intense speaking tour of America, giving lectures under such titles as "Why War Came," "The Extent of the Japanese Challenge," and "How We Must Fight to Defeat Japan."

"The Well of Liberty" Runs Dry

"To await the hoped-for discrediting in Japan of the Japanese Army and the Japanese military system is to await the millennium. The Japanese Army is no protuberance like the tail of a dog that might be cut off to prevent the tail from wagging the dog: it is inextricably bound up with the fabric of the entire nation."[6] This quotation comes from an entry in Grew's diary of December 1, 1939, which he often used in his aforementioned speeches. Until August 1943, when he began to turn toward the theme of peace, Grew constantly asserted that the military machine had penetrated into the heart of every sphere of Japanese society.

> The Japanese people have been accustomed to regimentation since the very birth of their nation. There are Japanese living today who were

born when their country was still a feudal land, when every feudal lord held the power of life and death over his so-called common people. We in the West shook off feudalism many centuries ago. In Japan it existed so recently that it has left a vast heritage of almost prostrate subservience to birth and authority. The men who rule Japan today have taken full advantage of the docility of the Japanese people to create a formidable military and economic machine.[7]

Japanese workers, subordinated by low wages and police oppression, were consistently denied freedom of expression. Alluding to Benjamin Franklin's observation that no one realizes there is a shortage of water until the well runs dry, Grew commented that he had "spent the last ten years in a country where the well of liberty has always been dry."[8] It was generally the Japanese peasantry who had to pay the price, both in the form of taxes and through the loss of their children in the war—their life of poverty formed the basis of Japan's competition in the world market. Moreover, the precarious situation of the Japanese middle classes could only be secured through state control. "When I arrived in Japan in 1932, Japanese business was still a model of comparative efficiency, drive, and inventiveness. By 1941, it had become an adjunct to the military regime."[9]

The whole philosophy of Japanese education also centered on an absolute obedience to the military. "If the visitor stayed long enough, he would soon come to realize that for Japan the years of peace were but years of preparation, and that from early childhood Japanese children were being reared for war, and reared with the thought that their greatest good fortune would be to die on the field of battle."[10] Further, in reference to emperor worship, Grew commented that "The people of Japan are wholly united in their support of the armed forces and of this war simply because it is declared to be the will of the Emperor. To oppose the will of the Throne, the will of the Son of Heaven, is unthinkable in Japan. Disloyalty to the Emperor, too, would shame their own ancestors; and ancestor worship, the patriotic faith called Shintoism, is the fundamental faith of the entire country."[11]

As has been seen, for Grew, Japanese militarism was no mere appendage of Japanese society, but rather a complete authoritarian structure that had permeated throughout Japanese life. The total dissolution of the military would therefore demand the dismantling and reorientation of the country's entire political and social systems.

Yet despite such views, Grew also told his audiences of how he had made many friends during his ten years in Japan, among them people of excellent character for whom he had nothing but the greatest respect. "They are not the people who brought on this war. As patriots they will fight for their Emperor and country, to the last ditch if necessary, but they did not want this war and it was not they who began it."[12]

Moreover, Grew opposed the idea suggested to him in a letter from one of his audience, James A. Scherer, in October 1942, that the Imperial Palace should have been bombed in the U.S. Air Force raid on Tokyo on April 18 of that year. Grew replied:

> ... I think that such action, under the circumstances then obtaining, would have ... more solidly united the entire Japanese people against us. ... There are a great many Japanese who, regardless of the war, entertain no intensive hatred against the United States and the American people. ... I do not, therefore, follow your argument that the bombing of the Emperor's palace, whether or not the Emperor himself had been injured or killed, would have put Japan out of the war once and for all.

Nevertheless, in 1942 Grew was naturally unable to express such opinions openly, and he rarely referred to his Japanese friends who opposed the war—the liberals and moderates. G. William Gahagan at the OWI warned him that audiences would feel let down by any expression of goodwill toward Japanese moderates. Grew agreed that, in the present climate, it would clearly not be wise to say anything that dampened "the angry and fighting mood" of his listeners. Accordingly, until the following summer of 1943, Grew concentrated his speech making on the condemnation of Japanese militarism, and it was against this background that *Report from Tokyo* was published.

Grew's Ghost-Writer

On comparing *Report from Tokyo* in detail with *Ten Years in Japan*, it is evident that the former is laced with vehement criticism of Japanese militarism and the Japanese people as a whole, while the latter adopts a sudden change of tone, expressing a high opinion of the emperor and the moderates. While the speeches compiled in *Report from Tokyo* were made during the very height of anti-Japanese feeling in the United States, directly after Pearl Harbor, I have felt for some time that this alone could not sufficiently explain the discrepancy between the tone of the two books.

On this point, I have recently obtained important information that has helped me to solve this puzzle, namely the records of Paul Linebarger. While most of Linebarger's documents are kept in Stanford University's Hoover Institution on War, Revolution and Peace, the material pertaining to his relationship with Grew is to be found in the library of Hitotsubashi University in Japan. I was surprised to find that a considerable number of the speeches Grew made during his lecture tour of the United States were in fact written for him by Linebarger. Of *Report from Tokyo*, one-third was composed by Linebarger and a quarter by another writer, Bradford Smith. Let us look briefly at Linebarger's career.

Paul Linebarger (1913–1966), a China expert and graduate of George Washington University, served in the Office of War Information during the Pacific War. His father, Paul M. W. Linebarger, was a friend of Sun Yat-sen and had taken part in China's 1911 Revolution. The young Paul learned Chinese from Sun's wife and gained a great knowledge of China through his many trips there with his father.

Even from this short account one can see that, in direct contrast to Grew, Linebarger would have held a pro-China, anti-Japan stance. It is said that the OWI chose him as a ghost-writer for the drafts of Grew's speeches on account of the outstanding ability he had demonstrated in propaganda warfare, but I also feel that he was used to ensure that the speeches of the pro-Japanese Grew remained in line with American policy.

Taking a fresh look at *Report from Tokyo* from this angle and reading through Grew's correspondence with Linebarger, it becomes clear that the whole of Grew's speech making in 1942–43 formed part of the State Department's and OWI's propaganda war against Japan. Although Linebarger and the other speech writers naturally referred to material provided by Grew, they went beyond this to incorporate the OWI's own views in the final speeches. This explains why the tone of *Report from Tokyo* is overwhelmingly hostile toward Japan, containing some harsh language Grew himself would have been unlikely to use.

If one were to attempt to identify those parts of *Report from Tokyo* written by Grew and those written by Linebarger, they could perhaps be divided as follows:

Written by Grew
"Introductory Note"
"Return from Japan"
"The Extent of the Japanese Challenge"
"How We Must Fight to Defeat Japan"

Written by Linebarger
"Why War Came"
"Why We Can No Longer Do Business with Japan"
"Is This a Racial War?"
"Our Allies in the Pacific"
"Building the Future—Postscript"

I am tempted to make a detailed comparison of the two writers in order to highlight their differences, but that will have to wait for another occasion. Here, we must examine the subtle changes to Grew's speeches that occurred in the years following the publication of *Report from Tokyo*, while Japan's defeat increasingly became simply a matter of time.

2

THE THEME OF PEACE
The Key Role of the Emperor System

A Carthaginian Peace?

IN FEBRUARY 1943 the German Army surrendered at Stalingrad. In the same month the Japanese were forced to retreat from Guadalcanal, and in May they fought a desperate battle on Attu Island, refusing to surrender. U.S. forces were gradually closing in on the Japanese in the Gilbert and Marshall Islands, and although the war was still far from over, in Grew's view the defeat of Germany and Japan was "approaching with a mathematical certainty."

Waldo Heinrichs has observed that from May 1943 onward, Grew changed from the theme of war to peace, pointing to a speech of May 20 as his evidence. But this is not strictly correct. If one looks at Heinrichs's description and the records of Grew's lectures in the *Department of State Bulletin*, it seems more accurate to regard Grew's speech of August 28 as his first public discussion of the theme of peace.

This address, entitled "For This We Fight," was given under the auspices of the Commission to Study the Organization of Peace, with the backing of NBC broadcasting. Grew indicated that it was the first time he had spoken in public about an eventual peace settlement with Japan. Let us look at the points Grew made in this speech.

As his main themes, Grew discussed the current state of the war against Japan and the issue of dealing with Japan after the final victory, in other words, the terms of surrender.

For Grew, the Battle of Midway had marked a decisive turning point in the war, followed by successive U.S. triumphs on Attu, Guadalcanal, the Gulf of Kula, Munda, and Salamoa. An American victory was now no longer a question of "if" but of "when." Talking of the future peace settlement with Japan, Grew maintained that "common sense dictates that the military terms of settlement shall prevent Japan from again becoming a menace to international peace."[1] This would require not only the disarmament of Japan, war reparations, and the punishment of war criminals and all those responsible for the maltreatment of prisoners, but also the permanent removal of the cult of militarism through the reeducation of the Japanese people themselves.

Grew was fearful, however, that the United States would seek revenge by imposing severely punitive, "Carthaginian" surrender conditions on Japan, which might even risk the survival of the entire population. Such an outcome had to be avoided, as Grew noted in a letter to his friend Norman Briggs: "The future peace settlement must be based upon practical common sense and must be approached with no attitude of vindictiveness" (January 14, 1943).

In "For This We Fight," he therefore attempted to dispel the prejudices and desire for revenge held by most Americans by pointing out the difference between the ruthless militarists and the ordinary Japanese: "Throughout Japanese history the pendulum has swung to and fro between aggressive and peace-seeking policies and action. . . . The Japanese people at home in their own land are not inherently the wolves in human form which some of our own people who do not know them believe. Once caught in the military machine they are taught brutality, cruelty, trickery, and ruthlessness."[2]

Since the start of the war with China in 1937, living conditions in Japan had become progressively worse. A growing number of families were receiving the little white box in which the ashes of their loved ones, killed on the mainland, were returned to them. Having come to realize just what "glorious sacrifice" really meant, the Japanese people were growing weary of the war, and Grew therefore believed that "when Japan's war with the United Nations is over, even in their defeat, the great majority of the Japanese people will give a sigh of profound relief."[3] In this way, Grew argued that once Japan had learned from experience that war crimes and acts of cruelty served no purpose, the honest Japanese he knew to exist would then use the opportunity to take control.

In conclusion, Grew turned to the issue of the peace settlement: "If an ancient tree is torn up by the roots and remodelled it will not live, but if the healthy trunk and roots remain the branches and foliage can, with care, achieve regeneration. Whatever is found to be healthy in the Japanese body politic should be preserved; the rotten branches must be ruthlessly cut away."[4]

What were the "healthy" parts of the Japanese government that Grew was referring to in this metaphor? This careful wording concealed the true aim of Grew's far sighted plans.

Looking to the Future—A Note of Caution

The emperor and emperor system were a central concern to Grew in his consideration of the possible terms of peace after Japan's imminent defeat, although at the time the emperor issue could not be discussed openly.

On this point, there is a very interesting Gallup poll conducted in June 1942. When asked, "Which do you see as our number one enemy, Japan or Germany?" 50 percent of Americans said it was Germany; 25 percent, Japan. ("Both" polled 23 percent, and "no reply," 2 percent.) In a similar poll in February 1943 after the German defeat at Stalingrad, however, the positions were reversed: Japan had 53 percent; Germany, 34 percent; and "no opinion," 13 percent.

The American people maintained an image of the emperor as the sovereign leader of the "land of the rising sun," now seen as the principal enemy of the United States. Hirohito was thus synonymous with the brutal Japanese military, and it was therefore taboo to make any favorable comments about him in public that might conflict with this popular view. Even Grew refrained from referring directly to the emperor until his speech in Chicago on December 29, 1943. Yet his correspondence shows that from March of that year he was placing his hopes on the moderates in Japan, which included Hirohito.

In a letter to Major Robert Spencer of the Air Intelligence School dated March 27, 1943, Grew wrote, "there are many healthy elements in Japan who will remain after we have cut out the cancer of militarism from that misguided country." Nevertheless, he warned that many uncertain factors remained, making it premature to predict the future situation. He made a similar point when writing to Paul Rowland, a MacMurray College lecturer, on July 9, 1943, but having said that, he went on to argue that "the Imperial Throne is the only substantial cornerstone on which something healthy can be built in the future.

While the present Emperor must of course be held responsible for the war I have very good reason to believe that he himself was definitely opposed to it and did everything in his power to avoid it."

Thus, Grew maintained the image, as portrayed in *Ten Years in Japan*, of the emperor as a pacifist. Indeed, he believed the wisest policy would be to preserve the emperor system in order to avoid the chaos and needless war of attrition that defeating the Japanese might entail. As noted, Grew did not share the expectation of his fellow Americans that this defeat would be easily achieved. He explained his reservations in a letter to John Cudahy, written on August 6, 1943:

> Mr. Leathem Smith [is convinced that] once the European Axis powers are deposed it will be only a question of a short time until the Japanese fall into our bag. . . . I wish I could agree with him, but I can't. . . .
>
> First of all, it might be pertinent to ask if Mr. Smith has lived for ten years in Japan as I have and whether he understands Japanese psychology, mentality, hardihood and fanaticism by long personal experience and observation as I do. Industrial capacity is by no means the only or indeed the prime factor in the problem.
>
> Let me say at once that I entirely agree with Mr. Smith that Japan is doomed. . . . I agree that Japan's shipping, including warships and supply ships, is her Achilles Heel and that . . . we shall eventually reduce her marine communications to practically zero. But I can conceive a situation where even after we have done this and have occupied Tokyo and forced the Japanese Government to flee and to set up elsewhere, the Japanese forces in the outlying areas—China, the Philippines, Hongkong, Indochina, Thailand, The Malay States, Singapore, Burma, Borneo, Java, Sumatra and the many islands extending to the south— . . . will continue to fight defensively. . . . The Japanese are fanatic, last-ditch, no-surrender fighters, and even with perhaps second-rate, inadequate equipment they can hold off better armed troops for considerable periods. . . . [They will] fight from their fox-holes . . . until annihilated to the last man.
>
> . . . I can't see how we can bring about their complete defeat in a short time after the European Axis powers fall. I assume that our war with Japan will not be over until we have cleaned the Japanese out from all the far-flung areas which they now occupy. . . .
>
> . . . Some of my foreign colleagues in Tokyo proved to their satisfaction several years ago that Japan must crack economically within six months. I disagreed. Unfortunately they left out of consideration several factors such as the fanatical psychology of the Japanese, their capacity to integrate the entire country in total war and their ability to subsist and to fight on a shoe-string.

Thus, Grew continued to criticize the groundless optimism of those who believed that, once Hitler was beaten, the "Japs" would be "easy meat." As the defeat of Japan drew closer, Grew became increasingly worried that the Japanese military might embark upon a fight to the death, as they had on Attu. It is worth noting that while Grew staunchly advocated the preservation of the emperor system, he continued to fear the possibility of mass self-sacrifice in the name of Hirohito.

Once victory was finally achieved, however, what was to be the future of postwar Japan? Grew expressed one of his central beliefs in a letter he sent to Stanley Hornbeck on September 30, 1943: "I have constantly held that when, through defeat in war and postwar measures, the Japanese military caste and cult have been rendered powerless, elements will be found in Japan who will welcome and who will cooperate in the building of a new and non-military national structure."

Hornbeck, the leading member of the China crowd within the State Department, was generally regarded as holding the most hard-line position on the Japanese emperor system. The problem of swaying Hornbeck's opinion was therefore one of Grew's major considerations in his formulation of surrender terms for Japan.

It has often been observed that Grew had great expectations of the moderates and the emperor, and while this is true, it is interesting to note the following argument he made in his letter to Hornbeck.

> [Once the Japanese military machine has been dismantled, healthy and cooperative elements will emerge.] I think it is nevertheless open to question whether, in planning postwar reconstruction in Japan we can confidently rely on any particular individuals or groups among the old so-called moderates or liberals since we cannot know in advance what effect the war itself may have had on their individual thinking and eventual attitude and position. It is of course possible that the impact of the war may have converted some or many of our old friends among the moderates to rabid extremists whose conversion may be difficult or impossible. . . . It seems to me to be risky to assume too much or to conclude too much at this stage as to what we shall find in Japan and what sort of material we shall be able to work with when the war is over.
>
> As to the institution of the Throne—as distinct from the person of the present Emperor—I am clear in my own mind that it should be preserved, for I believe that as a symbol it can be made to serve as a

cornerstone for healthy and peaceful internal growth as it did for the erstwhile cult of militarism, although the whole cult of militarism will first have to undergo a radical operation. I believe that for a long time to come, the alternative would be chaos. I do not believe that it will be wise to try to graft on the Japanese people a system or a national structure—such, for instance, as an outright democracy—for which they will be psychologically and politically wholly unprepared. I believe that future healthy growth will have to come from within, wisely guided in its initial stages by the United Nations.

British Prime Minister Churchill and U.S. President Roosevelt had agreed at the Casablanca conference in January 1943 that the war could only be brought to an end by the unconditional surrender of the Axis powers. As yet, however, there was no definite plan, and discussions on the exact meaning of "unconditional surrender" were still in progress within the U.S. State Department. These centered on the Inter-Divisional Area Committee on the Far East, set up in October 1942, which also dealt with the issue of the emperor system and the form of the future Allied occupation of Japan.

From early on, Grew held that the emperor system would be the key to an unconditional surrender. He frequently asserted that the psychology and character of the Japanese must not be measured by Western standards, thus challenging the basic assumption of most Americans that the emperor system and democracy were naturally incompatible. As Heinrichs observes, from summer 1943, Grew began to stress the idea of promoting development based on Japanese traditions, rather than imposing the reforms already established in the West. It was in his Chicago speech that he first ventured to broach this theme.

3

THE CHICAGO SPEECH
Grew Comes Under Fire

Changing Japan's Image

ON DECEMBER 29, 1943, Grew was a guest at the ninetieth anniversary dinner of the Illinois Education Association in Chicago, where he gave a speech entitled "War and Post-War Problems in the Far East." In this address, commonly called the "Chicago speech," Grew appealed to Americans to meet the coming peace with tolerance and the highest qualities of statesmanship. War criminals had of course to be severely punished, but peace talks should not be allowed to fall victim to feelings of revenge, arrogance, or prejudice.

The cornerstones of a secure and lasting order of world peace had been laid with the Atlantic Charter (1941), the Moscow "declaration" (1943), and the Cairo and Tehran conferences (1943). The policy for dealing with Japanese territories was decided by the "Big Three" (Churchill, Roosevelt, and Chiang Kai-shek) at the Cairo conference in late November 1943. They agreed to strip Japan of all areas it had occupied since 1914, return Manchuria and Taiwan to China, and ensure the independence of Korea. The fight against Japan would continue until its unconditional surrender.

Although Grew saw this policy as the basic framework for peace, it would be no more than an external precondition—it was fundamental that the reform of Japanese society and the reeducation of the people were ultimately accomplished by forces arising from within Japan itself. Thus, in the Chicago speech as previously, Grew made repeated references to the healthy elements existing in Japanese society.

> Although this subject is controversial, most of our people feel that we are chiefly fighting Nazis and the militaristic caste and cult and

doctrine in Germany and not the Germans as a whole. But today comparatively few of our people are able or willing to admit that there can be anything good in Japan or any good elements in the Japanese race. The prejudice is all-embracing.[1]

During Grew's lecture tour of the southern states, one gentleman had told him: "That was a very interesting talk you gave tonight. But you haven't changed my opinion in the slightest. The only good Jap is a dead Jap . . . they are all a barbarous, tricky, brutal mass that we can have no truck with ever again."[2] Grew often encountered such attitudes and was frequently told that Japan should be left to "stew in her own juice." But such opinions bore no trace of the "statesmanship" that Grew urged.

To his Chicago audience, Grew recounted various episodes demonstrating his experience of the kind and friendly nature of the Japanese people. There was, for instance, the *"Panay* incident," in which Japanese aircraft bombed and sank the U.S. gunboat *Panay* on the Yangtze River near Nanking on December 12, 1937. This dramatic event seemed likely to cause a breakdown of U.S.–Japanese relations, and Grew reacted swiftly, struggling to prevent the situation from deteriorating further. The Japanese government made a full apology and the incident was closed within about three weeks. During this time, Japanese people from all walks of life came to the U.S. Embassy to express their feelings of shame and regret for what the Japanese military had done. Letters of apology poured in. The most moving episode occurred when one young woman came to the embassy and asked to be lent a pair of scissors. On receiving them, she cut off her beautiful long hair and presented it with a carnation she had taken from her head. " 'Please give this to the Ambassador,' she said. 'It is my apology for the sinking of the *Panay*.' "[3]

One other tale came from the time of the embassy staff's six months' confinement following Pearl Harbor. A raucous demonstration, orchestrated by the police, was being held to celebrate the fall of Singapore on February 15, 1942, and a crowd had gathered in front of the American Embassy shouting, "Down with the United States!" Grew was concerned that they might climb the fence and invade the embassy itself. As the demonstration reached fever pitch, one of the embassy staff watching the rally from the balcony pulled a handkerchief from his pocket and waved it at the crowd. Naturally, this strange gesture surprised the Japanese, but after a short while the demonstrators stopped their shouting and, amazingly, began to take out their own handkerchiefs. Laughing, they cheerily waved them back in a gesture of friendship, enraging the police, who tried in vain to stop them. What had been a "whole pack of snarling wolves" went on their way, still laughing.[4]

Grew recounted the above tale as evidence to support his view of the Japanese as a docile people who, like sheep, could easily be guided and reorganized under new circumstances and new direction. It was also intended to show that, despite the propaganda war, among ordinary Japanese there was no fundamental hatred of, or desire for war against, the United States. From this, Grew moved on to his final and most important point.

> There are those in our country who believe that Shintoism is the root of all evil in Japan. I do not agree. Just so long as militarism is rampant in that land, Shintoism will be used by the military leaders, by appealing to the emotionalism and the superstition of the people, to stress the virtues of militarism and of war through emphasis on the worship of the spirits of former military heroes. When militarism goes, that emphasis will likewise disappear. Shintoism involves emperor-homage too, and when once Japan is under the aegis of a peace-seeking ruler not controlled by the military, that phase of Shintoism can become an asset, not a liability, in a reconstructed nation.[5]

Grew finished off his speech with a quote from Sir George Sansom. "'I should not be surprised if, in favourable conditions, [the Japanese] developed a more modern and democratic type of constitutional monarchy.' "

Criticism from the American Media

Grew's speech was received with great surprise by an America that imagined Shinto to be the religious root of emperor worship and Japanese militarism. Early in the next year, 1944, Grew was subjected to ruthless condemnation throughout the press. An editorial in the *New York Times* on January 2, for example, made the following criticism.

> The first [consideration] is that Japan is a theocracy in which all sovereign powers are vested, not in the people but in the Emperor as the

godhead of the nation. In ratifying the Kellogg pact outlawing war the Japanese government specifically declared that Japan ratified it not "in the name of the people," as the text provided, but in the name of the Emperor, since the people had no sovereign rights. Whether the Japanese want to live under a constitutional monarchy or some other form of government is their concern. But it would be contrary to our professions if we undertook to sponsor an autocratic theocracy incapable of developing a real democracy based on self-government by the people, and therefore always subject to domination by cliques which can dominate the Emperor.

The second consideration is that modern Shinto, like nazism, has become a doctrine of expansion under the principle of Hakko Ichiu, which calls for the "unification" of the entire world under the rule of the Japanese Emperor. This doctrine is propagated in Japan as both religious and political dogma . . . and has persuaded all Japanese that they are fighting "holy wars" against all who will not submit to it. It confronts us with even more difficult but no less dangerous problems than nazism and fascism which we are pledged to eradicate. . . . Anything resembling defence of Shinto and the Japanese emperor seems out of place while our forces in the Pacific are fighting against everything they symbolize.

Other newspapers also wrote sensational accounts of how Grew was trying to defend and utilize the emperor. The *Star Times*, for instance, wrote in its editorial, "Japan's Mikado, Source of Cruelty, Must Go," that "In his speech in Chicago, Ambassador Grew subsequently commented . . . that 'emperor-worship is not the root of all evil' and that Mikadoism may more prove more of an asset than a liability." On December 31, 1943, the *Philadelphia Record* reported Grew's arguments with heavy irony: "Grew says that the emperor did not seek a war with America, and it is clear that he was not able to make his advisers follow his wishes before Pearl Harbor. When the war is over, will Grew then be saying that the emperor was suddenly endowed with such power, as if by magic?" It went on to argue that the State Department should keep Grew silent to preserve the morale of the American forces fighting in the Pacific.

Faced with such vociferous criticism, Grew felt obliged to vindicate his opinions in a *New York Times* interview on February 2, 1944.

. . . [N]ever, either publicly or privately, have I expressed an opinion that the Emperor Hirohito should be or should not be retained on the throne of Japan after the war. Frankly, I do not think that any of us are yet in a position to determine what shall be or may be the precise political structure in Japan after our certain ultimate victory in the war. I fear that only harm and no good can come from reading into my public utterances views which I have never held and therefore have never expressed.

The newspaper reports of the Chicago speech were clearly a crude oversimplification and distortion of Grew's words, but it must nevertheless be said that the reviewers were able to detect some hidden intention behind Grew's words.

What, then, were Grew's real aims? There is a very revealing letter relating to this, which I would like to quote almost in its entirety. Addressed to John S. Piper of the *San Francisco News*, it was dated November 30, 1943, about one month before the Chicago speech.

> I know as a fact, from intimate and reliable information from my stay in Japan, that the Emperor of Japan sincerely desired peace and did what he could to preserve peace but he was simply over-ruled by the military extremists and he was obliged to sign the war rescript on the dotted line. That is, of course, one of the strange paradoxes of Japan, namely, that in spite of the fact that the Emperor is regarded as semi-divine. . . . he is in actuality little more than a symbol and he was powerless to withstand the militarists.
>
> With regard to our psychological warfare policy, my own opinion is that it is better to avoid mention of the Emperor altogether. The prejudice in our country against him is strong and perfectly logical because whatever the facts, the Emperor, if only as a symbol, must take full responsibility for the war. On the other hand, to attack the Emperor openly would simply result in welding all elements of the Japanese people against us in solid hatred, and I know that a good many elements in Japan, in spite of the propaganda of their military leaders, have no fundamental hatred against us whatever. Those are the elements that I hope we can work with in future and build something healthy after the Japanese military machine has been completely defeated and discredited in the eyes of the Japanese people, as I am convinced it will be. That is one reason why I am thankful that General Doolittle did not bomb the Emperor's palace as he had been urged to do.
>
> Whatever happens to the Emperor in future it is my firm belief that the institution of the Throne in Japan should remain. To try to graft a democracy on Japan would result in chaos whereas the Throne, which is the cornerstone and sheetanchor of Japanese life, can undoubtedly be

used as a foundation on which to build a healthy structure in future once we have purged the country of the poison of militarism. I myself have little doubt that we can and shall do this.

Grew enclosed an extra copy of this letter for Piper, "in case you wish to send it in confidence to the high official of our Government mentioned in your letter." He was thus beginning to express his personal views in a semipublic way.

Although the press unanimously received the Chigago speech with outrage, Grew had attempted to soften the impact of the speech by making a distinction between the emperor as an individual and the imperial institution as a whole, firmly believing that even if Hirohito were to abdicate, the emperor system should be retained.

Before making such ideas public, however, various political considerations had to be taken into account. In the Chicago speech, before moving on to discuss the postwar peace settlement with Japan, Grew said, "I must make perfectly clear the fact that I am speaking solely for myself. . . . I am presuming in no respect to reflect the official views of the Government." But this was not necessarily the case, for prior to delivering his talk, Grew showed the full text to the State and War departments and the OWI for their approval (as he later revealed in a letter to Erle Dickover, chief of the Japan section at the Office of Far Eastern Affairs, on January 19, 1944).

Most probably as a result of this consultation, Grew sent a telegram the day before the speech to B. I. Griffith, director of Public Relations at the Illinois Education Association, telling him that "The entire paragraph about the Emperor [in the] typewritten text . . . and the mimeographed text [for newspaper publication] is to be eliminated." This is why the speech made no mention of the emperor, referring only to Shinto, which is not surprising, considering that opinion within the U.S. government was still divided on whether or not to retain the emperor system at all. Any favorable comments about the emperor or the imperial institution would also have been a political blunder, being anathema to the American public at that time.

The After-Effects of the Chicago Speech

As Grew revealed in a letter to Undersecretary of State Edward R. Stettinius on January 21, 1944, Secretary of State Hull had requested him to suspend his speech-making activity. In his position as a public official, he was obliged to decline all future requests to speak and had already canceled some existing engagements. Enraged by the press coverage, Grew was further demoralized by Hull's instructions.

Thereafter, Grew had to approach the emperor issue with great caution, as he remarked to Admiral Harry E. Yarnell of the Navy Department (January 6, 1944): "In my Chicago speech last week, . . . I planted certain seeds which I am sure will spring up in due course, but having done that I am not going to continue to speak along those lines at the present moment."

Grew also wished to avoid any further distortions of his opinions by the media:

> With regard to the passage on Shintoism [in my article], I have deleted the final paragraph, not because I have any doubt as to the soundness of my opinion but because it involves a controversial theme. Certain newspapers have associated this passage in my Chicago address with my statement that Emperor Hirohito was opposed to the war and they have interpreted the passage as an expression of my opinion that Hirohito should be retained on the throne of Japan after the war. That interpretation is far-fetched. [6]

The Chicago speech once again clearly demonstrated how the animosity of American opinion toward the emperor and emperor system was much greater than Grew had anticipated.

Coming after almost 250 speeches since his return to the United States, the Chicago speech therefore marked an important turning point, after which he ceased to speak about the emperor issue in public. No doubt he found it very difficult to stomach the negative reaction of the press, and he frequently expressed his feelings of helplessness and pent-up anger in the many letters he wrote to friends and colleagues:

> There is obviously nothing in the speech to justify the assumption of some newspapers that I had advocated the retention of Emperor Hirohito on the throne of Japan after the war.[7]
> I have repeatedly warned our people against the danger of an inconclusive or compromise peace with Japan. . . . As a purely supplementary point, I have expressed my belief that once we have destroyed that military machine, . . . we shall find elements among the Japanese people who will welcome the return of their country to a peaceful and reputable

national and international life and I state this, not merely as a matter of opinion, but of knowledge because you can't live among a people for ten years without knowing them.[8]

Moreover, in a letter to the journalist James Young on February 25, 1944, Grew complained that "some of your unfounded statements and comments, as reported, with regard to my public addresses, have in my opinion had a destructive effect on the work that I have been trying to do in our war effort."

In Grew's view, the emperor, as the symbol of national unity, was being manipulated by the military for evil ends. During his time in Tokyo, Grew had received secret information that confirmed that the emperor himself had not desired a war with the United States, but rather had done everything in his power to prevent it. Influenced by these sources, it cannot be denied that Grew consistently viewed the emperor as a pacifist. He wrote the following in a letter to J. M. Ellicott, former captain in the U.S. Navy, on June 26, 1944: "If Hirohito had taken a stronger position and had refused to sign the [Declaration of War], he would in all probability have been assassinated or relegated with the Imperial Family to Kyoto as were his forebears and a new shogunate would have been established."

Moreover, Grew never considered himself to be eccentric in predicting dire consequences if the emperor system was abolished after the war: "I do . . . believe that to insist on the abolishment of the institution of the throne in Japan would result in chaos, and I find that most experts on Japan, men who have lived there for many years such as Sir George Sansom, Wilfrid Fleisher, Hugh Byas, Eugene Dooman, Hillis Lory and many others, agree with me on this point."[9]

In drafting the political shape of postwar Japan, Grew therefore believed that the smoothest path would be to allow the Japanese themselves to choose a political structure centered on the emperor and the moderates, rather than imposing a Western system from the outside:

> In the light of Pearl Harbor and especially the unspeakable atrocities in the Philippines and elsewhere, our people are quite naturally not in a mood at present to believe that there are any good elements in Japan or anything good in the structure of the Japanese nation. . . . Nevertheless, as we approach the eventual peace it is important that [we should

acknowledge] the fact that there were ... elements totally opposed to war [in Japan].[10]

Grew, Shinto, and Anti-Japanese Feeling

Grew also had his own particular view of the Shinto religion, which was the object of much criticism after the Chicago speech.

> [Shinto,] as you are well aware, is a very complicated subject. Out of the original simple religious aspects of Shinto the military caste in Japan have, through manipulation, developed what amounts to a national political cult, and they have used it to support their prestige and extremist ambitions. Emperor homage is a fundamental conception of that cult and that conception, in my belief can work both ways. The following paragraph in my Chicago address [that Shintoism can become an asset] is of course based on this *a priori* assumption that we are going to cut militarism out of Japan, wholly and permanently.[11]

> The Shinto cult (as distinguished from the old Shinto religion) is a purely artificial doctrine and it has been manipulated by the military extremists to support their megalomaniac ambitions. Since, however, the Shinto cult implies reverence of the emperor, it seems to me to be common sense to hold that if in future there is a peace-seeking ruler on the Japanese throne not controlled by the military, Shinto can become an asset rather than a liability. This does not, however, for a moment mean that I advocate maintaining the myth of the divinity of the Emperor of Japan. All that mumbo jumbo must go by the board through reeducation if we are to eliminate for all time the power and influence of the military caste in Japan.[12]

Certainly, it is true that, in origin, Shintoism is a deep native belief of shamanistic character, which historically took the form of spirit-, nature-, and ancestor-worship, and the peaceful farming culture that can be seen in village festivals.

Yet the fact remains that Shinto also embraced a "Japanocentric" view in which Japan, the land of the rising sun, was the center of the earth, and the Emperor, son of the gods, was the rightful ruler of the whole world. Through the teaching of scholars of National Learning and the Mito School, this aspect of Shinto was gradually formed into a chauvinistic nationalism, which grew rapidly during Japan's confrontation with the outside world at the end of the Tokugawa era (1603–

1867). When Shinto later became established under the Meiji state as the official religion—State Shinto—it was easily transformed into an ideology advocating the supremacy of the Yamato race.

The concept of *hakkō ichiu** was constructed around this ethnocentric aspect of Shinto, gradually developing into an ideology of invasion and conquest, as the fifteen years of war between 1930 and 1945 testify. For the average American during the Pacific War, Shinto was seen as the ideological pillar of Japanese militarism, inseparable from emperor-worship, and therefore the object of bitter hatred. On this point, it must be said that Grew's interpretation of Shinto oversimplified one historical aspect of the religion, which aroused much anger, being centrally linked to his support for the preservation of the emperor system.

The January 29, 1944, issue of the *Sunday School Times* of Philadelphia, for example, carried an article by Gordon Holdcroft under the title "The Menace of Japanese Shintoism," in which he warned of the "subtle danger of looking upon idol worship as an asset." The *Argonaut* on July 21, 1944, also severely criticized Grew in a piece entitled "Joseph Grew, Mythologist, Speaks for the Mikado": "Why does Mr. Grew wish to protect the person and position of this monstrous war criminal?"

But why, exactly, was there such vehement opposition to the emperor in the United States? The fact is that, as Grew had said, Americans of that period knew nothing about Japan, and their views were overwhelmingly based on prejudice. What is more, the memory of Pearl Harbor, which had become a byword for foul play, was certain to remain in the minds of Americans, forming the core of their hostility toward Japan.

At the same time, one should also note the influence on many Americans of the anti-emperor campaign pursued by the Chinese lobby. Anti-Japanese propaganda from various missionaries, scholars, and journalists who supported China, along with the condemnation of Japanese militarism by the Chinese people themselves, was relayed to the American people through the media.

For example, in a dispatch to the *Christian Science Monitor* (November

---

*Literally, "the eight corners of the world under one roof," or the unification of the world under the emperor.—Trans.

9, 1943) from Chungking, Gunther Stein reported that the Chinese public thought it imperative to destroy the imperial legend, abolish the monarchy, and exile all possible heirs to the throne.[13] Dr. B. A. Liu also argued in an article for *Contemporary China* that Emperor Hirohito bore direct responsibility for Japan's acts of aggression since 1931 and should be treated as the leading war criminal. Liu called for the emperor's abdication and preferably his execution; steps should then be taken to confiscate his property, using the proceeds to compensate, in some small measure, the victims of Japanese atrocities. Even more emphatic was the well-known Chinese author Lin Yutang, writing for the *Pacific Mail*'s "Post-War Forum" (February 9, 1943):

> Destroy the Emperor. Bomb the Palace.... We must blow up this belief that the Japanese Emperor is the descendant of God. Unless their myth of racial superiority and their worship of military power are destroyed, the culture and psychology which represents Japanese society will come up again and again to threaten the world as Hitler's Germany does.[14]

Finally, Dr. Sun Fo, son of Sun Yat-sen and president of the Legislative Yuan of the Chinese national government, argued in a letter to the *New York Times* on October 10, 1943, that victory over Japan would not prove lasting unless it cleared away the military caste, the emperor and emperor-worship, and established a democratic Japanese republic. In his opinion, this democratic system could only be introduced from outside, principally by the United States and China.[15]

At the forefront of the barrage of Chinese criticism of the imperial institution was Sun Fo's famous article "The Mikado Must Go," published in the October 1944 issue of *Foreign Affairs*.[16] In this, Sun Fo bitterly condemned Grew and his supporters, who had such influence over American opinion, for advocating the preservation of the "Mikado" after Japan's surrender. "I would like to say, as emphatically as I know how, that if there is to be an end of militarism and a beginning of democracy in Japan ... the Mikado must go. The Mikado must go because the imperial idea is the essence of Japanese aggression.... Militarism, the power of the military caste, and the institution of the Tenno [emperor] are inextricably interwoven in Japan."[17]

Appearing as it did in *Foreign Affairs*, the article caused a great stir, and it seems that several newspapers and journals expected Grew to write a rejoinder. The *Reader's Digest* requested an article, even in the form of an indirect reply, but after long consideration, Grew declined. He was not at all certain that the American people were at that point ready to understand his views.

Grew's feelings relating to this question are revealed in an interesting letter he wrote on October 25, 1944, to Ellery Sedgwick of the *Atlantic Monthly Press* in Boston. In this he said the following.

> Sun Fo' s article . . . [is based on] inaccurate and distorted versions of a speech which I made in Chicago nearly a year ago.
>
> My position about the emperor of Japan is roughly this: When we have finally defeated Japan we shall, I assume, have two main objectives; one, to establish some sort of order in Japan and, two, to render the Japanese impotent again to threaten world peace. In seeking those objectives we shall wish to use all available assets and to eliminate liabilities. If the institution of the Japanese throne is to be a liability and an incentive to a continuance of the military cult, it had better be scrapped. If, on the other hand, it proves to be the only cornerstone on which something peaceful and healthy can be built in future, we had better not scrap it through mere prejudice. I am inclined to think that the latter will be the case, but we cannot possibly answer this question until we actually get to Tokyo and I therefore feel that it is premature to try to solve that problem now and that, owing to many still imponderable factors, the situation had better be left fluid for the present.
>
> As for Hirohito himself, I personally don't see how he can stay, especially in view of the fact that in Japan the acceptance of responsibility for failure is traditional. In the case of an ordinary failure, some cabinet officer or other official would take the responsibility off the Emperor's shoulders by resigning or committing hara-kiri, but in view of the terrific cataclysm which Japan inevitably faces, I don't see how Hirohito could dodge the responsibility, for whether he wanted war or not he signed the Imperial Rescript declaring war. I don't think, however, that this matters much one way or the other as Hirohito is only a symbol and it is the institution of the throne that counts.*
>
> My alleged support of Hirohito springs chiefly from a paragraph in my Chicago speech in which I said that if in future there should be a peace-seeking ruler in Japan *not controlled by the military*, the Shinto cult (as distinguished from the Shinto religion) could become an asset

---

*Grew thought that if the emperor's abdication could not be avoided, then either Prince Chichibu or the Crown Prince should take the lead in a "New Japan"—N.M.

and not a liability in a reconstructed Japan. I distinctly said could and not would. The Shinto cult is really an artificial excrescence which has been artificially used and developed by the military caste to support their own desires, and everything that is artificial can be artificially remoulded under new circumstances.

All this seems to me to be common sense, but of course most of our people do not understand the problem at all and we can hardly blame them for believing that the Emperor, supported by Shinto, is the root of evil in that misguided country.

The summer of 1944 marked a great turning point in the Pacific War. In June the Japanese navy made their final stand in the sea battle off the Marianas Islands, falling to a crushing defeat. The war was now a lost cause for Japan. Further, in July the Japanese garrison at Saipan was destroyed, and that same month the Tōjō cabinet was forced to resign.

Just as Grew had predicted, Japan's defeat was drawing near with a mathematical certainty. How, then, could the United States bring about Japan's early surrender with minimum casualties? Grew's idea of maintaining and utilizing the emperor system became the basis for the U.S. "peace initiatives." Nevertheless, many obstacles still had to be overcome before Grew's opinion became the dominant view, not only within the United States but, more particularly, within the U.S. State Department.

TEN YEARS IN JAPAN

A Contemporary Record
Drawn from the
Diaries and Private and Official
Papers of

JOSEPH C. GREW

United States Ambassador
to Japan
1932–1942

19 44

SIMON AND SCHUSTER
NEW YORK

The first edition of Grew's *Ten Years in Japan*, autographed by the author.

REPORT FROM TOKYO

A MESSAGE TO THE
AMERICAN PEOPLE

JOSEPH C. GREW
UNITED STATES AMBASSADOR TO JAPAN, 1932 TO 1941

Grew giving a dinner speech, flanked by Sir Robert Craigie and Mrs. Grew.

A drawing of Grew in the *San Francisco Chronicle*, May 14, 1944.

滞日十年

TEN YEARS
IN
JAPAN

上 巻

ジョセフ・C・グルー

石川欣一譯

毎日新聞社

The Japanese translation of Grew's *Ten Years in Japan*.

Grew with Admiral Nimitz at Pearl Harbor in late 1944. (The photo is autographed by Nimitz.)

Truman   Byrnes   MacArthur

Grew   Dooman

4

THE PUBLICATION OF *TEN YEARS IN JAPAN*

Careful Timing

THE DATE of publication of *Ten Years in Japan* by Simon and Schuster on May 15, 1944, is an important point to note. As already stated, Grew began plans to publish the book after his return to the United States in the autumn of 1942, with various political aims in mind. This demanded that the book appear at precisely the right time. As Japan's defeat now seemed inevitable, Grew no doubt wished the publication to coincide with the start of the American government's formulation of concrete plans for postwar Japan. Indeed, the following letter, which Grew sent to Quincy Howe of Simon and Schuster along with the corrected galleys on January 31, 1944, confirms this.

> Now with regard to the date of publication. The American people, including myself, have been deeply stirred and shocked by the recent revelations of Japanese atrocities in the Philippines and elsewhere [for instance, the Bataan death march and the atrocities against British POWs in the construction of the Taimen bridge]. The public, quite rightly, is at present in no mood to hear or to read anything good about Japan or the Japanese, even the fair and accurate picture painted in my diary, and I fear that if my book comes out in April it may have a very bad press. Later, as our forces get nearer to Tokyo and as the Japanese army and navy come nearer to final defeat and the eventual showdown is in sight, I believe that my book may be helpful in preparing public opinion for a sane peace.
>
> My own inclination would therefore be to hold publication in abeyance for the present and to watch for a moment more favorable for the appearance of the book than now seems to me to exist. . . . Developments in the war may later tend in some degree to modify the acute

bitterness which now logically colors all public thinking, but if such a story as mine were published now I do not believe that it would be given a fair and objective reception. I think that the public reaction, except in the case of a small minority of intellectually honest thinkers, would at best be a shrug of the shoulders and at worst a condemnatory tirade, and as an officer of the Department of State I particularly do not wish to embarrass Mr. Hull. . . .

I know that [Simon and Schuster's] outlook in such problems is guided more by the importance of our national interests than by purely commercial considerations, and if they believe that my apprehensions with regard to a bad public reception of my book at this time are groundless, I shall be satisfied to leave the decision as to the date of publication in their good hands.

At the time he wrote this letter, Grew was coming under fierce criticism for his Chicago speech and had recently been ordered by Secretary of State Hull to suspend his speech-making activities. This had made him adopt a prudent and even fainthearted approach.

Grew's worries, however, seem to have been dispelled by his appointment as director of the Office of Far Eastern Affairs on May 1. He had now acquired a position that enabled him to realize his own ideas and plans for postwar policy toward Japan.

Yet in Washington this new appointment was greeted with some surprise, because it was thought that after Hornbeck, only China specialists would be selected for the post. On June 9, 1944, the journal *Amerasia* published a special issue entitled "A New Far East Policy? Japan vs China," immediately probing whether or not this new appointment indicated a shift in emphasis from China toward Japan in State Department policy on the Far East.

In addition to Mr. Grew, Joseph W. Ballantine, a former counselor of the American Embassy in Tokyo, has been made Deputy Director, Earle [*sic*] R. Dickover, a former first secretary in Tokyo, is chief of the Japanese section, and Frank Williams, former commercial attaché in Japan, is under Dickover. These appointments were generally taken to mean that the direction of American Far Eastern policy had been transferred from the so-called "China crowd" headed by Dr. Hornbeck, who had been in charge of the Far Eastern Division since 1928, to men whose Far Eastern diplomatic experience has been largely if not entirely in Japan.

Having reported this, *Amerasia* then severely criticized Grew, the leading figure of the Japan crowd, for his view of the emperor, his expectations regarding the moderates, and his conception of postwar policy for Japan. We shall look at that in more detail later.

Reviews of *Ten Years in Japan*—Mixed Reactions

Eventually published after painstaking preparation, *Ten Years in Japan* reached number two on the *New York Times* best-seller list for June and July, much as Grew and Simon and Schuster had expected. Nearly forty reviews were written, generally all favorable, as the following examples demonstrate.

Wilfrid Fleisher, writing in the *Baltimore Evening Sun* (May 13, 1944), found it to be an interesting personal and diplomatic record of the ten years preceding Pearl Harbor. Whereas Joseph E. Davies's *Mission to Moscow* and the memoirs of other diplomats, such as former Ambassador to Germany James W. Gerard, had all been written in retirement, this book was published when "Mr. Grew has just taken over the post of director of the Office of Far Eastern Affairs." It thus "has an important bearing not only on the past but on what the future may hold. [Grew] is in charge of American Far Eastern policy and while for the moment it is restricted to our relations with China, he will eventually have to deal with the whole complex problem of a Far Eastern peace. The book has had the approval of Secretary of State Cordell Hull. . . . Rarely has the American public had such an opportunity to acquaint itself so intimately with events that mold our destiny today."

Further, Kenneth C. Kaufman in the *Chicago Tribune* (May 14, 1944) gave the following review:

> Ambassador Grew's previous book, "Report from Tokyo," aimed at giving a realistic view of the strength of our Asiatic enemy and at combating undue optimism; the present volume goes further back and further forward, portraying and analyzing those complexities of national mentality and character which slowly pushed Japan into national hara-kiri, and building up a predicate for a solution of the peace problems.
>
> When he went to Japan it was obvious that the war mongers had embarked on a course of rule or ruin; they had seized Manchuria and were preparing to junk the Washington treaties, quit the League of

Nations, and bid for leadership in Asia. President Hoover appointed him on May 14, 1932; on May 15 a series of political assassinations culminated in the murder of Premier Inukai. Nevertheless, that first year led only to the recognition of Manchukuo, followed by a period of comparative calm. On the surface it looked as if the moderates—and they were many—might swing the country back to sanity. But in February 1936, hotheaded young army officers staged another series of murders; again they failed and some of their number were executed. Yet troops kept pouring into North China and in 1937 the China incident became open war. By 1940 the military were so firm in the saddle that they were able to align their country with the axis and begin the southward expansion. To that point, Mr. Grew, a career diplomat with forty years of experience [he had served in Mexico, Russia, Austria-Hungary, Germany, Denmark, Switzerland, and Turkey], had . . . a ringside seat at the struggle between the dual governments of Japan—civil and military. . . . Throughout are to be found shrewd glimpses of Japanese life and customs, amusing and pathetic incidents, portraits of outstanding personalities. . . . Probably Mr. Grew was unaware, in compiling his book, that he was doing his self-portrait.

Joseph Henry Jackson, in the *San Francisco Chronicle*, May 14, 1944, gave a similarly warm appraisal of the book.

Since he returned to the U.S., Mr. Grew has done his best to make two of his beliefs crystal clear. One of these is that all Japan did not want war with the U.S., did not even approve of the military clique's "Greater East Asia Co-Prosperity" program. It is unfortunate that this has led some Americans to take the attitude that Mr. Grew is trying to excuse Japan. . . . Indeed, he means just the opposite. And that is the second thing his book makes clear. Japan, he writes, must be "overwhelmingly beaten." And he adds, "However long this process may take, however much it may involve American blood, sweat and tears, there must be no relinquishing of this essential task until it is finally and effectively completed. There is no room in the Pacific Area for a peaceful America and a swash-buckling Japan." And Mr. Grew concludes, on the subject of Japan's defeat, "Of that final defeat I have not the slightest doubt. It seems to me as mathematically certain as the law of gravity." [In this way, Grew disposes] cleanly of the arguments of those who might point to his remarks on anti-war Japanese as a kind of softening of purpose. . . . Like the first-rate diplomat he is, Mr. Grew sees both points and knows that the American people must see them if their war is to have other than military success.

As is apparent from the above, *Ten Years in Japan* was favorably received in many newspapers. Moreover, all of these reviews appeared either one or two days prior to its publication. Grew and his publisher probably arranged through the State Department or the OWI to have advance press reviews. In that sense, the book went beyond the scope of being simply the personal record of a single diplomat, for it was also undeniably aimed to inform and persuade public opinion regarding the State Department's war aims and its postwar policy on Japan.

Nevertheless, when *Amerasia* warned of "a new Far Eastern policy," it had its own reasons for expressing concern about Grew's appointment as director of the Office of Far Eastern Affairs and about the publication of *Ten Years in Japan*. *Amerasia* published the writings of liberals and New Dealers such as Frederick Fields, Phillip Jaffee, Kate Mitchell, Thomas Bisson, Owen Lattimore, and Chi Ch'ao-ting, and it was regarded as taking an anti-Japan and pro-China position. Although even at its height it published only two thousand copies per issue, it was widely influential among specialists in Asian affairs.

"A New Far Eastern Policy?" expounded a long criticism of Grew, of which I shall quote the main points here.

> Additional light on Mr. Grew's views concerning Japan is provided by his recently published book, *Ten Years in Japan*. . . . Because of its semi-official character, however, it cannot be taken as a wholly accurate reflection of Mr. Grew's opinions since it has been carefully edited by the State Department and is strictly non-committal with regard to many vital though controversial issues." (p. 181)

Amerasia also criticized Grew's faith in the dangerous policy of entrusting Japan to the emperor system, Shintoism, and the moderates, as revealed in his Chicago speech.

> A perusal of the book makes clear that the "many Japanese" to whom Mr. Grew refers were prominent civilian members of the ruling oligarchy, including the Emperor himself, members of the Court circle, and foreign office officials with whom he was in close contact throughout his stay in Japan. At no point in his book does Mr. Grew refer to or analyze the more popular mass movements which constituted an important potential force opposing war. . . .
> . . . At no point in his record does he include an analysis of Japan's social and economic structure, which would reveal that the great busi-

ness and financial trusts, including the Imperial Household, were as fully committed to a policy of expanding Japan's political control to embrace all of Eastern Asia as were the most fanatical militarists. . . .

Mr. Grew's faith in the "moderates" . . . was such that even when the Konoye Cabinet fell on October 16, 1941, and General Tōjō became Prime Minister, . . . he accepted as reasonable Prince Konoye's explanation that he had resigned in the belief that "the conversations with the United States would make more rapid progress if our Government were dealing with a Prime Minister whose power was based on a commanding position in and on support of the Army." To this note in his diary, dated October 20, 1941, Mr. Grew added: "It would be logical to expect that General Tōjō, in retaining his active rank in the Army, will as a result be in a position to exercise a larger degree of control over Army extremist groups." . . . Thus until the very last, Mr. Grew clung to the hope that the "moderate" elements would prevail, even under Tōjō.

. . . But in view of the evidence of the last three years, . . . there would seem to be little reason for his continued efforts to justify his assiduous cultivation of the "moderate" wing of the Japanese oligarchy. (pp. 184–85)

Nor was *Amerasia* the only publication to criticize Grew's exaggerated expectations of Japan's "moderates" and the emperor. Orville Prescott, for example, in his review for the *New York Times* on May 15, 1944, wrote: "[Grew] knows that not quite every Japanese has succumbed to [the militarists'] propaganda. A few [liberals] are still uncontaminated and are ashamed of their country's crimes. But whether they would crowd a small room if they were all gathered together is doubtful."

Grew and the moderates—this is the key to Grew's understanding of Japan and a core element at the heart of his postwar plans for that country. But who really were the moderates?

5

THE MODERATES
Makino Nobuaki, Kabayama Aisuke, Yoshida Shigeru

Grew, the Moderates, and the "Pendulum Theory"

GREW'S diplomatic style could best be described as "court diplomacy." During his time in Tokyo, he regularly invited Japanese dignitaries to dine at the U.S. Embassy, and in return he was invited by friends to banquets, funerals, and other social gatherings. Among those who appear in Grew's diaries are Makino Nobuaki, Kabayama Aisuke, Konoe Fumimaro, Matsudaira Tsuneo, Hirota Kōki, Yoshida Shigeru, Debuchi Katsuji, Shidehara Kijūrō, Shigemitsu Mamoru, and Nitobe Inazo. In addition, the admiralty and leading businessmen from the zaibatsu, such as Mitsui and Sumitomo, also maintained contacts with the U.S. ambassador.

Heinrichs divides Grew's social circle into three groups: the admiralty, the business magnates, and the court entourage, his most important source of information. Grew's image of the moderates, who had all studied or served in Europe and the United States, was of modest, cultured, and dignified gentlemen.

Grew himself came from the Boston social elite, attending Groton School, where many of America's most prestigious families sent their children, and later graduating from Harvard. The great affinity Grew felt for the Japanese upper classes and the trust he placed in them were thus surely related to his own background, as clearly demonstrated in this diary entry for June 11, 1940, published in *Ten Years in Japan.*

> The Buddhist funeral rites for Prince Tokugawa today were intensely impressive, as all such ceremonies are in Japan. . . . After eight years in Japan I had the feeling today of being not outsiders but an intimate part of that group, almost as if the gathering were of old family friends in

> Boston and not in Tokyo. We knew well a great many of the Japanese and their wives who were sitting around us, members of the outstanding families and clans. The Tokugawas, Konoyes, Matsudairas, Mastukatas might have been Saltonstalls and Sedgwicks and Peabodys. We knew their positions, their influence and reputations, their personalities, and their interrelationships as well as those of a similar group in Boston. And we felt too that they regarded us as a sort of part of them. (pp. 319–20)

Indeed, Grew saw such social occasions as the best opportunity to meet Japanese who had a detailed understanding of the political situation. He had, however, been left with hearing difficulties following an attack of scarlet fever as a child, and he had not learned to speak Japanese himself. Therefore, the moderates, who all spoke English to varying degrees, represented a vital source of information for him. But these were not the only reasons that Grew was drawn to this political group—his bond with them was also closely linked to his view of Japan and Japanese history. For example, in both the original diaries and *Ten Years in Japan*, one often comes across the following ideas.

> Japanese history shows that the country has passed through periodical cycles of intense nationalism attended by anti-foreign sentiment, but these periods have always been followed by other periods of international conciliation and cooperation.[1]

> The pendulum in Japan is always swinging; the moderates say that it will soon swing back toward normal, but I fear not. I fear that it must swing still farther toward the extreme, and that if Konoye falls, either through resignation or through a coup d'etat, he is likely to be succeeded by a military dictatorship, even by a sort of revival of the shogunate. (*Ten Years*, p. 350)

> History has shown that the pendulum in Japan is always swinging between extremist and moderate politics, but as things stand today we believe that the pendulum is more likely to swing still further toward extremes than to reverse its direction. Konoye, and especially Matsuoka, will fall in due course, but *under present circumstances* no Japanese leader or group of leaders could reverse the expansionist program and hope to survive. (pp. 359–60)

In this way, Grew saw Japanese history since the Meiji Restoration as a swing from militarism to moderate politics and back again to extremism. This "pendulum theory" formed the framework of his view of Japan and explains why, in *Ten Years in Japan* and elsewhere, he frequently refers to the cyclical nature of Japanese politics, seeking to highlight the contrast between the moderates and the militarists.

Makino Nobuaki

Grew's diaries show that, of all the moderates, he placed the most trust in Makino Nobuaki (1861–1949), whom he constantly praises throughout *Ten Years in Japan*. "In every nation great gentlemen stand out, and during our entire conversation, which was by all odds the pleasantest I've had here, Count Makino impressed me as a really great gentleman. He is close to the Emperor but he doesn't, alas, carry much weight in these days of military domination. He referred, as nearly everyone does here, to the sentiment of the Japanese for Alice as a Perry" (p. 33).*

During the discussion in question, Makino talked to Grew about post-Meiji Japan and the "pendulum theory." Grew noted that "his talk was very similar to that which I had with Ambassador Matsudaira in London with regard to the swing of the pendulum" (p. 32). Thus, it was in fact Makino and the other liberals who gave Grew this image of modern Japanese history as a process of fluctuation between extremist and moderate politics at home, and correspondingly in external affairs, between xenophobic nationalism and a spirit of international cooperation. Grew was no doubt attracted by the convenience of this perspective.

In addition, the moderates frequently described the vital role played by the emperor in Japan's complex decision-making process, something Grew himself experienced in his contact with many members of the political elite. This was a further reason why he sought to preserve close links with the moderates and court officials.

Grew's frequent references to the emperor in *Ten Years in Japan* consistently present him as a pacifist and the leading Japanese moderate.

---

*In 1904, Grew married Alice D. P. Perry, a descendant of Oliver Hazard Perry, whose younger brother, Commodore Matthew Galbraith Perry, had landed at Uraga, near Tokyo, in 1853, demanding that Japan open its borders. Partly because of this connection, Alice was a popular figure in Japanese social circles.—N.M.

This is nowhere more clear than when Grew says, "The highest influences in the country are pacific. The Emperor is a man of mild and peaceful character. The era of his reign is characterized by the word *Shōwa*, which he himself chose and which means 'enlightened peace'" (p. 118). Yet one cannot imagine Grew holding this view of the emperor had he not maintained such regular contact with the court.

On May 22, 1935, Grew attended a Japanese banquet at the Maple Club given by the grand master of ceremonies, Viscount Matsudaira, and his wife. The diary entry for that day, entitled "A Great Japanese Gentleman on Japan," is often quoted, and I include a substantial part of it here.

> After dinner I sat with Count Makino and had an interesting talk, in the course of which he told me of a conversation he had just had with Dubosc, editor of the Paris *Temps*, who has been traveling in Japan. Dubosc apparently told Count Makino that he considered the political situation in Japan as "dangerous" owing to the strife and corruption among the political parties and the risk of military Fascism on the one hand and of Communism on the other.
>
> Makino said to Dubosc ... , "When you return to Paris and make your report or write your editorials on the domestic situation in Japan, cut out the word 'danger' from your vocabulary. We have a safeguard in Japan which other countries do not possess in the same degree, namely the Imperial Household. There will never be 'danger' from military Fascism or Communism or from any other kind of 'ism' simply because the Emperor is supreme and will always have the last word."
>
> I have never heard the old man speak so emphatically or exhibit so much patriotic emotion; his eyes filled with tears and he had to wipe his glasses. The manner in which he talked tonight—his emphasis and emotion—gave a momentary revelation of the intensity of their devotion to the Throne, and I think that the force of that devotion throughout the nation—in spite of all the bickering and the political agitations and even the assassinations—or perhaps because of them—is stronger, much stronger, than foreigners generally appreciate. At any rate, I was greatly impressed tonight by this momentary glimpse into the mind of the usually suave, courteous, and eminently gentle Count Makino, whom I shall always regard as one of the world's greatest gentlemen. (pp. 155–56)

Nine months after this conversation, on February 26, 1936, the so-called 2–26 incident erupted with the revolt of a faction of army officers.

Makino narrowly escaped with his life. The day after the uprising, Grew noted in his diary: "These assassinations have stirred us terribly—Saitō [Makoto], Takahashi [Korekiyo], Watanabe [Jōtarō] dead and Suzuki [Kantarō] probably fatally wounded. Thank heaven that Count Makino escaped" (p. 171). This event highlighted the differences separating Makino and the court group from the military fascists and no doubt further confirmed Grew's image of the court elite as liberals.

Grew's diary shows how he saw his contacts with the court as an indispensable means of influencing the emperor. He would, for instance, discuss the U.S. viewpoint with Makino "in the hope that [their] conversation [would] be reported to the Emperor" (p. 31). He also recounted how he once "asked for an interview with the Prime Minister [Konoe] . . . I insisted and finally got a half-hour between 1 and 1:30, just before he went to see the emperor on another matter, which was all to the good" (p. 264).

Kabayama Aisuke, the Go-Between

Another member of the moderate group to gain Grew's trust was Kabayama Aisuke (1865–1953). Son of Admiral Kabayama Sukenori, at the age of fifteen he went to the United States where he studied for five years at Wilbraham Junior High School in Massachussetts. He went on to Wesleyan University in Connecticut but transferred to Amherst on the death of his tutor. Returning to Japan at age twenty-seven in 1891, Kabayama had the opportunity to gain an inside view of politics when he became personal secretary to his father, who successively held the posts of navy, home, and education minister. Around 1907, at the age of forty-two, he entered the world of business, founding Anglo-Japanese Hydro-Electric, the first ever joint venture between the two countries. He became a director of Chiyoda Fire and Life Insurance in 1913; the following year, executive director of Japan Steel. For over forty years he managed the running of these two companies as president and chairman, and later as a consultant. In 1923 he succeeded as head of the family on the death of his father. He was elected to the House of Peers in 1925, at age sixty. He also became vice-chairman of the Japanese–U.S. Association of Foundations in 1924 and in 1940 succeeded Tokugawa Ietatsu as chairman.[2]

Some Japanese said the aged Kabayama was too pro-American, while U.S. diplomats variously described him as an "international glad hander" and an "incorrigible busybody."[3] Grew knew of these opinions and tolerated them. Kabayama frequently visited the U.S. Embassy and became an important source of information for Grew as well as his mediator in contacts with the court.

The following passage, which appears in *Ten Years in Japan* under the entry for October 18, 1932, confirms that the court elite were emphasizing to Grew the strength of the moderate element.

> Dinner at the Uchidas' [Foreign Minister Uchida Yasuya], including Mrs. Woodrow Wilson, the Debuchis, Count Makino, Count Kabayama, Prince Tokugawa, the Aritas, the McIlroys, and so on. Both before and after dinner I had long talks with Count Makino, who spoke very much along the lines of ——'s talks this afternoon, emphasizing the existing "undercurrent" of moderate thought, and then we talked of the results of the Versailles Peace Treaty. Later I sat down with ——, who spoke along precisely the same lines as Makino. They are all trying to get this idea across to me. (pp. 51–52)

Who, one wonders, do the deletions refer to? By looking at the original diaries, we can see that the first was Yoshida Shigeru and the second, Kabayama Aisuke. Grew later admitted that he had attempted to conceal Yoshida's name throughout *Ten Years in Japan*, but Kabayama was another whom Grew evidently felt he had to shield. This is because, as Grew's general go-between with the court, Kabayama regularly reported back to the ambassador with confidential information that was necessary for making top-level political decisions.

In *Ten Years in Japan*, there are many passages where Grew conceals someone's name, attributing his information to "a highly reliable source," "a famous Japanese liberal," or "my sources." Several of these refer to Kabayama; for instance, it was he who told Grew that the formation of the Okada Keisuke cabinet in July 1935 was a victory for the moderates, and that Okada's position after the North China crisis in 1935 was more secure than that of any prime minister in recent years. While maintaining that he was unable to give his full support to this assessment, Grew nevertheless wired the State Department with the message that "the moderates have gained the upper hand."

On July 19, 1935, Grew went to the United States for an extended holiday, returning to Japan in December. About two weeks before leaving, he wrote the following in his diary, which was not included in *Ten Years in Japan*: "Count Kabayama came in for a long talk. He had seen the Prime Minister in order to bring me a direct message about the situation before my departure. Kabayama talked much about domestic politics and said categorically that the strongest influences in Japan today were those of Prince Saionji and Count Makino and that they were absolutely supported by the emperor who is more moderate in his views than any of his predecessors."[4]

The court elite—Makino, Kabayama, and the others—constantly fed Grew with the image of the emperor as a pacifist, asserting that it was the moderates who were the true force of political stability in Japan and who were advancing peaceful diplomacy between Japan and the United States. Undoubtedly, Grew's association with the moderates exerted a great influence on his later plans for postwar Japan.

Nevertheless, Kabayama and Makino were old men and Grew would not be able to rely on them indefinitely. He therefore also wanted to maintain regular contact with those moderates who would shoulder the future responsibilities of the nation. One of these was Makino's son-in-law, Yoshida Shigeru.

Grew's Friendship with Yoshida

As indicated, Grew sought to conceal Yoshida's name when he published *Ten Years in Japan*, and many of the deletions in the text in fact refer to Yoshida. The following extract, from an entry made on October 18, 1932, is one example.

> In the afternoon —— came to see me by appointment. He said he wished merely to thank me for our dinner, but that is generally done by merely leaving cards, and it was obvious that he wanted to talk. He said a good deal to the effect that the moderate element in Japan is stronger and more widespread than is generally known, because their views do not get into the press or public speeches; the people who do the most talking and writing in the newspapers are not always the ones who carry the most weight, and that the moderate thinkers will be heard from in due course. (p. 51)

Yoshida, who was Japan's ambassador to Italy, had returned to Tokyo on October 9, 1932, intending to resign his post, and immediately established contact with Grew through his father-in-law, Count Makino. The above discussion took place shortly after the signing of the Japan–Manchuria Protocol, by which the Japanese government officially recognized the puppet state of "Manchukuo." Yoshida was well informed on the situation in China, having served as consul general in Tianjin from 1922 to 1928 and later in Mukden. He therefore represented a desirable contact for Grew, who was keenly interested in the future development of Japanese policy toward China, following its recognition of Manchukuo. For his part, Yoshida hoped to gain information from Grew on how Britain and the United States perceived such policy, and what form their future involvement might take.

Ever since his first meeting with Grew, Yoshida had established himself as a moderate, adopting a pro-British, pro-American stance and speaking frankly about the domestic and external situation facing Japan. He also put himself forward as an intermediary between Grew and the Japanese political elite; for instance, Grew noted in his diary on October 24, 1932, about two weeks after their first conversation, that he had been able to gain an interview at short notice with Shidehara Kijūrō through the good offices of Kabayama and Yoshida. (During his two periods as foreign minister [1924–27, 1929–31], Shidehara had sponsored a policy of nonintervention in the Chinese civil war; his successor, Tanaka Giichi, had reversed this policy, but Grew was hoping for a possible return to "Shidehara diplomacy.")

Almost a year later, Grew noted that, again through Yoshida, he had managed to establish a close personal relationship with Hirota Kōki, minister for foreign affairs. They had apparently chosen to meet at Hirota's own residence rather than at the Foreign Ministry. All these facts were omitted, however, when *Ten Years in Japan* was published.

In his diary, Grew described Yoshida as "one of the few Japanese to whom one can speak with the utmost frankness" (September 30, 1933), and "a good friend of the United States and a good friend of mine" (April 2, 1936). Behind this friendship lay the establishment of a secret information channel, as Yoshida gradually became an indispensable element in Grew's diplomatic work. Consequently, they kept in frequent contact with each other from October 1932 until April 1936, and then from January 1939 until Autumn 1941. In the interim, Yoshida went to serve as ambassador to Britain and consequently rarely appears in this section of Grew's diary.

Grew and Yoshida's first period of contact spanned from Japan's withdrawal from the League of Nations to the military's establishment of its predominance following the "2–26" affair. The latter period comprised three years of upheaval leading to the Pacific War, as U.S.–Japanese relations rapidly deteriorated, through termination of the American trade treaty with Japan (July 1939) and the formation of the Tripartite Pact (September 1940), followed by the banning of U.S. exports of scrap iron to Japan (October 1940), the freezing of Japanese assets (July 1941), and finally, the embargo on sales of aviation fuel (August 1941).

Throughout this time, Yoshida, along with Kabayama Aisuke and others, helped Grew to maintain his links with the Japanese political elite. The diaries reveal how important these two men were for Grew as reliable mediators and informants.

In a long talk after dinner Yoshida told me that Prince Konoe was being groomed eventually to succeed Prince Saionji as Genro or elder statesman and as close adviser to the Throne and the Government, and that the main purpose of his visit to the United States was for his own education so that he might be familiar with American thought and institutions in preparation for the important political position which he would eventually fill. It was therefore of the utmost importance that his impressions should be happy ones. He was not going in any respect as a "goodwill envoy" or to indulge in Japanese propaganda. I gathered that this was an indirect message to me from highest sources that they would be glad to have me pave the way for his visit to Washington. Yoshida naturally reflects these thoughts, and perhaps sometimes the messages, of his distinguished father-in-law Count Makino who is very close to the Emperor. Have written fully to Mr. Hull. (April 25, 1934)

To dinner came Mr. and Mrs. Yoshida, former Ambassador to London, Matsukata (the elder), Jirō Shirasu, Mrs. Parsons ... and Max Schmidt. After dinner I talked for a long time to Yoshida and Shirasu about the state of American public opinion towards Japan and the reasons therefore; they urged me to tell all this to the Prime Minister and said that they would arrange a meeting; I said that I did not wish to make representations over the head of the Foreign Minister but that if the Prime Minister should send for me I would of course come and would talk with the utmost frankness. They likewise urged a talk with Prince Konoye who appears to have been responsible for the choice of the present Cabinet. (October 13, 1939)

Shirasu Jirō was the son-in-law of Kabayama Aisuke and also belonged to Konoe's circle of contacts. Yoshida had made his acquaintance during his time as ambassador to England, and after the Japanese surrender Shirasu was to act as a link between GHQ and Yoshida in his position as vice-chief of the Central Liaison Office. One can see from the above, however, that their relationship had already been established before the war.

By arranging important meetings through his various personal contacts, passing on inside political information, and so on, Yoshida consistently sought to convince Grew that the moderates remained a strong political force.*

Concealing the Moderates

When I compared the index of names in the translation of *Ten Years in Japan* with the English version, I noticed something rather strange. Under the "Y" heading in the English version, all I found was "Yoshida, Admiral, 178–79, 427," but no mention at all of Yoshida Shigeru. "Admiral Yoshida" of course indicates Navy Minister Yoshida Zengo (August 1939–September 1940). What, then, is recorded under these entries?

> March 5, 1936
> To our astonishment, Hirota immediately announced the make-up of his new cabinet, including Yoshida as Minister for Foreign Affairs, and the press said that Yoshida was acting as his chief of staff in choosing the various Ministers. This seemed to us precisely like waving a red flag at a bull because not only is Yoshida a pronounced liberal but he is the son-in-law of Count Makino. But naturally the Army wouldn't accept him for a moment, and it was soon announced that Hirota . . . was having difficulty in forming his cabinet. (p. 178)

---

*John W. Dower's *Empire and Aftermath: Yoshida Shigeru and the Japanese Experience 1878–1954* (translated into Japanese in 1981) also reveals the close relationship that existed between the two men.—N.M.

September 6, 1941

Prince Konoye told me that from the inception of the informal talks in Washington he had received the strongest concurrence from the responsible chiefs of both the Army and the Navy. Only today he had conferred with the Minister of War, who had promised to send a full general to accompany the Prime Minister to the meeting with the President; the Minister of the Navy had agreed that a full admiral should accompany the Prime Minister. Prince Konoye added in confidence that he expected that the representative of the Navy would probably be Admiral Yoshida, a former Minister of the Navy. (p. 427)

The first extract refers to the formation of the Hirota cabinet directly after the "2–26" affair; the second, to the tense negotiations between Japan and the United States three months before the start of the war. The Yoshida in the former passage is clearly not Yoshida Zengo, but Yoshida Shigeru.

I cannot believe that this is simply an error. It was Grew who proposed to Simon and Schuster (in a letter of January 1944) that an index of names should be included in Ten Years in Japan, and one can therefore only conclude that the removal of Yoshida Shigeru's name from this index was a deliberate decision on Grew's part. It seems strange that the name Yoshida should appear only twice in all the 554 pages of the book, and stranger still when one discovers that although one of these references is to Yoshida Zengo and the other to Yoshida Shigeru, they are listed together under the index entry for the former.

Three reasons come to mind as to why Grew performed this complicated deception. The first and major factor was his promise of confidentiality to his "trustworthy Japanese sources": he wished to avoid laying the moderates open to attack from the military and right wing. As Grew wrote in a letter to his friend, George M. Brill, on December 30, 1944: "while I was frequently in touch with Count Kabayama during the last four years of my stay in Japan, I especially avoided mentioning his name in my diary during those years as any Japanese who maintained contact with us during that period invariably came under suspicion of the military police and I did not wish harm to come to Kabayama through any published record of mine."

Furthermore, on April 21, 1945, in a letter to George Bilankin of the Royal Empire Society in England, Grew said that following Pearl

Harbor, he had received letters from two Japanese friends, but in order to protect them, he had purposefully concealed their names. But who were the "two Japanese friends," and what did these letters say?

Tokyo, December 17, 1941
Dear Mr. and Mrs. Grew:

No one could have forseen this tragic end of our longstanding friendly relations, although so many unfortunate events occurred in recent years. I well remember that you always tell me that to promote the friendship of our two countries is your lifework. I know also how hard you worked to prevent the breaking up of the talk in Washington even till the very last moment. It is a very sad thing that even your unfatigued efforts could not save the peace. But you can rest assured that we will never forget your friendship to our country and to us. Before ending my letter I must add one thing. Whenever I told the progress of our talk in Washington to my wife at her sick bedside during the last summer, she always tried to strain her weakening nerves not to have escaped any words from her ears. She is happy not to have witnessed in her lifetime this tragic end of our good relations.

Please accept my gratitude for your personal friendship and kindness to me and to my family, and I beg to remain,

Yours most sincerely. (p. 508)

Tokyo, December 30, 1941
Dear Mr. Grew:

It is with a sense of great grief that I write you this letter. In spite of our sincere and sustained endeavors to avert the rupture of our relations, the awful eventuality has at last come. I do not want to say much on the causes and circumstances that have led to this war; I only wish that the present struggle may prove but a brief episode in the long annals of our relations, which I hope will be quickly restored.

You and Mrs. Grew have won numerous friends among my compatriots by your able and admirable work extending over nine long years. As you well know, it is not the habit of our people to forget their friends easily, especially when they are so highly esteemed as you are, and I assure you that there are many of us who tender their deep sympathy to you in your great difficulty.

Perhaps it is unnecessary for me to say that I consider it a great privilege to have enjoyed your genial and generous friendship. I look forward keenly to the happy day when we shall once again co-operate heartily for the advancement of the relations of our two countries.

As I have been transferred, I am leaving for my new post within a few days' time. I wish Mrs. Grew and your good self a happy new year and safe voyage home.

Yours very sincerely. (pp. 508–9)

I immediately consulted the diaries, where I found that the first letter had come from Yoshida Shigeru and the second from Shigemitsu Mamoru. John Dower quotes Yoshida's letter, but because he worked from the original diaries throughout, he does not mention the fact that Grew concealed Yoshida's and Shigemitsu's names in *Ten Years in Japan*. I was able to discover this, however, because my research led first from the Japanese translation to the English version and then on to the original diaries.

The second reason behind Grew's concealment of these names was Yoshida's involvement in peace initiatives from June 1942 to April 1945. I will not go into the details of this period here, as Dower describes them fully in chapter 7 of his book ("The Yoshida Anti-War Group and the Konoe Memorial, 1942–1945"), but Grew was probably aware of Yoshida's activity. Not surprisingly, Grew and the State Department therefore considered that it would be highly dangerous to reveal Yoshida Shigeru as a principal informant in *Ten Years in Japan* when it was published in May 1944.

Third, as demonstrated, *Ten Years in Japan* was designed to be more than a personal memoir—it also represented a public statement by the State Department in preparation for establishing peace with Japan. The names Grew replaced with a dash in the text were, as stated earlier, all those of moderates: Yoshida and others, whom the Japan crowd in the State Department hoped would become the political leaders of postwar Japan. In 1944, with Japan's defeat drawing closer, Grew saw the value of protecting them in order to realize these plans. After the end of the war, Yoshida Shigeru did indeed become prime minister and the champion of Japanese conservative politics; one can surmise that his friendship with Grew from 1932 onward was a major factor in his success in postwar politics.

Yoshida mentions Grew in his own memoirs, *Kaisō jūnen*, published in 1957.[5] In the context of the occupation's preservation of the emperor system, he says, "I believe that [Ambassador Grew's] opinions and proposals have been very influential. The Ambassador surely is a 'true friend of Japan.' "[6]

Defining the "Moderate Element"

It must be said that throughout *Ten Years in Japan*, Grew's tendency is to lavish excessive praise on the moderates, overstating their real political power. As a consequence, he repeatedly misjudged the Japanese political situation, one prime example being his failure to predict Japan's withdrawal from the League of Nations on March 27, 1933. Six weeks prior to that, on February 14, 1933, Grew wrote in his diary: "Of course I may be proved to be wrong, because one can never be sure of the strength of the military, but withdrawal from the League would first have to be approved by the cabinet, the Privy Council, and the Emperor, and with such outstanding men as Saito, Takahashi, and Makino fighting against it, as I know they are, the step will at least not be taken without counting the cost" (p. 60).

But Grew's prediction proved to be completely mistaken. Six days later, the cabinet of Saitō Makoto resolved to withdraw from the League, and Grew was forced to accept that the moderates had suffered a fundamental defeat. He even remarked in his diary, "The Genro [Saionji] himself is practically helpless before the military clique and will presumably be overridden right along" (p. 75).

The formation of Okada Keisuke's cabinet in July 1934, however, and the retention of Hirota Kōki as foreign minister were seen by Grew as signs that the moderates had recovered their strength. As he commented on July 6 of that year:

> Cabled the [State] Department an extensive estimate of the new cabinet given me by an eminent Japanese liberal. He regards it as an outstanding victory for the moderates, as indeed it is, because the chauvinists were pressing hard for an ultranationalist line-up. Saionji, Makino, and their group are clearly in the saddle.... My informant told me that the decision had come like a "thunder clap" and that if the United States had had the privilege of choosing the cabinet in its own interests, it could not have done better. (p. 139)

The "eminent Japanese liberal" in this extract was in fact Kabayama Aisuke, who, as seen from this example, presented Grew with a glowing picture of the moderates. History undeniably shows, however, that under the Okada cabinet, the power of the moderates in fact declined, while that of the military and the right wing steadily expanded. When, in the February following the cabinet's formation, the "emperor-as-organ" issue arose, Prime Minister Okada himself announced to the Diet, on March 4, 1943, that he opposed Dr. Minobe Tatsukichi's "organ theory."* Moreover, on two occasions in August and October, the cabinet made a declaration on *kokutai meichō* (clarification of the national polity), denouncing Minobe's ideas as a heresy "against our sacred national polity."

Similarly, although the Okada cabinet initially pursued Foreign Minister Hirota's policy of "peaceful cooperation" with China, Hirota gradually indicated his shift toward the military's line. In October 1935 he presented Chinese Ambassador Jiang Zuobin with his so-called three principles, which demanded an end to the anti-Japanese boycott, the tacit recognition of Manchukuo, and the prevention of communism as the preconditions for good relations between China and Japan. In so doing, he openly declared his submission to the will of the armed forces. One should also not forget that it was Okada and Hirota who oversaw the establishment of the Jidong regime by forcing through the North China partition policy.

In that case, who were the moderates for whom Grew had such high hopes? Were they really the genuine antimilitarist force that Grew describes? Within the U.S. State Department, opinion was divided on the issue. I have already indicated several times how Grew's Japan crowd (which included Ballantine, Borton, Dooman, Blakeslee, and Dickover) defined the moderates as liberals: a pacifist influence and the single stabilizing force within Japanese politics. The China crowd, however (Cordell Hull, James Byrnes, Dean Acheson, Stanley Hornbeck, and others), did not agree. Rather, they asserted that while it appeared on the surface that the moderates and the militarists held entirely conflicting opinions, their differences were in fact concerned simply with questions of strategy, and not with Japan's fundamental war aims.

This view was developed more fully by American liberals and left-wing scholars, for instance, Andrew Roth, author of *Dilemma in Japan*:

---

*Minobe's interpretation of the Meiji Constitution described the emperor and the official branches of government as "organs" of the state and sought to establish the primacy of the legislative branch. During the 1920s it furnished theoretical legitimization for political party rule.—Trans.

The term "moderate" has been used by a generation of British and American diplomats and journalists to describe the businessmen and other members of the Japanese oligarchy who have not been outspokenly and obviously anxious to precipitate war with the United States and Britain. It has been usual, however, to exaggerate the differences between the more cautious economic imperialists and the brash and adventurous military extremists.

This concept of the Japanese so-called liberals or "moderates" as virtual angels of peace battling valiantly against the militarist devils will probably go down in the history of American Far Eastern relations, along with the quaint notion of Japan's "moderate" navy, as one of the most important, persistent and dangerous bits of folklore in American thinking about Japan.[7]

Roth went on to comment that the "moderates" and the militarists were totally united in seeking Japanese hegemony in the Far East; it was simply that "[the moderates] disagreed on the need for using military force *until all other means had failed.*"

The New Dealer and Asia specialist Thomas A. Bisson, who had written numerous splendid articles in the journals of the Diplomatic Association and the Research Committee of the Institute of Pacific Affairs, also launched a severe attack on Grew's defense of the moderates, in a review of *Ten Years in Japan* that appeared in the *Nation* on June 3, 1944.

The court circle and the business leaders, making up the "moderates" with whom Ambassador Grew had his main contacts, do not provide the safest foundation on which to build post-war hopes. They are not pillars of democracy; if they are taken for such, the end will be disillusionment. They are much more closely allied to the militarists, whom we are asked to concentrate on eliminating, than to the people as a whole.

Further, literary critic Edmund Wilson, writing in the *New Yorker* on the same day, expressed his surprise at the way Grew simplistically divided all the people he had met during his long stay in Japan into just two groups: "liberals" or "militarists." For Wilson, the fact that Grew seemed to have had no contact with ordinary Japanese, never once mentioning industrial or agricultural life, or indeed young students influenced by Western ideas, only served to demonstrate the parochial nature of his diplomatic activity. This criticism reveals how Grew's excessive expectations of the moderates were a product of the extremely limited "court diplomacy" he pursued.

Diplomats from other countries were also critical. On December 4, 1944, the *Pacific Mail* carried an article by former Argentine Consul Ramon Lavalle condemning Japanese "liberalism." Lavalle had been transferred from Hong Kong to Tokyo following the Japanese invasion, but he resigned his post and left Japan in January 1943 in protest at Argentina's policy of neutrality. The main points of his critique of Grew are as follows.

> British and U.S. tories declare that the emperor must be kept in a beaten Japan as a safeguard against Communism. The problem in Japan is not and has never been Communism. It is feudalism.
>
> The dangers we must take into consideration are exactly the same dangers that, for 70 years, have led Japan along the war path. These dangers do not spring from the masses; they come exclusively from the ruling class.
>
> If we are to be on the side of forward-looking democracy as against backward-looking feudalism, if we are for a Pacific visualized by Vice-President Wallace instead of the Pacific suggested by Ex-Ambassador Grew, then Japan will cease to be a danger.
>
> ... British and American tories ... like to talk about the Japanese industrialists' traditional "opposition" to the armed forces and speak of certain Japanese "liberals" with whom we could cooperate in the rebuilding of Japan.
>
> It's time to expose this phony Japanese "liberalism."
>
> ... These are the propaganda pitfalls we must watch:
>
> — that the imperial institution may help us at the time of peace.
>
> — that the so-called liberals are our friends at heart and would help us to rebuild a new Japan.
>
> — that unless we proceed to keep the emperor and work with the liberals, Japan will go Communistic.
>
> All these points are untrue. The only hope in postwar Japan exists in the democratic re-education of the people, and the removal of all feudal institutions and past leaders.
>
> ... If we solve the distress of the masses and show them that the war against Japan was a war for their own liberation, the Japanese people would side with us.

In this way, Roth, Bisson, Wilson, and Lavalle all accurately identified the shortcomings of Grew's biased perception of Japan's moderate element. But Grew was unable to understand the true nature of the moderates or, perhaps more accurately, did not attempt to comprehend it, as his diplomatic approach mirrored theirs exactly.

Under the diary entry "Why America Must Stand Firm in the Far East" on December 27, 1934, Grew expressed his opposition to the growing opinion within the United States that they should withdraw from the Far East and renounce all U.S. interests there, to reduce the danger of getting involved in a war with Japan. "[We should] insist, and continue to insist, not aggressively yet not the less firmly, on the maintenance of our legitimate rights and interests in this part of the world and, so far as practicable, to support the normal development of those interests constructively and progressively" (p. 145).

Grew was related by marriage to American financial baron J. P. Morgan, and he had many contacts with other U.S. businessmen who were advancing into the markets of Japan and China. Given such personal links, Grew saw that the protection of American interests in East Asia was a vital part of his diplomatic mission; he sought to assuage the occasional frictions that arose between the United States and Japan, without sacrificing U.S. government principles, most notably the "open door" policy. Grew's approach was thus one of "aggressive yet not the less firm" "economic imperialism" or so-called "covert methods." (These phrases are used by Japanese historians to contrast with "military imperialism" or "overt methods.")

While it is undeniable that Grew felt a real and deep hostility toward Japanese nationalism and military extremism, the fact remains that, coming as he did from the Boston elite, he made no attempt to understand the life of ordinary Japanese workers, farmers, or the urban population. As Edmund Wilson pointed out, ordinary Japanese only receive a mention in *Ten Years in Japan* when Grew quotes as amusing asides some of the letters written in broken English to the U.S. Embassy.

Grew seems to have directed practically all his attentions toward the upper classes and the moderates, who, for their part, consistently exaggerated their own importance to Grew, asserting that their time would soon come. Grew noted, for instance, that Yoshida "always predicts the rainbow just around the corner."[8] Certainly, the ambassador had reservations about the optimistic predictions often made by Yoshida and others, and frequently expressed his doubts. In drawing an absolute distinction between militarists and moderates, however, and by entrusting the success or failure of his diplomacy solely with the latter, it is only natural that Grew was overindulgent toward them.

Yet even if one grants that these two groups were divided not over fundamental policy, but rather over lesser considerations of strategy and timing, then the scope for change within Japanese politics was remarkably narrow. As long as Grew continued to adhere to the "pendulum theory," which ignored this reality, his judgment of the Japanese political situation would inevitably swing like a pendulum itself.

As Waldo Heinrichs points out, Grew's weakness lay in his reporting of the diplomatic situation. He lacked "the broad intellectual curiosities, passion for detail ... [and] sophisticated techniques of the modern analyst" and "depended more on feel than on fact."[9]

6

THE FORMATION OF POSTWAR POLICY FOR JAPAN
Grew's Plan

Grew as Director of the Office of Far Eastern Affairs

AT THE BEGINNING of 1944, as Grew was coming under fierce criticism from the press following his Chicago speech, the State Department began serious discussion of postwar policy for Japan. On January 15, the Committee on Postwar Programs (PWC) was established, along with the Office of Far Eastern Affairs under the directorship of Stanley Hornbeck.

On May 1, among various other staff changes within the State Department, Grew was appointed to replace Hornbeck, thus gaining a position at the heart of the State Department where he would be responsible for the development of U.S. policy on Japan. Grew appointed Joseph Ballantine as his deputy, and Erle Dickover, formerly his first secretary at the embassy in Tokyo, as chief of the Japan section. As discussed in chapter 4, articles in *Amerasia* and other publications expressed concern over the new appointments. Indeed, it seems puzzling that although Grew had been ordered by Secretary of State Hull not to give any further public speeches following his Chicago address, he was nevertheless appointed to such an important post. This is not as strange as it may seem, however.

In spring 1944 the attention of U.S. leaders was still focused on Europe, and while the U.S. government was in the process of discussing postwar plans for Japan, it was tacitly understood that such policy would not be finalized until after the fall of Nazi Germany.

At the Cairo Conference held the previous November, however, the three leaders of the United States, Britain, and China had reaffirmed as their ultimate war aim Japan's unconditional surrender. The State Department therefore had to make an urgent decision on what an "unconditional surrender" would mean. Hull could not exclude Grew from this basic policy discussion, but if Grew's proposals were too lenient on Japan, they could always be rejected or revised. In this way, Grew was able to return to an active position within the State Department.

Therefore, to study Grew's activities after the Chicago speech, one must refer to the official State Department records, for instance by looking at Grew's correspondence during this period. Yet what kind of policy proposals was Grew formulating in the State Department, following his withdrawal from public life? On this point it is important to note a report that the PWC had been preparing since the end of 1943, entitled "Japan: Political Problems: Institution of the Emperor" (PWC–116 series), which was sent to Grew directly after he took over at the Office of Far Eastern Affairs. Drafted by H. Borton, E. Dickover, and E. Dooman, this document examined the position that the occupation forces should adopt toward the emperor after Japan's surrender. Shortly before its completion, on April 26, 1944, it was sent to Ballantine and Grew so that they could register their opinions.

I shall omit here the details of this document, which have already been discussed by scholars such as Takeda Kiyoko, Takemae Eiji, Hata Ikuhiko, and Iokibe Makoto. Principally, it involved a discussion of the three alternative policy options that lay open to the Allies after Japan's occupation, namely, (1) to suspend all powers exercised by the emperor, (2) to leave these powers intact, or (3) to suspend the majority of his powers. There were also proposals, if circumstances so demanded, to place the emperor and his immediate family in protective custody and to transfer the court away from Tokyo to a safer place, such as the Hayama imperial residence.

Ballantine was the first to voice his opinions on document PWC–116a, which formed part of the above series. Over many months of discussion, he became aware of the variety of opinions that existed within the PWC, and he began to express openly his support for the ideas of well-known British academic Geoffrey Gorer.[1] Ballantine quoted Gorer thus:

> [The Japanese] have as much knowledge, experience, and success in internal politics as any contemporary society. During the two centuries of isolation, a great deal of their energy and ingenuity was put into political experiment; this knowledge has been extended over the inter-

vening period. . . . It would seem reasonable to employ such abilities to produce an orderly Japanese society; for without an orderly Japan, a cooperative Japan can never emerge. . . . Because an Imperial Rescript can do more than many regiments, the power of the Imperial Rescript is a political device with which it would be shortsighted to do away.[2]

Ballantine then continued:

We have considered the lessons of history and we have been impressed by the number of instances in which the deposition of sovereigns has been followed by the establishment of dictatorship. . . . [Given the continuing resilience of Japanese adoration of the emperor] we feel that permanent change—whether reform or elimination of the institution—must for the most part be a development coming from the will of the Japanese themselves and not from force imposed from outside. . . .

We have presented . . . a flexible [procedure] capable of being modified in the light of [changing circumstances].

Thus Ballantine advocated a policy of caution, expressing his support for the preservation of the emperor system.

Grew then spoke, describing his own position in the form of a statement he had prepared in advance. Regarding the problem of handling the emperor system after occupation, Grew pressed for both the long-term and short-term perspectives to be considered. In the short-term view:

First of all, I wish to make clear that . . . I am referring to the institution of the Japanese throne and not to Hirohito himself. . . . Hirohito . . . signed the Imperial Rescript of December 8, 1941, declaring war and calling on the Japanese people to destroy the United States and Great Britain, and it is difficult to see how, in defeat, he could fail to accept responsibility. . . . We know, . . . based on what I still regard as reliable information, that Hirohito was always opposed to the war with the United States. . . . I was interested in reading the following item in the London *Times* of March 24:

"Sir Robert Craigie, British Ambassador in Japan until the outbreak of war . . . said that he was convinced that the Emperor of Japan, who acted on the advice of his counselors, was never in favor of the present war. During the time Sir Robert Craigie was in Tokyo the Emperor showed many indications of his personal desire to avoid plunging his country into war."

But this is all water over the dam now, and the point is not of great importance anyway. Facts alone count, and whatever Hirohito's wishes may have been, we cannot with any certainty foresee what the effect of the impact of the war and of defeat may be on the thinking and attitude of the so-called liberal elements in Japan, including the Emperor himself. Until we learn these things, some of our plans for occupation of Japan should only be tentative. If Hirohito has disappeared at the time of our occupation, it is not impossible that a regency may have been set up with the minor Crown Prince as Emperor. This point does not seem to me to be of prime importance. It is the *institution* of the Throne with which we shall have to deal. . . .

The Japanese people, through long-inculcated habits of regimentation and discipline, are somewhat like sheep in following leaders. Without intelligent leadership, they tend to disintegrate. . . .

Nevertheless, an early step after occupation will be to explore the possibilities of enlisting the cooperation of Japanese civil elements . . . the enlistment of such cooperation . . . will be a thousandfold more easily secured if [it] springs from the authority of the Throne. Indeed, without the endorsement of the Throne it seems highly doubtful if the desired cooperation and civil leadership can be secured at all. . . .

Now as to the long-term haul, the point has been advanced that . . . [the Emperor] will personify and perpetuate . . . the cult of military aggression.

. . . [But] the Emperor has quite simply been used as a convenient facade to justify and to consecrate that cult in the eyes of the people. . . .

. . . Parts of [my Chicago speech] were misreported and distorted in the press and aroused considerable editorial controversy . . . Admiral Yarnell, whose thinking and policy have been about as hardheaded as those of any of us . . . heard my speech and told me afterwards that he agreed with every word of it. . . . Any cult which has been *artificially* created, as has the Shinto cult, can always be molded to suit new conditions, . . . The Japanese are past masters at executing the maneuvre [*sic*] of right-about-face.[3]

Grew thus presented a long discussion of the relationship between the emperor and the Japanese people. As a short-term objective, he situated the emperor as the key figure in Japanese cooperation with the future occupation forces. In the long term, Grew predicted, concluding here as in the Chicago speech with the words of Sir George Sansom, that Japan would develop a "more modern and democratic type of constitutional monarchy." This, then, formed the essence of Grew's view of the emperor, a position he maintained consistently thereafter.

The Emperor Institution—Three Currents of Opinion

The upper echelons of the State Department, however, were puzzled by Ballantine and Grew's plans to preserve and use the emperor; some, for instance, Assistant Undersecretary of State Long even expressed open indignation. Hornbeck also sought to call Secretary of State Hull's attention to the range of differing opinions on the imperial institution in a memorandum he sent three days later, on April 29, entitled "Japanese Emperor Institution: American Policy Regarding It: 'Expert Opinions': Three Schools of Thought."

In this document, Hornbeck said that within the United States and throughout the world, there existed the following three basic views on the emperor system.

1. To abolish the emperor system.
2. To preserve and use it.
3. To preserve it, but suspend the emperor's power and functions.

But which of these should be seen as the dominant view? On this, Hornbeck stated, "the number who propose that the occupying authorities should attempt to destroy the institution appear to be few in number. Those who advocate protecting and using the institution appear to be in the majority." The real problem lay not between the first and third viewpoints above, but rather between the second and third. To summarize Hornbeck's assessment: while the majority of opinion seemed to favor preservation of the emperor system, it was divided over whether to utilize or to suspend the emperor's powers.

The tone of the debate within the United States on the emperor issue at that time was dominated, however, by the conflict between the first and second schools of thought. According to Hornbeck's memorandum, those wishing to see the emperor system maintained and used included Geoffrey Gorer, Sir Robert Craigie, John Morris, Hugh Byas, and Sir George Sansom. These men were prominent diplomats, academics, and journalists, and interestingly, all were British. According to Hornbeck's analysis, within the United States it was the Japan crowd, headed by Joseph Grew, that supported their ideas.

Against this, Hornbeck said that those advocating abolition or opposing utilization of the emperor system were "not as impressive as are those mentioned above, but . . . they are not lacking in numbers and should not be ignored or disregarded." He cited the following names: Willis Church Lamott (who spent nineteen years in Japan, six of them as lecturer at Meiji University, Tokyo); Kate L. Mitchell (an editor of *Amerasia* and author of "The Industrialization of Japan" and "India Without Fable"); Lawrence K. Rosinger (writer of "People—Not Emperor—Hold the Key to Peaceful Japan," *Foreign Policy Bulletin*, January 7, 1944); Gordon Holdcroft (theologian, author of "The Menace of Japanese Shintoism," *Sunday School Times*, January 29, 1944); John B. Powell (for many years editor of the *China Weekly Review*, Shanghai, with personal experience of imprisonment and ill-treatment at the hands of the Japanese); Ramon Lavalle (former chargé d'affaires at the Argentine Embassy in Tokyo and author of "Have We Any Friends in Japan?" *Free World*, April 1944); and Thomas A. Bisson (noted Asia scholar, writer of "The Price of Peace for Japan," *Pacific Affairs*, March 1944).

I will not attempt here to present each of these people's views individually, but, briefly stated, it was argued that the policy of preserving and utilizing the emperor would ultimately leave room for a revival of militarism through an emperor system designed for political manipulation. It would also serve to impede the development of democracy in Japan.

By this time, the anti-emperor campaign in China was also becoming increasingly influential, and the main points of this argument even reached the heads of the State Department. Hornbeck focused in particular on "The Mikado Must Go," written by Dr. Sun Fo in collaboration with Dr. Liu and others, which I mentioned in chapter 3. Hornbeck was convinced that it was impossible to discuss policy on Japan without taking the views of the Chinese side into account, although he himself knew little about Japan. He therefore sought to weaken the influence of the Japan crowd by impressing upon Hull the deeply rooted opposition existing within the United States and elsewhere to the idea of making use of the emperor system. In his memorandum, Hornbeck states that "Mr. Grew is unquestionably an expert; what he thinks and what he says commands our respect and carries weight," but it would be unwise to accept this at face value.

Three days after presenting this document, Hornbeck was replaced by Grew as director of the Office of Far Eastern Affairs. After this, in what direction did Grew focus his actions?

The "Queen Bee" Speech—Grew Consolidates His Position

By the summer of 1944, on June 15, U.S. forces had landed on Saipan and within three weeks the Japanese garrison of thirty thousand men had perished in a fight to the death. June 19 saw the start of the sea battle off the Marianas Islands, the largest of the Pacific War, which ended in Japan's crushing defeat and the loss of three aircraft carriers and 430 planes. The battle for Leyte began on October 24; the following day, the Japanese Navy's *kamikaze* special attack force launched the first of its suicide missions against U.S. warships. Grew's fears of a "last-ditch," "do-or-die" campaign by the Japanese Army thus seemed to have been realized.

In the course of these events, on November 21, Secretary of State Hull resigned his post due to illness and was succeeded by his deputy, Edward Stettinius. The Hull era, which had lasted for twelve years, had finally ended. Unlike Hull, Stettinius, who had been president of U.S. Steel, had little diplomatic experience or knowledge of Japan, and for this reason he chose Grew to be his undersecretary. Grew's position within the State Department was thus further elevated.

The appointment of Grew, the Japan crowd's leading figure, ran into trouble, however, when it came before the U.S. Senate for approval. Senator Joseph Guffey cast doubts upon Grew's suitability, reading out for the Senate record an editorial from the *Philadelphia Record* that denounced Grew for "doing business with Hirohito." Guffey was supported by a number of liberal senators, and Grew's nomination was returned to the Foreign Relations Committee.

Grew was then called to a committee hearing on December 12, where he gave his famous "queen bee" speech to the assembled senators. The speech included the following passages: "Japan has never lost a war in modern times. We therefore have no yardstick to measure the eventual impact on the Japanese mind of the cataclysm of destruction and defeat. Before we allow any Japanese authority to emerge in the post-surrender period, we can, and I hope we will, require it to demonstrate that it will be cooperative, stable, and trustworthy."[4]

Grew then went on to comment on the function of the imperial institution. "To understand the position of the Emperor . . . it might be useful to draw a homely parallel. As you know, the queen bee in a hive is surrounded by the attentions of the hive, which treats her with veneration and ministers in every way to her comfort. . . . if one were to remove the queen from the swarm, the hive would disintegrate."

With this forthright statement, Grew was able to quell the opposition and was duly approved by the committee, taking up his post on December 19.

Yet Grew had not been inactive in the period leading up to his official promotion; while on a fact-finding tour of Hawaii, he visited Admiral Chester Nimitz at Pearl Harbor in mid-November, gathering details of the U.S. Navy's battle plans and propaganda tactics, which probably included top secret information on the U.S. strategy for Iwo Jima and Okinawa. Grew was certainly horrified at the prospect of a gruesome mopping-up operation costing the lives of countless American soldiers. A report on Grew's visit to Hawaii describes his comments to Nimitz: "Mr. Grew believes that no direct action should be taken at the present time against the Emperor, such as a special bombing mission to hit the palace, . . . It is just possible that the Emperor will be the only one who can force the Generals on the mainland to give up, . . . As we cannot tell what the situation will be until we are in Japan, it would be better to leave the final decision on the Institution of the Emperor until later."[5]

Nimitz apparently agreed with Grew on this, and on his return to Washington Grew reported on his Hawaii trip and his meeting with the admiral to the 169th meeting of the Inter-Divisional Area Committee on the Far East (IDACFE), stressing the confidential nature of this information. Furthermore, several days later, he was also pleased to describe to Stettinius how Nimitz had shared his own views.

Amidst this, in an attempt to exclude the influence of the ailing President Roosevelt, Secretary of War Stimson had revived the so-called Committee of the Three (made up of the heads of the State, War, and Navy departments), effectively forming a "war cabinet" of the leaders of the government and armed forces.[6] Thus Navy Secretary James Forrestal and Secretary of State Stettinius joined Stimson on the Committee of the Three. From around the time of the Yalta conference in February 1945, however, Grew, as undersecretary, regularly attended meetings in Stettinius's place, as the secretary himself was then rarely present in the State Department, spending most of his time abroad at various international conferences. From mid-December 1944 until April 1945, Grew therefore acted as de facto secretary of state.

A State–War–Navy Coordinating Committee (SWNCC) was set up on December 29, 1944, under the Committee of the Three on the assistant undersecretary level, thus creating one of the central pillars in the structure of policy making on postwar Germany and Japan. On January 5, 1945, the State–War–Navy Coordinating Subcommittee for the Far East (SFE) was established under SWNCC, with Eugene Dooman, Grew's right-hand man, as chairman.

The SFE's main task was to draft the U.S. occupation policy for Japan. Once again, this working committee included Blakeslee and Borton, the Japan specialists from the State Department. During the period between Yalta and Potsdam, therefore, a time of crucial significance in the formation of policy on Japan, the Japan crowd had managed to secure an unprecedented influence in the State Department and were therefore deeply involved in shaping that policy.

In a letter to former Secretary of State Hull on December 4, 1944, Grew expressed his regret at Hull's resignation and added that "It is doubly reassuring to know that he (Ed Stettinius) and the rest of us can count on your vision and wise advice in the years ahead."[7] No doubt Grew was sincere in saying this, but on the other hand, Hull's departure also represented a release from the pressure of having to work under him, as Grew had for the past ten years. In addition, come 1945, Stettinius's frequent absences from the State Department, as he traveled to the Yalta Conference and discussions on the establishment of the United Nations, meant that Grew served as acting secretary from April 24 until the appointment of the new secretary of state, James Byrnes, on July 3.

Here, at the culmination of his forty years as a diplomat, came the greatest opportunity of his career. From late May 1945 until the middle of June, Grew launched himself into furious activity concerning the Potsdam Declaration, which was to decide the fate of postwar Japan.

7

THE POTSDAM DECLARATION
Grew's Struggle

Preparing for Victory—Grew Takes Urgent Action

JAPAN'S position was becoming increasingly hopeless by 1945. On February 19, the U.S. task force had begun its assault on Iwo Jima, where in March twenty-three thousand Japanese were killed. The invasion of the main island of Okinawa followed on April 1. Observing the progress of the war, Grew wrote a letter to Randall Gould, editor of *The Shanghai Evening Post and Mercury*:

> I personally don't see how Hirohito can very well remain as I should think he would have to take the responsibility of defeat, especially in a country [like Japan] where personal responsibility is an important factor in any situation.... If [the emperor institution] is to be a liability, I should think it would have to go....
> The really important point in all this, however, seems to me to be just this: ... that [there] will be no guarantee whatsoever that the millions of Japanese soldiers throughout East Asia will stop fighting, and the mopping up of those tremendous areas would of course be a very long and costly process. If at that time however the Emperor could be led to issue an Imperial Rescript, ... that is the one thing that might do the trick and it might save the lives of tens of thousands of our own fighting men. That of course is a pure gamble, but it is a gamble worth considering, and I think we would make a great mistake to ... [determine] in advance to eliminate the Emperor merely through prejudice....
> Of course, it would be unwise and unhelpful to publish all this just now....
> ... I have discussed this problem thoroughly with Admiral King and Admiral Nimitz, both of whom have expressed to me their complete concurrence in my views...." (April 14, 1945)

Three weeks after this letter, on May 7, 1945, the German Army declared its unconditional surrender. The next day, War Secretary Stimson informed Grew about the secret "Yalta agreement" and the atomic bomb project. As Stimson noted in his diary: "After the normal business was over . . . I shooed out everybody except Forrestal and Grew and told them of the Interim Committee for S–1 [the atomic bomb] that I am forming."[1]

As is now well known, at Yalta Stalin had promised the U.S. and British leaders that the Soviet Union would join the war against Japan three months after the German defeat. If this promise was upheld, Soviet influence over postwar Japan would increase considerably. Furthermore, by the end of May, Tokyo had already suffered three intensive air raids, in which even part of the Imperial Palace had burned down. Use of the atomic bomb on the capital would mean the death of those moderates who were expected to play a central role in any future peace negotiations, thus making it even more difficult to obtain Japan's unconditional surrender at an early date. Grew felt there was not a moment to lose, and he spent the last weeks of May and the first half of June attempting to secure a rapid end to the war.

Grew's actions during this period require no more than a brief outline here, as they have been described in detail by various authors, including Takeda Kiyoko (in *Tennokan no sokoku*), Iokibe Makoto (*Beikoku no nihon senryo seisaku*, vol. 2), Arai Shinichi (*Genbaku toka e no michi*), and Yamagiwa Akira (*Potsudamu sengen no soan ni tsuite*). What I would like to focus on, however, is the question of who drafted paragraph 12 of the Potsdam Declaration, the section concerning the emperor. This is an issue that has also recently been examined by Yamagiwa.

Persuading the President—and the Japanese

On May 26 Grew called in Eugene Dooman and urgently asked him to draw up a statement on Japan for inclusion in a speech by President Truman scheduled for May 31. Dooman spent the weekend of May 26 and 27 working on his draft, which he handed to Grew on the morning of May 28. Grew gave his immediate approval and took the speech to the State Department Secretary's Committee meeting that morning to seek further opinion.

The reaction from those attending the meeting was much stronger than Grew had anticipated, the opposition being led by two deputies, Dean Acheson and Archibald MacLeish. Acheson later wrote: "I was soon engaged in a sharp difference of opinion with Joe Grew regarding the future of the Emperor of Japan. Grew argued for his retention as the main stabilizing factor in Japan; I argued that he should be removed because he was a weak leader who had yielded to the military demand for war and who could not be relied upon."[2]

MacLeish also criticized Grew for advocating any mitigation of the unconditional surrender terms. Thus Grew's policy had immediately met with fierce opposition from some of his closest colleagues within the State Department. Undaunted, he went on to a meeting later that same morning with Truman, "on my own initiative as acting secretary of state," accompanied by the president's special counsel, Judge Samuel Rosenman. Here, Grew implored the president:

> In waging our war against Japan. . . nothing must be sacrificed. . . to the attainment and maintenance of our main objective, namely to render it impossible for Japan again to threaten world peace. . . . it should be our aim to accomplish our purpose with the least possible loss of American lives. We should, therefore, give most careful consideration to any step which . . . might render it easier for the Japanese to surrender unconditionally now. . . . The greatest obstacle to unconditional surrender by the Japanese is their belief that this would entail the destruction or permanent removal of the Emperor and the institution of the Throne. If some indication can now be given the Japanese that they themselves. . . will be permitted to determine their own future political structure, they will be afforded a method of saving face without which surrender will be highly unlikely. It is believed that such a statement would have maximum effect if issued immediately following the great devastation of Tokyo which occurred two days ago. The psychological impact of such a statement at this particular moment would be very great. . . . Once the military extremists have been discredited through defeat the Emperor, purely a symbol, can and possibly will be used by new leaders who will be expected to emerge once the Japanese people are convinced that their military leaders have let them down. The institution of the Throne can, therefore, become a cornerstone for building a peaceful future for the country.[3]

Having said this, Grew submitted Dooman's draft statement on Japan to Truman to be included in his May 31 speech.

At the time, Grew was four years older than the president, who was sixty. Truman had been promoted from vice-president just six weeks before, following Roosevelt's untimely death on April 12. Grew, on the other hand, was a veteran career diplomat of forty years' standing, and he was widely considered to have the deepest understanding of the Japanese mind. Truman therefore listened intently to what Grew had to say: "The President said that he was interested in what I said because his own thoughts had been following the same line. He thereupon asked me to arrange for a meeting to discuss this question in the first instance with the Secretaries of the War and Navy, General Marshall and Admiral King, and after we had exchanged views he would like to have the same group come to the White House for a conference with him."[4]

Grew immediately contacted Stimson and arranged a meeting for eleven o'clock the following morning in Stimson's office at the Pentagon. Grew's proposal, however, was rejected at that meeting "for certain military reasons," which in fact concerned the atomic bomb. Stimson, who was responsible for the bomb project, fully accepted Grew's views on the utility of the emperor system, but he thought that it would be premature for the president to make a statement at that stage. Grew was naturally disappointed by this decision.

In the meantime, a tremendous land battle had developed on Okinawa, and on June 16 Grew paid a second visit to the White House, recommending that Truman make a statement on Japan to coincide with the fall of the island. The president said that he would consider it a second time if Grew prepared a draft, which Grew duly handed to Rosenman at the White House that same evening. This top-secret memorandum is fairly long, but the main point is as follows.

> The campaign in Okinawa is likely to be finished in the not distant future and I am wondering whether, with the announcement of its fall, a suitable opportunity would not be present for us to make some sort of public statement again calling upon the Japanese to surrender. As we are bearing the brunt of the war in the Pacific, I am not convinced that there is any good reason to defer such action until the meeting of the Big Three, and in my opinion the sooner we can get the Japanese thinking about final surrender the better it will be and the more lives of Americans may ultimately be saved.
>
> As I have said to the President and to you, we must at every step make it abundantly clear that we propose to cut out the cancer of militarism in Japan once and for all. Having stated our position in that

respect . . . [we must] give the Japanese a clearer idea of what we mean
by unconditional surrender.

With this, Grew argued that it was necessary to impress two points
upon the Japanese. First, that once the Allies had rendered Japan incapable of rebuilding a military machine, and the Japanese had convinced them of their commitment to fulfill Japan's international
obligations and cooperate toward building world peace and security,
decisions on the nature of the country's future political structure would
be left in the hands of the Japanese people themselves. Second, when
these matters had been settled, Japan should be guaranteed the opportunity to construct a suitable peacetime economy to protect its people
from starvation, and should be allowed gradually to regain its place in
the family of nations.

A meeting between Truman and the Joint Chiefs of Staff was scheduled for the afternoon of June 18, and Grew was very much hoping
that they would agree to include his draft in the presidential statement.
For Grew, it was vital that such a statement be made promptly, either
with the imminent fall of Okinawa or, at the very least, before the U.S.
invasion of the Japanese mainland. He therefore visited Truman again
on the morning of June 18, to find out what the president thought of his
proposal. But Truman's response was not positive, as Grew noted in a
memorandum: "The President said that he had carefully considered yes-
terday the draft statements which I had given to Judge Rosenman. . . .
While he liked the idea he had decided to hold this up until it could be
discussed at the Big Three meeting." Grew's hopes had once again
been dashed. More important, he now appeared to have lost almost all
influence over the president's decisions.

That afternoon, Truman held his planned meeting with the heads of
the armed forces, who included Admiral William Leahy, General
George C. Marshall, Admiral Ernest J. King and I. C. Eaker from the
Joint Chiefs of Staff, Navy Secretary Forrestal, War Secretary Stimson, and Stimson's assistant secretary, McCloy. In retrospect, this
meeting is of crucial significance, for it delineates the complete picture
of the U.S. strategy for the defeat of Japan.

In brief, the meeting discussed the following crucial points: (1) the
planned invasion of Kyushu, the southernmost of Japan's four main
islands, scheduled for November 1 (code-named "Operation Olym-
pic"); (2) Soviet participation in the war with Japan; (3) the use of the

atomic bomb; and (4) a statement on whether or not to give the Japanese an indication that the emperor system would be retained. Items 3 and 4 were not entered in the official records of the meeting, but, judging from McCloy's memoirs and other sources, it is certain that U.S. government and military leaders had begun to envisage these four factors as the key to achieving Japan's ultimate defeat.

Grew's idea of inducing an early Japanese surrender by promising the preservation of the emperor thus had to be revised with regard to the broader military strategy, in particular the plan to use the atom bomb. The U.S. government's strategy for the end of the war was now out of Grew's hands and firmly in the grasp of Stimson in the War Department. But in what direction would Stimson's plans lead Japan? After the war, Stimson wrote an article, "The decision to use the Atomic Bomb," in *Harper's Magazine* (February 1947), in which he said:

> We held two cards to assist us in such an effort. One was the traditional veneration in which the Japanese Emperor was held by his subjects and the power which was thus vested in him over his loyal troops. . . . The second card was the use of the atomic bomb in the manner best calculated to persuade that Emperor and the counselors about him to submit to our demand for what was essentially unconditional surrender, placing his immense power over his people and his troops subject to our orders.

Drafting the Potsdam Declaration

Stimson wrote two important documents that were to form the original draft of the Potsdam Declaration. These were the "Memorandum for the President—Proposed Program for Japan" and the accompanying draft for a "Proclamation by the Heads of State U.S.–UK–[USSR]–China," which Stimson presented to Truman on July 2, 1945.[5] It is not possible to deal with the entire contents here, but paragraph 5 of the memorandum and paragraph 12 of the draft proclamation are especially pertinent to the present investigation. Let us first look at the memorandum.

> The withdrawal as soon as the above objectives of the Allies are accomplished, and as soon as there has been established a peacefully inclined government, of a character representative of the masses of

Japanese people. I personally think that if in saying this we should add that we do not exclude a constitutional monarchy under her present dynasty, it would substantially add to the chances of acceptance.

This was the first time Stimson had used the phrase "we do not exclude a constitutional monarchy under her present dynasty." On the basis of this memorandum, the committee drafting a statement on Japan, which included McCloy (War Department) and Dooman and Ballantine (State Department), produced a draft of the Potsdam Declaration, which contained a more polished version of Stimson's words:

> (12) The occupying forces of the Allies shall be withdrawn from Japan as soon as our objectives are accomplished and there has been established beyond doubt a peacefully inclined, responsible government of a character representative of the Japanese people. This may include a constitutional monarchy under the present dynasty if it be shown to the complete satisfaction of the world that such a government will never again aspire to aggression.[6]

Thus we see that it was in fact Stimson, not Grew, who wrote the first draft of the Potsdam Declaration. Yet many authors have implied that it was written by Grew, notably Iokibe Makoto in *Beikoku no Nihon senryo seisaku* (vol. 2); John K. Emmerson (*The Japanese Thread: A Life in the U.S. Foreign Service* [New York, Holt, Rinehart and Winston, 1978]); Kobori Keiichirō ("Saisho Suzuki Kantaro," *Bungei Shunju*, 1982); and Hirakawa Sukehiro (*Heiwa no umi to takai no umi* [Shincho Sha, 1983]).

As Yamagiwa Akira convincingly demonstrates, however, this is clearly mistaken;[7] through my own research, I have been able to confirm his theory that it was Stimson who was responsible for the draft. This may at first appear to be a trivial matter, but in my view it relates to the image one creates of Grew, and that is why I venture to discuss it here.

In any case, many previous works have traced in detail how the draft declaration went on to be revised further at the Potsdam Conference. I would therefore like to examine briefly Grew's actions leading up to Potsdam.

On July 3 James Byrnes, a member of the China crowd, replaced Stettinius as secretary of state. Grew saw that his time as undersecretary was now limited. At a State Department Secretary's meeting on July 7 that he himself chaired, Grew sought opinions on the Stimson memorandum. As usual, both MacLeish and Acheson called for the deletion of all phrases that suggested the preservation of the emperor system.

In response, Grew expressed "his belief that it is absolutely impossible to abolish the institution [of the emperor]. . . . He emphasized again that such a statement could in no way be interpreted to be a modification of the terms of unconditional surrender."[8] Because of Acheson's request that the meeting leave no record that could give the impression of having approved the draft statement, however, Grew was not only unable to persuade the secretary's meeting to agree with him, but was also obliged to record the results of the meeting himself.

Shortly before his departure for Potsdam, the newly appointed Byrnes rang former Secretary of State Hull to ask his opinion. Hull replied that the emperor stipulation seemed "too much like appeasement." But Hull did not consider a reply by telephone to be sufficient, and on July 16 he sent the following secret telegram via Grew to Byrnes, who was already in Potsdam.

> The proponents [of article 12] believe that this step might shorten the war and save allied lives. . . . The other side is that no person knows how the proposal would work out. The militarists would try hard to interfere. Also should it fail the Japs would be encouraged while terrible political repercussions would follow in the U.S.. Would it be well first to await the climax of allied bombing and Russia's entry into the war? Hull.

Having already left the State Department, Hull doubtless had little alternative but to send the telegram through Grew. This does seem rather harsh, however, considering that Grew had repeatedly argued for a statement on Japan to be made before the Soviet Union's entry into the war or the use of the atomic bomb. Grew not only fundamentally disagreed with Hull's telegram, but would hardly ever use the word "Jap" to refer to the Japanese.

This episode added to Grew's desperation. In a final effort to have his own views incorporated in the Potsdam Declaration, Grew had passed a memo to Byrnes just before he departed for the conference, only managing to slip the note into the secretary of state's pocket as he was on his way to the airport.

With Stimson already in Europe, Grew then sought out the undersecretary at the War Department, John McCloy, and asked him to convey his concerns over this issue to the war secretary. The situation indicated that much had been decided already, and therefore, during this period, "Grew displayed a remarkable enthusiasm, verging on obstinacy,"[9] in a last attempt to influence the decision makers. He was in fact secretly considering resigning as undersecretary of state at the end of the war and withdrawing from diplomatic life altogether.

One day before the start of the Potsdam Conference (July 17–August 2, 1945), a secret telegram reached Stimson reporting the success of the atomic bomb test, upon which Truman swiftly adopted a tough stance against Stalin. (The details of this have been vividly described by Arai Shinichi in his book *Genbaku toka e no michi*). Paragraph 12, the issue in question, was altered as follows at the summit meeting.

> (12) The occupying forces of the Allies shall be withdrawn from Japan as soon as these objectives [of the occupation] have been accomplished and there has been established in accordance with the freely expressed will of the Japanese people a peacefully inclined and responsible government.

The phrase "this may include a constitutional monarchy under the present dynasty," which had appeared in the draft declaration, was deleted due to Byrnes's and the military's intractable opposition. Hull's telegram had no doubt also played a part.

Japan's Surrender and Grew's Resignation

On July 26 the Potsdam Proclamation was officially declared. The Japanese government responded on the 28th with Prime Minister Suzuki Kantarō's declaration of a policy of *mokusatsu* [lit., to kill with silence]. This was apparently intended to restrain the hard-line military, who were calling for a final battle on the mainland, but it clearly left the Japanese powerless to control the timing of the end of the war.

Truman used the Japanese response as an excuse to drop the atom bomb, causing the tragedy of Hiroshima on August 6 and Nagasaki on August 9, the day after the Soviet Union had joined the war against Japan. After the war, Grew himself noted that "The action of Prime Minister Suzuki in rejecting the Potsdam ultimatum by announcing on July 28, 1945, that it was 'unworthy of public notice' was most unfortunate."[10]

On August 10, 1945, the Japanese government finally decided after intense debate to accept the Potsdam Declaration on the condition that the "Sacred National Polity" be preserved: "with the understanding that the said declaration does not comprise any demand which prejudices the prerogatives of His Majesty as a Sovereign Ruler." This no doubt made an impression on Stimson, for the Japanese response was exactly as Grew, and indeed he himself, had expected. On the same day, U.S. leaders met at the White House, and Stimson insisted that they should reply according to the Japanese demands. He noted in his diary for August 10, 1945: "something like this use of the Emperor must be made in order to save us from a score of bloody Iwo Jimas and Okinawas. . . . He was the only source of authority in Japan under the Japanese theory of the State."

Truman and Byrnes were opposed, however, to making any clear commitment to the Japanese government, fearing a violent reaction from the American people should they sanction preservation of the emperor system. According to a Gallup poll in the summer of 1945, more than 70 percent of Americans favored severe punishment of the Japanese emperor, either by execution or by life imprisonment. In other countries, such as Australia, New Zealand, and China, there were also increasing calls for the emperor to be treated as a war criminal.

Given these circumstances, the debate at the White House continued for several hours. Eventually a compromise was proposed by Navy Secretary Forrestal, and the White House finally settled for a reply in line with the existing wording of the Potsdam Declaration, thus avoiding as far as possible any public outcry.

It fell to Byrnes to write this reply, which included the passage "From the moment of surrender the authority of the Emperor and the Japanese Government to rule the state shall be subject to the Supreme Commander of the Allied powers." These words did not directly answer the demands of the Japanese government for guarantees on the emperor's position, but Byrnes's reply did state that "The ultimate form of government of Japan shall, in accordance with the Potsdam Declaration, be established by the freely expressed will of the Japanese people," thus hinting that even after occupation, the emperor system could remain if the Japanese people so wished.

On August 11 the Byrnes reply was sent by the United States via the Swiss in the joint names of the United States, Britain, China, and the Soviet Union. Upon receiving it, the Japanese held an Imperial Conference (*gozenkaigi*) on August 14, where they finally decided to accept the Potsdam Proclamation. At noon the following day, the emperor's radio broadcast told the Japanese people of their country's defeat.

Now that he had seen the final outcome of the war, Grew handed notice of his resignation as undersecretary of state to President Truman on August 15, 1945. On September 2, reflecting on his retirement in a letter to his daughter Elsie, Grew said, "I was immensely happy to get out, feeling that my job was really done in having started the ball rolling for the Potsdam Proclamation . . . and in having persuaded the Administration to keep the Emperor."

Further, on October 15 Grew sent a letter to his friend, Colonel Stanley Washburn, a journalist with expert knowledge of Japan who shared Grew's pro-emperor stance. In his youth, Washburn had spent a year and a half as a war correspondent attached to the Japanese Army during the Russo-Japanese War, and in the Second World War he had served as an army intelligence officer. Grew's letter to him reads in part:

> I am immensely gratified by the [letter] published in this evening's *Washington Star* in which you give me credit for having advocated the right policy toward Japan. In the face of the many attacks on me from all over the country, in books, articles and broadcasts, your public endorsement of my attitude is very helpful indeed and I thank you for it. . . .
>
> You will be interested in an excerpt from a personal letter received today from Mr. Stimson: "The position which you and I took almost alone in regard to the treatment of the Emperor of Japan and the entire Japanese problem is certainly now proving of enormous value. I agree with you that it has saved many thousands of American fighting men."

Secretary of State Byrnes would subsequently push through personnel changes within the State Department that would effectively sweep away the Japan crowd. Nevertheless, after the occupation of Japan under MacArthur had begun, Grew continued to involve himself in the issue of the emperor.

8

GREW AND MACARTHUR

Listing the Japan Experts—Support for Dooman

WITH JAPAN'S surrender in August 1945, Grew felt that his diplomatic career of forty-one years had come to an end. Byrnes had suggested that he should go to Japan as MacArthur's political adviser, but Grew declined. In letters to various friends, including one to his son Harry on August 21, 1945, he gave the following reasons for his decision.

First, MacArthur had made an excellent start on the occupation of Japan, and being "something of a prima donna," he was not the type of person who would listen readily to other people's opinions. Second, having lived in Japan for over ten years and made many friends there, Grew was not keen to return in the new guise of conqueror. Moreover, Grew was also having gallstone trouble and was in no fit state to travel to Japan.

Nevertheless, Grew considered that if a military government was to be established in Tokyo, then before the end of the war, a political advisory section would have to be formed within the military administration to work in close cooperation with the theater commanders. This idea is contained in the following portions of a secret memorandum sent to Byrnes on August 7, 1945.

> The end of the Pacific War might come suddenly and unexpectedly; . . . in the interests of establishing successful teamwork between the political adviser and the theatre commander or commanders there should be developed mutual understanding and confidence well in advance of operations within Japan.
>
> It is understood that the assignment of Mr. Murphy as Political Adviser on German Affairs to General Eisenhower was not made as a

result of specific requests either by the Department or by the Army; it was the result of the gradual development of a situation extending from the landing in North Africa to the fall of Berlin, which rendered desirable the presence of a political adviser with the armed forces. . . .

It is believed that the political adviser in the Pacific area should be an officer fully conversant with Japanese affairs and that he be supported by a staff of political, economic and financial officers who are not only specialists in their fields but also conversant with Japanese matters.

Grew followed this with his list of seventeen possible candidates for the position of political adviser. These men, who all had experience in the diplomatic service, included Joseph Ballantine, Eugene Dooman, Erle Dickover, Cabot Coville, Max Bishop, and John Emmerson. Of these, Ballantine, Dooman, and Dickover were the three men Grew recommended most strongly.

Grew also suggested the names of several private businessmen and bankers with long experience of Japan, whom he regarded as sufficiently qualified to be economic or financial advisers. These were: Clarence E. Meyer (Standard Vacuum Oil Company); Kirk Fowler (International General Electric Company); Robert F. Moss (formerly with Oriental Steel Products Company); John F. Curtis (National City Bank of New York); Daniel Waugh (National City Bank of New York); John T. S. Reed (National City Bank of New York); and F. M. Gibson (Bethlehem Steel Corporation).

Last, Willis Lamott, Joe Mickle, and Russell L. Durgin were named as specialists who would be able to assist the military government in educational and cultural matters. This extremely detailed list of recommendations therefore represents an invaluable record of those men who were seen by Grew to be the Japan specialists of the day.

When MacArthur was appointed Supreme Commander of Allied Powers on August 15, 1945, however, Byrnes still had not decided who was to be his political adviser. Neverthless, following the wide-ranging personnel changes within the State Department that accompanied the Japanese defeat, Grew and the rest of the Japan crowd were destined to fade into the background. On August 22, Byrnes gave Grew's post as undersecretary of state to the radical reformer Dean Acheson, and this was followed by Ballantine's replacement with John Vincent, a pro-China diplomat, as head of the Office of Far Eastern

Affairs. Eugene Dooman, Grew's right-hand man, also retired, and thus, with the end of the war, the influence of the Japan crowd had been all but totally removed.

Grew, who was contemplating Japan's unconditional surrender as an opportunity to withdraw from diplomatic life, immediately sent a telegram to Dean Acheson in Ottawa, Canada, to congratulate him on his new appointment. But the choice of George Atcheson, Jr., of the China crowd as MacArthur's political adviser seems to have surprised Grew. As he stated in his secret memo to Byrnes of August 7, Grew believed that the success or failure of the Japanese occupation would depend entirely on whether or not the commander in Japan could obtain a talented political adviser. Any mishandling of the emperor issue by MacArthur not only would give rise to needless chaos, but might also prolong the occupation itself.

Grew therefore made up his mind to write directly to MacArthur recommending Dooman's services. In this letter, dated August 22, Grew wrote the following:

> The purpose of this letter is to say to you unofficially, because I have recently retired from public office after forty-one years of service, that if you should wish to have at hand during your occupation of Japan a man who knows and understands the Japanese probably better then any living American, I would unhesitatingly recommend Eugene H. Dooman. Dooman was Counselor of our Embassy during several years prior to Pearl Harbor; he was born in Japan, has spent the greater part of his foreign service in Japan and he speaks and reads Japanese thoroughly and fluently. During those momentous years before war broke out he was my right-hand man and I sought his mature and sound advice on all occasions. . . .
>
> . . . [Unlike] armchair statesmen who have never lived in Japan and who know little of Japanese life and psychology, [Dooman has an in-depth knowledge of Japanese affairs]. We have both known that the Emperor was the only man who could stop the war because the Japanese armies in the field would never have listened to an order from any Japanese government, but we also both know that a great many fundamental changes must be wrought in the whole Japanese system before that misguided country can take its proper place among the peace-loving nations. I wish merely to pass his name on to you in case you should have occasion to seek his mature advice in connection with some of the problems that will face you. I believe that Mr. Stimson appreciates his qualifications. I understand that Dooman is also retiring from the Foreign Service shortly.

Grew probably did not expect MacArthur actually to take Dooman on—for a start, he doubtless would have clashed with George Atcheson. It therefore seems most likely that the real aim of Grew's letter was to advise the smooth execution of the occupation by referring indirectly to the utility of the emperor and emperor system. It is not known whether or not MacArthur made any reply to this—all that is known for certain is that he did not appoint Dooman as his adviser. Meanwhile, in Tokyo, MacArthur's occupation reforms were proceeding not only faster than Grew had imagined, but also in a surprisingly radical direction.

Occupation and the Emperor System: Grew's Links with MacArthur

MacArthur's headquarters issued a series of orders from October 4, 1945, starting with a memorandum concerning the removal of restrictions on political, civic, and religious freedoms. This included provisions for free discussion about the emperor, the release of political prisoners, the abolition of legal restrictions, and the disbanding of the thought police and dismissal of all members of other secret and special branches of the police force. This was followed, on October 10, by the release from prison of around five hundred Communist party members and others imprisoned by the military regime, and on October 11, with the "five great reforms" (emancipation of women, promotion of labor unions, and democratization of the education, legal and economic systems).

Grew cannot have viewed these developments with complete peace of mind. Indeed, during October he wrote a particularly large number of letters discussing the emperor issue. One of these, sent to Rear Admiral J. F. Shafroth in Tokyo on October 18, 1945, includes the following extract.

> It is a sad picture of Tokyo and Yokohama that you paint, yet I doubt if victory could have been achieved at any lesser price and, as you say, it was the atomic bomb that broke the camel's back, even though the Japanese were thoroughly licked before it was ever used. Without the use of the atomic bomb by us, the Japs might well have fought to the last ditch and might have made our invasion by force exceedingly costly.
>
> I shall always be glad to have taken two positions. First that the Japanese Emperor should be kept on ice as the only man who could, and did, stop the war. . . .

[Second is] the initiative for the Potsdam Declaration which helped to bring about the surrender. I broached the matter to the President at the end of May and he liked the idea but asked me to consult Stimson, Forrestal, Marshall and King, which I did. They also liked the idea but for military reasons they wanted another couple of months before acting, and the action was carried out at Potsdam just about as I had envisaged. I am not trying to take any personal credit for this, especially as Stimson, Forrestal and I had talked it over from time to time and I think we all saw the matter eye to eye. It would have been stupid to have told the Japanese that they must throw out the Emperor and the institution of the throne, for we cannot occupy Japan permanently and in all probability the Japanese would have put the Emperor right back again the moment our backs were turned. Anyway, the surrender was greatly helped by our telling the Japanese that they themselves would be free to choose their own eventual form of government. They may still throw the Emperor overboard, especially if the communists get control, but my guess is that some kind of constitutional monarchy will develop. From what I know of the Japanese, an outright democracy with an elected President, would bring about political chaos and would leave the field wide open for would-be dictators to get control.

As is apparent, while describing his own role prior to Japan's defeat and its acceptance of the Potsdam Declaration, Grew repeatedly warns against adopting the wrong policy on the emperor system. He sent a similar letter to his friend, the Reverend Charles Reifsnider:

October 19, 1945
Our Embassy residence was . . . saved [from war damage], but the 63 cases . . . containing the lovely things we had picked up during our ten years in Japan, were all opened and unpacked by the first group of soldiers who were sent up to Tokyo to get the Embassy ready for MacArthur . . . Alice was fit to be tied when she heard of it, but I was finally to get the story to the personal attention of MacArthur himself and although I told him to keep anything that he and Mrs. MacArthur needed for the Embassy, he is now having everything repacked and returned to us. "It's a way they have in the Army"!
I fully appreciate your support of the position I took about the Emperor. [Grew goes on to describe the drafting of the Potsdam Declaration as in the previous letter, which I shall omit here.] Stimson was splendid through it all—a really great statesman with a thorough understanding of Japanese mentality and great vision. . . .
[The Japanese] had better keep the throne as the one stabilizing influence. The old feudalistic system can best be destroyed by breaking

up the Zaibatsu and ensuring the farmers a new deal and a higher standard of living. The evils of state shintoism will largely disappear once the militarists are out of the way. All that is purely an artificial growth, as you well know.

But I don't think any American can rest until those responsible for Pearl Harbor and the utterly barbarous treatment of our prisoners have been tried and, if found guilty, adequately punished. Then our people will be able to take a more realistic and objective view of the whole scene as it shapes up.

Yet Grew remained a conservative, and considering what he actually did, it is doubtful how genuine he was in supporting the dissolution of the zaibatsu and advocating a new deal for farmers. Perhaps his intention was to give encouragement to Reifsnider and his colleagues now that the occupation reforms were progressing apace. Indeed, when I discussed this point with an American specialist on the Japanese occupation, he remarked, "In English, we call that 'whistling in the dark.' "

Further, in a letter of October 25, 1945, Grew wrote to his friend William Wharton (in Massachussetts) as follows:

> By and large it has seemed to me that MacArthur is doing a very good job in Japan. . . . He can accomplish his task much more effectively if he moves slowly and doesn't try to do everything at once. . . .
>
> . . . I knew Shidehara and Yoshida and some of the other members of the present Cabinet very well and they were bitterly opposed to militarism and all its works.
>
> . . . I dare say that Hirohito will have to go, for I can't see how he can dodge the responsibility of having signed the declaration of war even though I happen to know that he didn't want war. If he had refused to sign, he would unquestionably have been assassinated or thrown out. . . . That doesn't excuse him, however, and somehow or other I should think that he would have to take responsibility. The institution of the throne is another matter; it can be a power for great good as well as evil; it all depends on who controls. I don't see how the military can ever get control again. . . . If they ever try to build up a military machine again . . . all we need to do is to cut off their imports of iron, coal and oil.

As stated previously, Grew distinguished between the imperial institution and the emperor as an individual; he felt that even if Hirohito's abdication were inevitable, the institution itself could become a healthy stabilizing element in Japanese society, provided that the militarists were swept away. But, if so, in what form should it be preserved? This of course represented a major problem not only for Grew, but for MacArthur as well.

General MacArthur figures in only two passages in *Ten Years in Japan*, the more important of these under the entry for February 1, 1937. The previous evening, MacArthur, accompanying President Manuel Quezon of the Philippines on his visit to the United States, stopped off in Tokyo. Grew met the two men at Tokyo station and conducted them to the U.S. Embassy, where that evening an informal welcoming dinner was held in their honor. The next morning, Grew introduced Quezon to the emperor, with whom they later attended a luncheon at which Prince Takamatsu, Matsudaira Tsuneo, and others were also present. The banquet proceeded in a relaxed atmosphere; when Grew remarked that Japan was a "golfer's paradise," the emperor apparently expressed great interest. Grew wrote in his diary for that day that he had "seldom seen the Emperor so affable," and he probably recounted this tale to MacArthur, whose view of the imperial household was reinforced by such minor episodes.

Grew and MacArthur—up until now little significance has between attached to the relationship between these two men, yet personally, I cannot help thinking that they are connected by an invisible thread. By pursuing this, I hope, in the next chapter, to shed some light on the origins of the word "symbol" in the "symbol emperor system."

9

ORIGINS OF THE "SYMBOL"
Three Sources

Constitutional Theory and the Emperor System

CONCERNING the origins of the word "symbol" in the first article of the Constitution of Japan, there have generally been two hypotheses: either that it came from the British Statute of Westminster, 1931, or that it was proposed by one of the drafters in the constitutional drafting group of Government Section, General Headquarters, led by Charles L. Kades. My research has shown, however, that the source of this word is in fact much more complicated. I shall therefore trace three aspects of the origins of the "symbol," by looking in turn at the U.S., British, and Japanese perspectives.

Starting with the U.S. side, the focus naturally falls upon Grew. As far as is known to date, after Grew, the earliest reference to the emperor as "a symbol of Japanese national unity" was made by Max Bishop, while serving on the staff of the State Department's Office of Far Eastern Affairs, in a memorandum to Hornbeck dated December 14, 1942. Being one of the group of Japan experts, Bishop was heavily influenced by Grew, and it is highly possible that he picked up this idea through his regular conversations with Grew. Later, Grew wrote in a letter addressed to Hornbeck dated November 30, 1943: "As to the institution of the Throne—as distinct from the person of the present Emperor—I am clear in my mind that it should be preserved, for I believe that as a symbol it can be made to serve as a cornerstone for healthy and peaceful internal growth as it did for the erstwhile cult of a militarism."

Further, in a letter of February 22, 1944, to his friend Eugene R. Shippen, Grew referred to an essay by Helen Mears, saying that he agreed with her comment that "the emperor is a symbol of national unity." Mears was a Japanologist born in New York in 1900. Her works include *The Year of the Wild Boar** and *Mirror for Americans—Japan.*[1] The essay in question is an article entitled "The Japanese Emperor," which appeared in the *Yale Review* in December 1943. In it, Mears asserted the differences between nazism and Japan's imperial system. The following are some of her more important passages.

> The Emperor . . . as the titular head of state, is the connecting link between traditional and modern Japan.[2]

> It is necessary to remember that the Emperor is not an actual leader but a symbolic leader. He stands for the idea of national unity and the continuity of Japanese traditional civilization.[3]

> The Emperor is a powerful dual symbol to an army conscripted largely from the peasantry. He makes an emotional bond between Japan's primitive agriculture and her mechanized army by performing the rituals of traditional Shinto on the one hand and of Pure Shinto on the other.[4]

> Because of his importance, the current tendency in America to link the Emperor with Hitler as one of a partnership of aggressive political leaders is extremely unfortunate. The often urged proposal that, once the Japanese military have been defeated, troops of the United Nations must march to the imperial palace and arrest the Emperor is dangerous.[5]

> The way to discredit the military in [the Japanese people's] eyes is not to depose the Emperor but to use him.[6]

Mears's views thus had much in common with Grew's own opinions, which is no doubt why he commended her article to his friends. The central issue is contained in the second quotation above: there is no difference in meaning between Mears's phrase, "He stands for national unity," and Grew's words, "the Emperor is a symbol of national unity."

---

*This is an impressive discourse on Japan. The title is taken from the Chinese year–name for 1930, when Mears first went to Japan.—N.M.

Having established this, let us return to the issue raised earlier, namely, by whom and what process the word "symbol" came to be used in Article 1 of the Japanese Constitution. In October 1945, when Grew was in frequent correspondence with Shafroth and Bishop at GHQ, the emperor's war responsibility had become a highly controversial issue both in Japan and internationally. Indeed, on September 18, 1945, a resolution was introduced in the U.S. Senate that Emperor Hirohito of Japan be tried as a war criminal. In response, on November 25, the State–War–Navy Coordinating Subcommittee for the Far East (SFE) drew up a document on "Treatment of the Emperor of Japan" (SFE document 126), advising MacArthur on the position GHQ should adopt on the issue.

After receiving these orders from SWNCC, GHQ immediately started to investigate whether or not the emperor should be brought to trial, on the assumption that he bore responsibility for the war. One of those involved was Brigadier General Bonner F. Fellers, a soldier with expert knowledge of Japan who had served from 1943 as General MacArthur's military secretary and head of the U.S. Army's psychological warfare unit during the Pacific War. (It was also Fellers who, along with Major F. Bowers, was one of the two men ordered by MacArthur to receive Hirohito in the entrance hall of the U.S. Embassy at their first meeting on September 27, 1945.)

The following document, which Fellers sent to MacArthur on October 2, 1945, is of crucial significance. I have picked out the important passages.

> The attitude of the Japanese toward their Emperor is not generally understood. Unlike Christians, the Japanese have no God with whom to commune. Their Emperor is the living symbol of the race in whom lies the virtues of their ancestors. He is the incarnation of national spirit, incapable of wrong or misdeeds. Loyalty to him is absolute. . . .
>
> The Imperial War Rescript, 8 December 1941, was the inescapable responsibility of the Emperor who, as the head of a then sovereign state, possessed the legal right to issue it. From the highest and most reliable sources, it can be established that the war did not stem from the Emperor himself. He has personally said that he had no intention to have the War Rescript used as Tojo used it.
>
> It is a fundamental American concept that the people of any nation have the inherent right to choose their own government. Were the Japanese people given this opportunity, they would select the Emperor as the symbolic head of the state. . . .

If the Emperor were tried for war crimes the governmental structure would collapse and a general uprising would be inevitable. The people will uncomplainingly stand any other humiliation. Although they are disarmed, there would be chaos and bloodshed. It would necessitate a large expeditionary force with many thousands of public officials. The period of occupation would be prolonged and we would have alienated the Japanese.[7]

Not only did Fellers's views of the emperor and the Japanese people thus coincide exactly with those of Grew; they also came to exert a strong influence on MacArthur.

Of course, by the following year, the issue of the constitution had rapidly gained prominence. On December 27, 1945, the allied countries (comprising the "Big Four"—the United States, Britain, USSR, and China—along with Italy, Holland, Canada, Australia, New Zealand, and the Philippines) had agreed to establish a Far Eastern Commission, thus bringing the possibility of allied intervention in Japan's constitutional problems one step closer. MacArthur, however, wished to draw up a draft constitution on his own initiative before this committee set to work. Accordingly, the emperor's position under the new constitution had to be resolved without delay, and this would require a high-level political decision in advance, to discount the emperor's war responsibility and settle the issue of his abdication.

This, then, is what lay behind the famous secret telegram that MacArthur sent to U.S. Army Chief of Staff Eisenhower on January 25, 1946. Two days previously, a memorandum had come to MacArthur from the Joint Chiefs of Staff reporting that the Australian delegation at the United Nations War Crimes Commission meeting in London had begun to make preparations for the prosecution of Emperor Hirohito and sixty-one other wartime leaders as major war criminals. Furthermore, a rally to welcome home the Communist party leader, Nozaka Sanzō, was to be held in Hibiya Park, Tokyo, on January 26. It was indeed a time of great excitement and rapidly changing circumstances.

The contents of MacArthur's telegram have been quoted by a great many scholars, so I will not present it in detail here, save to focus on the following passage:

If [the emperor] is to be tried great changes must be made in occupational plans and due preparation therefore should be accomplished in preparedness before actual action is initiated. His indictment will unquestionably cause a tremendous convulsion among the Japanese people, the repercussions of which cannot be overestimated. He is a symbol which unites all Japanese. Destroy him and the nation will disintegrate.[8]

It is apparent that, by this time, MacArthur had already situated the emperor as "a symbol which unites all Japanese." This is effectively the same as Grew's "a symbol of national unity," a point I shall explore in more detail later on.

In addition, there are whole sections of MacArthur's cable that resemble very closely Fellers's words in his aforementioned memorandum, particularly the second half. It is of course true that passages such as the following are typical of MacArthur's exaggerated style:

[If the emperor were removed,] it would be absolutely essential to greatly increase the occupational forces. It is quite possible that a minimum of a million troops would be required which would have to be maintained for an indefinite number of years. In addition a complete civil service might have to be recruited and imported, possibly running into a size of several hundred thousand.

From the above, it seems fairly certain that MacArthur's telegram was in fact based on Fellers's memorandum. But what, exactly, was the connection among MacArthur, Fellers, and Grew?

First, as Morita Hideyuki observes, "MacArthur was, along with Grew and Washburn, a member of what we may call the moderate group within the Republican party who were Japan experts,"[9] and I think it is fair to say that the two men's views of the emperor were essentially the same or, perhaps more accurately, that Grew, with his ten years' experience in Japan, exerted a powerful influence on the views of MacArthur. As I have already pointed out, even after retiring from public office, Grew continued in his letters to MacArthur to give indirect warnings against mishandling the issue of the emperor system.

Second, Fellers would no doubt also have been in constant contact with Grew at the State Department over the prosecution of the propaganda war against Japan, during his time as chief of psychological warfare intelligence; clearly, he and Grew held identical views on the emperor.

Thus, on the American side, the use of the word "symbol" obviously progressed from Grew through Fellers to MacArthur. The next problem, then, is to establish how the ideas of these three men went on to be connected with the definition of the symbol emperor in the present constitution of Japan. Before examining that, the British angle should be explored, for although Grew was the first American to define the emperor as a "symbol," one must consider his original source for the word. Let us therefore take a look at the representative English theory of the monarchy, namely, Walter Bagehot's *The English Constitution*.

Bagehot, Balfour, and the Statute of Westminster, 1931

Walter Bagehot (1826–1877) was a celebrated English journalist, political theorist, and economist. Although *The English Constitution* (1867) is regarded as his finest work, he also wrote various other books, including *Physics and Politics* (1872) and *Lombard Street* (1873.)*

As I was reading through *The English Constitution*, I came across the following phrase: "The queen bee was taken away, but the hive went on."[10] This was surely the source of Grew's own reference to the "queen bee," as quoted in chapter 6, here referring figuratively to the way in which the British people managed to carry on much as normal, despite the royal family's withdrawal from public life after the death of Queen Victoria's husband, Prince Albert, in 1861. Thus Grew considered that while the loss of the "queen bee" in Britain might not affect the normal life of the people, this did not apply to Japan, where, if the monarch were to be removed, the entire society would collapse. One might therefore expect the words "a symbol" to appear somewhere in Bagehot's work, and I duly combed *The English Constitution* in search of this phrase, finding it used in the following two passages:

> The crown is of no party. Its apparent separation from business is that which removes it both from enmities and from desecration, which preserves its mystery, which enables it to combine the affection of conflicting parties—to be a visible symbol of unity to those still so imperfectly educated as to need a symbol.[11]

---

*Bagehot's name was known in Japan from the Meiji era; Sanseido published his *Biographical Studies of Eminent English Statesmen and Economists* in English in 1909.—N.M.

The fancy of the mass of men is incredibly weak; it can see nothing without a visible symbol, and there is much that it can scarcely make out with a symbol. Nobility is the symbol of mind.[12]

It is of course the first example that is the most important here. Bagehot defined two aspects of the British political structure: the "dignified parts," referring to the monarchy and House of Lords, and the "efficient parts," as represented by the Cabinet and the House of Commons. In the late nineteenth century, when Bagehot was writing, Britain had already undergone an industrial revolution; the old aristocratic order was being displaced by the rise of the industrial capitalists and working classes. For Bagehot, the best means of maintaining stable political rule under these circumstances was to leave politics in the hands of the elite.

The uneducated masses, on the other hand, had little but the symbolic and theatrical existence of the monarchy upon which to focus their aspirations. Bagehot believed that human behavior was not always based upon reason or self-interest; people were, rather, often motivated by irrational factors such as instinct or tradition. He therefore regarded that the growing political voice and participation of the common people could be held in check by relying on the "dignified" role of the monarchy. Yet Bagehot's book is certainly not a simple eulogy to the British royal family—he also points out the possible dangers of any constitutional monarchy that is centered on an irresponsible sovereign. Bagehot's ideas clearly correspond, however, to Grew's view of the Japanese monarchy and Japanese people, and I feel that he must have influenced Grew in some way. But does the influence of *The English Constitution* extend beyond this?

I should add at this point that the version of Bagehot I have referred to up until now has been the fourth edition published in 1885. In my university library, however, I also discovered a smaller, pocket-sized version, from the 1928 "World's Classics" series published by Oxford University Press. This edition, reprinted seven times, has been widely read around the world, and from here on I shall deal with the most recent (1952) edition.

The text of the two versions is of course the same, but the 1952 edition contains an added introduction. The introduction's author, the First Earl of Balfour (1848–1930), was a Conservative politician who served under his uncle, Prime Minister Lord Salisbury, as secretary for

Scotland and chief secretary for Ireland (1887–91), later becoming prime minister himself from 1902 to 1905. Balfour went on to hold the posts of first lord of the admiralty and foreign secretary during the First World War, after which he became president of the council (1919–22 and 1925–29). In 1926, he presented to Parliament a report defining the relationship of equality between Britain, as the mother country, and its self-governing territories, which was later to become law in the 1931 Statute of Westminster. In my view, Balfour was a remarkable figure.

On reading Balfour's commentary, parts of the 1885 edition that I had previously not understood became clear to me. Of particular importance are phrases such as "a shrine symbolic of his country's unity and continuity," and "Our King, in virtue of his descent and of his office, is the living representative of our national history."

These words immediately reminded me of those used by Grew, Mears, and Fellers; indeed, I was surprised at how much these American writers echo Balfour. For Grew's phrase "a symbol of national unity," Mears's "He stands for the idea of national unity and the continuity of Japanese traditional civilization," and Fellers's "the living symbol of the race" can all be seen as alternative ways of expressing the words of Bagehot and Balfour. It therefore seems more than likely that they read the "World's Classics" version of *The English Constitution*.

In what way, then, was the word "symbol" used in the Statute of Westminster? In the preamble, it appears as "the Crown is the symbol of the free association of the members of the British Commonwealth of Nations."

We should note here the use of the words "the symbol" rather than "a symbol." The statute thus declared that it is the Crown alone that symbolizes the British Commonwealth.

From the above, we can probably draw the following conclusions. Having no monarchy of their own, Americans were obliged to use the British royal family as their point of reference in order to understand the nature of the Japanese emperor system. Moreover, Grew knew from his time in Japan that the emperor was hoping to preserve and develop the Japanese monarchy along the lines of the British royal family.

From this overall picture, it is not surprising that Grew had a strong admiration for the authoritative English theory of the monarchy. Throughout his many discourses on the Japanese emperor, however, Grew, who was not an academic, never once revealed the original source of his theories. This made my work all the more difficult, but when I found that the idea behind Grew's "queen bee" speech came from Bagehot, my long-standing suspicions were finally confirmed.

The same probably applies to Mears and Fellers as well. In other words, the emperor theory held by the Japan experts in the United States was influenced to a greater or lesser degree by the ideas of Bagehot and Balfour. This, coupled with their own experiences of Japan, led them to develop a concept of the Japanese emperor as the symbol of national unity.

The Debate within GHQ:
MacArthur's "Three Principles"

It remains unclear, however, how far British theories of the monarchy influenced the GHQ constitutional draft team (comprising Whitney, Kades, Hussey, Rowell, and others). According to Tanaka Hideo's *Kenpō seitei katei oboegaki* (Notes on the process of enactment of the constitution), "both Rowell and Hussey say that there was no particular inspiration for their use of the word 'symbol,' " but I find this rather hard to believe, as it seems extremely likely that they would have come across, if not Bagehot, then at least the Statute of Westminster. In any case, even if one grants that they had not, we have already seen how MacArthur was using the word "symbol" before the GHQ draft was written. It therefore seems more appropriate to conclude that, far from the GHQ committee receiving "no particular inspiration" over the use of this word, it was in fact suggested to them in many different ways.

I shall now sum up this investigation by finally turning my attention to GHQ, following what may be called a "second thread" on the American side.

I shall start by looking at the first clause of the present Japanese Constitution.

> Article 1: The Emperor shall be the symbol of the State and of the unity of the people, deriving his position from the will of the people with whom resides sovereign power.

This is phrased in far more rigid and emphatic terms than the afore-mentioned words of either MacArthur or Grew. For one thing, "a symbol" is replaced by "the symbol" and "is" by "shall be." What does this signify, and how did the article come to take its present form? While a full explanation of this is beyond the scope of the present study, I would like to make the following points.

First, the phrase "the symbol" is clearly more limiting than "a symbol." The use of "a symbol" implies that although the emperor is one symbol of Japanese national unity, other such symbols might also exist (the national flag or Mount Fuji, for example). The use of "the symbol" makes such an interpretation impossible, however, for it strongly conveys the meaning that nothing other than the emperor can symbolize the unity of Japan and the Japanese nation.

Next, what about the replacement of "is" with "shall be"? The word "is" simply indicates an objective fact and carries with it no prescriptive meaning. Yet in all countries where there is a constitution, the supreme law of the land, this is not a simple statement of facts, but rather a set of prescriptions about that country's institutions and the actions of its people. It is therefore natural to see "shall be" used instead of "is" in the Japanese Constitution. Moreover, in stylistic terms, "shall be" carries a more severe tone. Consequently, it seems clear that the legal experts within GHQ had a hand in this choice of wording.

The key to this is clearly to be found in the period between February 4, 1946, when MacArthur presented his "three principles," and February 12, when he completed his draft constitution. I shall thus focus my attention on these nine days, based on the information in the book by Takayanagi Kenzō, Ōtomo Ichirō, and Tanaka Eiji, *Nihonkoku kenpō seitei no katei — I. Genbun to honyaku.*[13]

First, we need to look at the instructions given to MacArthur in directive SWNCC 228, "Reform of the Japanese Governmental System" (January 7, 1946), which concerned the drafting of the Japanese Constitution.

This document stated, on the basis of paragraph 12 of the Potsdam Declaration, that "though the ultimate form of government in Japan is to be established by the freely expressed will of the Japanese people, the retention of the Emperor institution in its present form is not considered consistent with the foregoing general objectives." It went on to say that "the Japanese should be encouraged to abolish the Emperor institution or to reform it along more democratic lines." Thus if the Japanese people wished to abolish the emperor system, GHQ was to give its support to such moves. As debate over the emperor's war guilt increased in Japan and abroad, however, MacArthur, judging that the occupation would progress more smoothly if he made use of the emperor rather than indicting him as a war criminal, sent his secret telegram to Eisenhower. This was a decisive factor in turning the U.S. government and GHQ toward a policy of absolving the emperor and preserving the emperor system.

Having established this, we must now look at the so-called three principles that MacArthur stressed to GHQ Government Section Chief Courtney Whitney in directing him to draw up GHQ's draft constitution on February 4, 1946.

> I. Emperor is at the head of the state.
> His succession is dynastic.
> His duties and powers will be exercised in accordance with the Constitution and responsive to the basic will of the people as provided therein.
> II. War as a sovereign right of the nation is abolished . . .
> III. The feudal system of Japan will cease . . .[14]

Many Japanese constitutional scholars, including Takayanagi et al., have translated MacArthur's words in paragraph I to mean "The Emperor is the head of the state." Yet this is not strictly accurate, as it does not make a clear enough contrast with article 4 of the Meiji Constitution, which states that "The Emperor is the head of the Empire, combining in himself the rights of sovereignty, and exercises them according to the provisions of the present Constitution." MacArthur's use of the preposition "at" implies that the emperor is at the apex of the state, but not necessarily the "head of state."

Even supposing that MacArthur had intended to mean "the head of the state," his idea would certainly not have been a head of state in the traditional sense, but rather a monarch with no formal power. For MacArthur specifically stated, in the second half of paragraph I, that "His duties and powers will be exercised in accordance with the Constitution and responsive to the basic will of the people as provided therein." Without being aware of this, it is impossible to understand fully the contents of the discussion that followed within the Government Section of GHQ. (Incidentally, my interpretation here is certainly nothing unusual; there are several constitutional experts who have used translations other than "head of state."*)

The Emergence of the Symbol Emperor Clause

Having received MacArthur's orders, Whitney immediately called a meeting of the Government Section to discuss the general's three principles. It was resolved that "In drafting the new constitution our emphasis should be upon placing sovereignty squarely in the hands of the people; the Emperor's role will be that of a social monarch, merely."[15] In other words, although MacArthur had said, "[The] Emperor is at the head of the state," it was affirmed through open discussion that this actually meant a monarch without power: a so-called social monarch.

Had MacArthur in fact intended his three principles to define the emperor as a head of state, the meeting surely would not have proceeded so smoothly. It is probably for this reason that the clause on the emperor did not, apparently, become a major problem.[16]

Following this, a Steering Committee was set up, comprising Charles L. Kades, Alfred R. Hussey, Milo E. Rowell, and Ruth Ellerman (as secretary), all of whom, apart from Ellerman, were legal experts. Under this committee, seven subcommittees were formed: Legislative; Executive; Civil Rights; Judiciary; Local Government; and Finance, together with a Committee on the Emperor, Treaties, and Enabling Provisions, which consisted of Navy Lieutenant George Nelson and Ensign Richard Poole.

On February 4, work immediately started on preparations for a draft constitution. Each committee was required to operate under strict rules: all work was to be carried out in absolute secrecy, using code names, with "a tentative draft" to be completed by the end of that week.

---

*Through the kind introduction of Mr. Furukawa Jun, I was by chance able to ask the opinion on this point of Professor Theodore McNelly of the University of Maryland while he was visiting Japan in July 1989. Professor McNelly expressed his agreement with Mr. Furukawa's view, saying that in this case, "at the head of the state" meant "at the top of the state." I then asked whether he thought MacArthur had intended his words to mean this, and he replied that he did not know. For this reason, I have adopted an approach in this book that leaves room for both interpretations.—N.M.

As early as February 6, discussions on the emperor clause were held between the Steering Committee and the Committee on the Emperor. "In the initial discussion of the Chapter on the Emperor, the Steering Committee consistently pressed for a strict delimitation of all powers of the Emperor, and the absolute clarification of his merely decorative role." They therefore expressed their objection to the use of the word "reign" in defining the role of the emperor and insisted that the words of the subcommittee's draft clause (code-named B1) be altered to "The emperor is the symbol of the state and of the unity of the people."[17]

Takayanagi et al. also quote the text of a draft B2, which was a "Memorandum for the Chief, Government Section, the Committee on the Emperor and Miscellaneous Affairs" (chairman Poole and co-author Nelson). It gives the following definition of the emperor's position.

> Article An Imperial Throne shall be the symbol of the State and of the Unity of the People, and an Emperor shall be the symbolic personification thereof, deriving his position from the sovereign will of the People, and from no other source.

Both drafts B1 and B2 on February 6 thus used the words "the symbol," and it is clear that they were both written by Poole and Nelson. Nevertheless, this still does not indicate who it was that chose this phrase. Let us therefore look at the subject in a little more detail.

The important day was Friday, February 12, when the Steering Committee reviewed the draft constitution that had been provisionally completed on the 10th. It was this meeting, also attended by Courtney Whitney, that examined draft B2, and the following comments were made.

First, that the use of both the words "An Imperial Throne" and "an Emperor" together in the first paragraph of the article on the emperor would raise the problem of a dual symbol. The wording should be made more concise by removing the phrase "symbolic personification thereof," which had a somewhat mystical sense, and replacing it with "The Emperor shall be the symbol of the state and of the unity of the people."

There were of course issues under discussion that day other than that of the emperor clause, and once this business was finished, the Government Section draft was presented to MacArthur. The general made one or two minor revisions and immediately approved the document, which now became the "MacArthur draft."

The following morning, at ten o'clock, Whitney, accompanied by Kades, Rowell, and Hussey, arrived at Foreign Minister Yoshida Shigeru's residence and handed the GHQ draft constitution to him and Minister of State Matsumoto Jōji, who was also chairman of the Japanese government's Committee on Constitutional Problems. The first Article of Chapter 1 of this draft read as follows.

> The Emperor shall be the symbol of the State and of the Unity of the People, deriving his position from the sovereign will of the People, and from no other source.

Thus it seems fair to say that this first paragraph of MacArthur's draft constitution was a revised version of proposal B2. But what exactly was discussed at the meeting of February 12?

Kades's Letters

Having got this far, I found that I had reached a dead end. The aforementioned book, *Nihonkoku kenpō seitei no katei*, is the best source available to us at present, but beyond this, it is impossible to obtain further information. I therefore ventured to write to Charles Kades (then eighty-three), the former deputy chief of Government Section, in an attempt to clear up some of these points. My acquaintance with Mr. Kades was limited to our meeting at the International Conference on the Occupation of Japan at Amherst University in 1980, and an informal talk we had had with Takemae Eiji and others at the New Otani Hotel on Kades's visit to Japan in the summer of 1988. I nevertheless received a swift and lengthy reply to my letter.

My inquiry concerned two main points. First, had Kades known that Grew, Fellers, and MacArthur had already been using the word "symbol" before the formulation of GHQ's draft constitution? Second, what was discussed concerning proposal B2 at the meeting of February 12, 1946, between the Steering Committee and the Committee on the Emperor?

Kades replied along the following lines. First, he had no knowledge that Joseph Grew ever used the words "The Emperor is a symbol of national unity." My letter was the first time he had ever seen that stated. He remembered, however, that Fellers used the word "symbol" in a memorandum to MacArthur, though there was no evidence that MacArthur ordered the word inserted in Article 1. He thought the language was changed on the initiative of the Steering Committee and that, when objections were raised to the term "symbolic personification," Poole probably might have proposed substituting "Emperor" for "Imperial Throne" before the word "symbol." And he suggested that I contact Poole directly.[18]

I was not completely satisfied with this, however, and wrote to Kades a second time, describing my ideas in more detail and asking for his comments. Two weeks later, I received the following reply:

> [First], much as I would like to help you, I don't think I can shed much more light on the origin [of the word "symbol" in] the beginning of Article 1 of the Constitution ... I agree with you that MacArthur's cable of January 25th, 1946, to the Joint Chiefs of Staff seems to draw some of its phrases from General Bonner Fellers' memorandum to MacArthur of the previous November. I don't know whether Fellers was aware of Undersecretary Joseph Grew's views on the Emperor's position or not, but apparently you are satisfied that he was. My recollection is that Fellers was in the Southwest Pacific Theater of Operations while Grew was at the State Department but, of course, he may have had a tour of duty in Washington D.C. when Grew was there or maybe they corresponded with each other. Be that as it may, neither the Steering Committee (Lt. Col. Rowell, Commander Hussey and me) nor the Committee on the Emperor & Miscellaneous Affairs (Ensign Poole and Lt. Nelson) were aware, so far as I know, of either Grew's views, Fellers's memo, or MacArthur's cable when Article 1 was being drafted during the week of February 3rd, 1946.
>
> [Second], the notes handed to me by General Whitney on February 3rd containing points that Whitney told me MacArthur wanted included in the draft of a model for a constitution do not describe the Emperor as a "symbol" [but rather as "at the head of the state"].
>
> [Third], although I think I read some of Walter Bagehot's writings while I was taking a course on "Government" under Professor Cushman of Cornell University, I do not believe I ever read his book on *The English Constitution*. However, in 1926 and 1927 I was a Senior Editor of *The Cornell Daily Sun*, the University's daily morning newspaper which was a member of the Associated Press. The Editor-in-Chief of the paper was Jervis Langdon, Jr. [born 1905], a distinguished lawyer later, who during World War II advanced from Captain to Colonel in

the U.S. Army Airforce and was Assistant Chief of Staff in the India–China Theater and Chief of Staff of the Southwest Pacific Wing of the Air Transport Command. Langdon became intensely interested in the British Commonwealth of Nations which was proposed at that time and wrote a series of editorials which analysed it, and I read avidly, concerning the proposal that resulted eventually in the Statute of Westminster in 1931, which you refer to and he may have read the Balfour Report to Parliament. Professor Theodore McNelly has a theory that Langdon may have described the British monarch as a "symbol" and that I was so impressed by Langdon's editorials that subliminally I may have carried the thought in my subconscious mind when we were searching for a word to substitute for Poole's "symbolic personification" description of the Emperor that I felt was too turgid. I just don't know the source but it's possible it was Jervis Langdon, Jr.[19]

This letter clarified the situation considerably. In particular, it explained how the original draft presented to the Steering Committee on February 12, which read, "An Imperial Throne shall be the symbol of the State . . . and an Emperor shall be the symbolic personification thereof," was revised through a process of discussion to a wording resembling the present constitution: "The Emperor shall be the symbol of the State and of the Unity of the People." Moreover, it clarified that this proposal was the work of Poole and Kades, among others.

The Statute of Westminster, as I have noted, similarly stated that "the Crown is the symbol of the free association of the members of the British Commonwealth of Nations." This does not refer to the actual person of the monarch himself, but rather to an abstract concept of the "Crown" as "symbol." It is not known for certain whether Poole and Nelson were inspired by this, but they likewise used the abstract idea of "An Imperial Throne" as "the symbol of the State" in their original draft. Not only did the use of both "An Imperial Throne" and "an Emperor" in the same clause imply a double symbol, but the phrase "symbolic personification" also had a turgid and obscure feel to it, and so the article was eventually altered to its present form.

To sum up, Grew, Fellers, and MacArthur, who represented the first thread on the American side, clearly saw the emperor as a "symbol." There is no clear evidence, however, that this had a particularly strong influence on the constitutional draft team. Instead, a second chain of people independently developed a "symbol" definition of the emperor, based on an apparently diverse set of influences.

Kades, former deputy chief of Government Section, seems to have been subconsciously inspired by the ideas of Jervis Langdon, Jr., and by the Statute of Westminster, which he studied during his time at Cornell University. It is not known, however, if Rowell and Hussey were similarly influenced by this piece of British legislation. In his letter to me, Kades made a point of noting that these two men had both been to law school, which I took to imply that they must have been familiar with the statute, although this remains uncertain. As far as Hussey is concerned, it emerged from my discussion with Professor McNelly that he was possibly influenced by the proposal of the Investigational Committee on Constitutional Issues on the Japanese side, which I shall discuss below. Nevertheless, it can be concluded that the two threads in the origin of the "symbol" on the U.S. side were connected in some form or other to the British theory of the monarchy; from Bagehot through Balfour to the Statute of Westminster, and it seems highly probable that it was by this path that the word "symbol" came to be chosen.

The "Symbol" from the Japanese Side

How, then, did the Japanese side receive the word "symbol"? Matsumoto Jōji's famous response to the "symbol" definition of the emperor on receiving the "MacArthur Draft" on February 13 is as follows: "I was really quite surprised; I thought it was a very literary choice of words to use for something like a constitution." But I would suggest that the Japanese were not entirely unprepared for the new definition. By this I mean that if one looks at several of the independent draft constitutions that were written, one can see that, even before the GHQ draft, there were attempts made to define the emperor as a "symbol."

The "constitutional draft outline" prepared by the Constitutional Research Group (which included Iwabuchi Tatsuo and Murobushi Takanobu) is a good example of this. Their final draft did not specifically define the emperor as a "symbol," but rather stated that "The Emperor does not participate in government himself but only presides over state ceremonies." During the process of discussion by the committee as to how to describe the position of the emperor once his political powers had been removed, the critic Sugimori Kōjirō, proposed the use of the word *shōchō* (symbol), and when the committee presented their draft to GHQ, Sugimori also gave an explanation of the use of this word.[20] Indeed, according to Professor McNelly, Rowell sent him a letter in which he wrote "This no doubt refers to the time when Lowell heard Sugimori's explanation."*

Koseki Shōichi has recently revealed in *Shinkenpō no tanjō* that even within the Japan Socialist party there was a movement to situate the emperor as "the symbol of national harmony." Its author was Katō Kanjū, who was highly regarded by GHQ. Here is part of what Katō had to say about the emperor.

> In view of the history of its genesis, the Emperor should always exist for purposes of festivals and ceremonies.... [Historically,] the reason why the Japanese have maintained the emperor's position is not because he is an absolute being. Rather, they have thought that by embracing the emperor they could maintain their national unity and avoid the confusion which arises in the common feeling and interests of the race in different periods when the emperor, an historical entity, is abolished. From this sort of perspective, I believe I can conclude that the emperor symbolizes national harmony and that the maintenance of his position as the head of state, who represents national ceremonies and honor, while leaving him politically powerless, is neither unnatural nor irrational.

The word "symbol" obviously did not just fall from the sky: it came from the Japanese side as well. Moreover, more than 90 percent of Japanese public opinion surveys around that time supported the "symbol emperor." Consequently, despite the fact that the literary word "symbol" was used, it was not in the least fantastic, because it was also a word rooted in Japan's long history.

---

*Recently, after my return to Japan, Professor McNelly sent me an essay he had written in 1969 entitled "The Role of Monarchy in the Political Modernization of Japan," in which he praises the Constitutional Research Group's draft outline for incorporating the principle of popular sovereignty. He also commented that "It was Hussey who was the main proponent of the emperor as symbol." The basis for this seems to have been a letter Rowell wrote to McNelly on July 26, 1967, there being no other explanation for this claim.

In the end, the use of the word "symbol" was something that came out of the discussion within the constitutional drafting team at GHQ Government Section; there does not seem to be much point in attempting to seek out a particular individual to whom it is attributable. Rather, it seems more pertinent to establish the context in which the wording was used.—N.M.

Finally, let us look briefly at the views that were exchanged in the Imperial Diet after the Japanese received GHQ's draft constitution. To anticipate: I have traced the process of change in the definition of symbol in Article 1 as follows:

1. The Japanese government's "March 2 draft"—"Article 1: The Emperor has the position of the symbol of Japan based on the supreme general will of the Japanese nation and he is the emblem of Japanese national unity."

2. The "Revised Draft Outline of the Constitution" announced on March 6, 1946—"Article 1: The Emperor shall be the symbol of Japan based on the supreme general will of the Japanese nation and of its national unity."

3. The revised draft of the Imperial Constitution, submitted to the Imperial Diet on June 20, 1946—"Article 1: The Emperor is the symbol of Japan and of its national unity and His position is based on the supreme general will of the Japanese nation."

4. The revised version that was voted on in the Lower House of the Diet on August 24 and in the House of Peers on October 6, 1946— "Article 1: The Emperor is the symbol of Japan and of its national unity, and His position is based on the general will of the Japanese nation in which sovereignty resides."

From the above it is apparent that the Japanese accepted the definition of the emperor as a symbol but, until the very last, tried to make the locus of sovereignty vague. Particularly troublesome was the phrase "and his position is based on the supreme general will of the Japanese nation." The Japanese would not use the words "sovereign power" and tried to obfuscate this by the word "supreme." Because their ploy was spotted by the translators and the military and civilian officials of Government Section, however, the expression finally settled on is what one sees in the present constitution. Since Thomas Bisson has brought new facts to light concerning these details of constitution making, readers may consult his book, *Nihon senryō kaisōki* [Reform years in Japan, 1945-47: Occupation memoir], translated by Nakamura Masanori and Miura Yōichi (Tokyo: Sanseido, 1983).

I have now carried out a complicated demonstration of the origins of the "symbol," searching for its roots from many angles, including the American, British, and Japanese sides. Figure 1 is a schematic summary of this search. Although complicated and intertwined, these

Figure 1. Origins of the "SYMBOL"

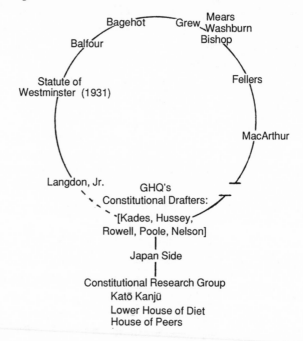

three currents ultimately traced a single circle that may be said to have converged in chapter 1, article 1 of the Constitution of Japan. A long historical background was required to make the Japanese Constitution in its final form, and the monarchical, political, and constitutional thought of the people of those three countries was reflected in that background. It is unwise, therefore, to hold fast to particular persons when asking the question, "Who used the word 'symbol.'" Rather, it is far more important to turn attention to the context in which Britons, Americans, and Japanese used the word.

10

ESTABLISHMENT OF THE SYMBOL EMPEROR SYSTEM

Article Nine and the Symbol Emperor

WITH THE PROMULGATION of the Constitution on November 3, 1946, the pre-1945 absolute monarchy was converted into a symbol-monarchy, and sovereignty shifted from the emperor to the Japanese people. The changes that accompanied this transfer of sovereignty can be called truly revolutionary, in the sense of a "revolution from above" or a "revolution from outside" by the occupation administration.

Articles 1 through 8 of the Constitution of Japan define the emperor's position: Article 3 states that "The advice and approval of the Cabinet shall be required for all acts of the Emperor in matters of state, and the Cabinet shall be responsible therefor," and article 4 clearly stipulates that "The Emperor shall perform only such acts in matters of state as are provided for in this Constitution and he shall not have powers related to government." Thus, unlike the emperor under the Meiji Constitution, the postwar constitution requires him to obtain "the advice and approval of the cabinet" even to perform the ten acts in matters of state defined in article 7 (which include promulgation of constitutional amendments, laws, cabinet orders, and treaties, convocation of the Diet, and dissolution of the House of Representatives). He is clearly not to have any powers whatsoever related to government.

Yet despite this definition of the emperor as a powerless "social monarch" performing only state ceremonies, international opinion in 1945–46 considered the retention of the emperor system itself to be extremely dangerous. Countries such as China, the Philippines, Australia, and New Zealand, which had experienced the rule of the Japanese Army, feared that if the emperor system remained, Japan might revive the militarism with which it had once sought to control the world and make a repeated bid for global domination. To eliminate these fears, a guarantee was needed that Japan would never again become a threat to world peace. Article 9 was devised to meet that need.

There have been various arguments over whether Article 9 originated with Prime Minister Shidehara Kijūrō or General MacArthur, although recent studies seem to conclude that it came out of collaboration between the two men.[1] On January 24, 1946, when Shidehara visited MacArthur, he is believed to have said: "Since I am old and do not know when I shall die, while I am alive I want you to allow me to maintain the imperial institution. I would appreciate your cooperation." On this occasion Shidehara also surprised MacArthur by saying that since Japan had lost world trust because of the war, "We have no choice but to abandon war." Shidehara, it seems, was merely thinking of issuing an international declaration along the lines of the 1928 Antiwar Treaty (Kellogg-Briand Pact). However, on February 4, in the second of his "three principles," MacArthur wrote that "War as a sovereign right of the nation is abolished," and that phrase, to Shidehara's apparent astonishment, was incorporated into chapter 2, article 8 (later changed to article 9) of GHQ's draft constitution.

On March 5, 1946, the Shidehara cabinet fiercely debated whether to accept the GHQ draft constitution with its two distinguishing features: the symbol emperor and the renunciation of war. It reached no decision, and during the meeting Shidehara left to visit the emperor. Judging that unless he accepted the draft, the existence of the monarchy would be endangered, the emperor told Shidehara that "Since matters have come this far, it cannot be helped." With this the cabinet finally decided to approve the GHQ proposal. Hirohito judged that unless he accepted this GHQ draft constitution, the existence of the monarchy itself would be in danger.

Shidehara also recorded in his 1955 biography, *Shidehara Kijūrō*: "I thought that at this time we had to take a bold step in abandoning war and establishing a peaceful Japan in order to preserve the imperial institution and protect the national polity." In this way, Articles 1 and 9 of the Constitution of Japan stand in a barter relationship: the retention of the symbol monarchy is (in the worlds of the preamble) predicted on the determination of the Japanese nation "to preserve our security and existence, trusting in the justice and faith of the peace-loving peoples of the world."

The Emperor's "Declaration of Humanity"[4]

On January 1, 1946, when the issue of his war responsibility had become acute, Emperor Hirohito issued his "Declaration of Humanity." This imperial rescript denying his divinity stated that "The ties between U.S. and Our people have always stood upon mutual trust and affection. They do not depend upon mere legends and myhs. They are not predicated on the false conception that the Emperor is divine." The rescript was drafted by Harold G. Henderson, head of the Education, Religions, and Cultural Resources Division within GHQ's Civil Intelligence and Education Section (CIE), and Reginald H. Blyth, an English professor at the Peers School. On the Japanese side, Yamanashi Katsunoshin, the president of the Peers School, Prime Minister Shidehara, Education Minister Maeda Tamon, and others are also said to have examined and written comments on the Japanese and English texts.[2] However, Professor Hirakawa Sukehiro has argued that the idea of the rescript itself came from Yamanashi Katsunoshin.[3]

Whichever view is correct, according to a State Department document dated December 18, 1945, as early as mid-1945 the American government had begun to consider ordering the Japanese government to issue some form of a document denying the emperor's divinity.[4] In the words of PR-34,

> (3) Extreme measures to keep the person of the Emperor mysteriously distant from the public and veiled in awesome secrecy should be abolished. . . . The Supreme Commander should exert every effort to influence the emperor voluntarily to demonstrate by word and deed to his people that he is an ordinary human being not different from other Japanese or from foreigners, that he himself does not believe in the divine origin of the imperial line or the mystical superiority of Japan over other lands, and that there is no such thing as the 'imperial will' as distinct from government policy.

This document was written by Edwin O. Reischauer, a specialist in Japanese history who was at the time an army intelligence officer assigned (at the request of the State Department) to head a working group under the auspices of the State–War–Navy Coordinating Subcommittee for the Far East. In this capacity, he came to participate in the drafting of the aforementioned "Treatment of the Institution of the

Emperor." Reischauer headed a working group that included Lieutenant Colonel Hendrick, dispatched from the Army Department, and Lieutenant Commanders Hackett and Sheppard, from the Navy Department.

After the deliberations of the Inter-Divisional Area Committee 242 on December 18, a second draft of PR–34 was made which differed principally from the first version in that all matters concerning the emperor as an individual, such as the issue of war crimes, were deleted. It is not clear whether this second draft was actually transmitted to SCAP in Tokyo and incorporated in the "Declaration of Humanity." Judging from Reischauer's statement, however, that "any attempt to persuade the emperor to participate in his own 'debunking' would have to be made in such a manner as to be unknown to the Japanese people and should be handled with such diplomacy as to give no suggestion of compulsion," the possibility cannot be denied that this document was sent to SCAP in some form.[5]

The division of GHQ in charge of this problem was CIE, headed by Brigadier General Dyke. In a diary entry of December 23, 1945, Kinoshita Michio recorded a strange string of names: "Dyke-Blyth-Yamanashi-Ishiwata-O-Shidehara-Suzuki." "O" indicates the emperor, and "Suzuki" is Suzuki Kantarō.[6] In short, the seven people noted by Kinoshita can be seen as having participated directly in drafting the "Declaration of Humanity." Moreover, it is clear that the declaration was drafted after it had received MacArthur's approval, for Kinoshita has written that MacArthur changed the words "the Japanese" to read "Emperor" in the English original where it said "the Japanese are descendants of the gods."[7] Thus, it seems more reasonable to see the declaration as having been drafted on the basis of a mutual agreement between GHQ and the Japanese, rather than originating in a spontaneous proposal from the Japanese side.

The *Washington Evening Star* of January 2, 1946, wrote that the Imperial Rescript was "remarkable proof of the revolution from above that was being planned by MacArthur."[8] And in his *Prospects for Democracy in Japan*, T. A. Bisson pointed out that "On January 1, 1946, undoubtedly in response to a 'suggestion' from Supreme Headquarters, the Emperor also issued a statement to the Japanese people disavowing his divinity."[9] Ōhara Yasuo, too, has written that "At the drafting stage, one might be able to call it a "Japan–U.S. joint production, but on the whole it is clear that GHQ took the initiative."[10]

If that was the case, then how did the emperor contribute to the drafting of the Imperial Rescript as mentioned in Kinoshita's strange list of names? Education Minister Maeda said that when he visited Emperor Hirohito on December 19, 1945, and showed him the original draft of the "Declaration of Humanity," the emperor insisted strongly on inserting the "Imperial Oath of Five Articles" in the opening paragraph of the rescript. The first article of the oath stated that "Deliberative assemblies shall be widely established and all matters decided by public discussion." It was declaring, in effect, that the future politics of Japan would be carried out in accordance with the principle of democracy. As for Emperor Hirohito, he sought to place the emphasis not on his transition for the first time from god to human being, on the basis of the "Declaration of Humanity," but rather to stress that ever since the Meiji period the Japanese monarchy had been compatible with democracy.

Looking back on the period in which he had issued the rescript, Hirohito remarked at a news conference on August 23, 1977, that:

> It [the Imperial Oath of Five Articles] was the main aim at the time of the Imperial Rescript. Divinity and other problems were secondary issues. The reason I issued it was because in those days, when the power of the United States and other foreign countries was so strong, I was very worried that the Japanese people might be overwhelmed by their influence.
>
> We adopted democracy because of the will of the Meiji Emperor. . . . The Meiji Constitution was made on that basis; and therefore I thought there was a great need to show that democracy was never something that had been imported.[11]

The Emperor's intention was clear. In his New Year's Day rescript he encouraged the defeated Japanese nation not to allow itself to become "overwhelmed" or submissive in the face of United States influence; at the same time, he wanted to appeal to the people that the substance of the Potsdam Declaration, which GHQ wished to implement, could be realized satisfactorily under the old constitution and that the monarchy had been constitutional from its inception.[12]

As already noted, Joseph Grew considered that efforts to force American democracy onto Japan would only produce chaos. As he wrote in the following extracts from letters to his friends in March 1944 and October 1945 respectively, "I myself should think that to try to graft a full-fledged democracy on Japan at the start, would certainly lead to chaos in short order."[13] Further, "From what I know of the Japanese, an outright democracy with an elected president, would bring about political chaos and would leave the field wide open for would-be dictators to get control."[14]

Later, however, MacArthur's occupation reforms advanced at a speed much greater, and with far more sweeping aims, than Grew had anticipated, and its contents were even more radical. A traditional conservative, Grew probably never dreamed that a radical constitution of Japan, which deprived the emperor of almost all his powers, would be enacted. As I shall explain later, in 1948 Grew was appointed honorary chairman of the Japan lobby's American Council on Japan and came to play a part in the reversal of U.S. occupation policy in Japan. For Grew, who thought of the throne as the surest safety device against communism, a bulwark preventing the spread of Soviet influence in Japan, that policy reversal was an inevitable development.

Thus, the emperor's "Declaration of Humanity" was a collaborative Japanese–U.S. strategy for prolonging the life of the imperial institution. At the same time, it was a product of a reform based on the emperor's strong belief that monarchy and democracy could be compatible. The "Declaration of Humanity" was warmly received in both the United States and Japan. The *Pacific Stars & Stripes* of January 4, 1946, reported the editorial opinion of many newspapers under the headline "Emperor's Rescript Draws Much Attention in U.S." The *New York Times* in its lead editorial said that the emperor by issuing the rescript "made himself one of the great reformers in Japanese history" and "opened the way for political reforms which may convert Japan into a real constitutional government." *Time* had commented that "Having accomplished his own transition from god to man, Hirohito now faces the task of completing the project which his grandfather, Meiji, initiated—the transformation of Japan from an oriental despotism to a modern democracy."

But the emperor's position was by no means secure yet, for in 1945 and 1946 the international and domestic debate on his war responsibility reached a peak. Hirohito was obliged to take action in order to deflect this criticism.

Imperial Tours of Local Areas

On February 19, 1946, the emperor began his first postwar tour of local areas. Starting in Kawasaki, Yokohama, Yokosuka, and other places in Kanagawa Prefecture, he visited factories and houses for overseas evacuees, giving encouragement to demobilized soldiers. Thereafter he made monthly visits to the provinces accompanied by several Imperial Household officials and protected by Military Police jeeps. Before the war, the Japanese people had seen only the figure of the emperor in military uniform, a saber at his side, sitting astride a white horse. Now he appeared before them in a business suit, smiling and shaking hands, and wherever he went, large crowds welcomed him. Some were puzzled by this sudden transformation, but the tours certainly narrowed at a single stroke the distance between the emperor and the people. From the time of his visit to Chiba Prefecture in June 1946, Hirohito's local inspection tours ceased to be one-day affairs as they had been up to that time.

As the emperor's popularity rose, some officials within GHQ warned that the imperial tours were a "strategic movement" aimed at maintaining the emperor system. The Japan Communist party, at its party convention in February 1946, passed a resolution opposing the imperial tours, declaring that "The emperor is avoiding his own war responsibility." Even in a meeting of the Far Eastern Commission in Washington, the Soviet Union, Australia, and New Zealand all expressed their opposition to the tours, saying that the old-guard forces were stubbornly scheming to protect the emperor system. Although these imperial visits were a highlight of 1947, they suddenly ceased the following year.

From February to March 1948 the Japanese political situation changed dramatically: the Socialist party cabinet of Katayama Tetsu resigned and was replaced by a Democratic party government under Ashida Hitoshi. Prime Minister Ashida, judging that the emperor's great popularity actually endangered the imperial institution, carried out a change in the personnel surrounding the emperor within the Imperial Household, which had been the driving force behind the imperial tours. Ashida appointed Tajima Michiji, chairman of the Japan Scholarship Foundation, as grand steward of the Imperial Household and Mitani Takanobu, the Christian vice-president of the Peers School, as grand chamberlain. Notwithstanding his personal affection for the emperor, Tajima nevertheless believed that the emperor should assume moral responsibility for the war and abdicate. In making these appointments of the emperor's close attendants, Ashida visited GHQ to seek MacArthur's opinion. The General agreed that the democratization of the court was necessary to avoid criticism from the Soviet Union, which advocated abolition of the emperor system. Moreover, it was anticipated that the final verdict in the Tokyo War Crimes Trial would be delivered in the autumn of that year, and that if the emperor maintained too high a profile it might rekindle discussion of the issue of his war crimes. Thus, when Tajima became grand steward of the Imperial Household, he put a temporary stop to the imperial tours.[15]

The Emperor Refuses to Abdicate

On November 12, 1948, the Tokyo War Crimes Tribunal handed down guilty verdicts on twenty-five defendants, and on December 23 seven of them, including Tōjō Hideki, were hanged. On November 18 the "Liaison Officer of the Imperial Household," Terasaki Hidenari, handed W. J. Sebald, the State Department's political adviser to MacArthur, a letter from the emperor to MacArthur. The letter was dated November 12, the day of the Tokyo Trial verdicts. The emperor's message, conveyed on his behalf by the grand steward of the Imperial Household, read:

> November 12, 1948
> Excellency,
> By Imperial command I have the honor to transmit to Your Excellency a message from His Majesty as follows:
> "I am most grateful for the kind and considerate message Your Excellency was good enough to send me by Prime Minister Yoshida the other day. It is my lifelong desire to serve the cause of world peace as well as to promote the welfare and happiness of my people. I am determined now more than ever to do my best in concert with the people to surmount all difficulties and speed the national reconstruction of Japan." [Remainder omitted—N.M.]
> Michiji Tajima

As has been frequently noted, Hirohito on three different occasions after the war considered making a statement in some form concerning his abdication or his war responsibility. The first was right after the defeat; the second came at the time of the Tokyo trial verdicts; and the third was when the San Francisco Peace Treaty came into effect. But in the first instance abdication alone was not enough in view of the political situation at home and abroad immediately after the defeat. On the contrary, with republicanism being hotly discussed, the emperor's close advisers judged that even the preservation of the imperial institution itself was in doubt and therefore he and his close advisers abandoned the idea of expressing the emperor's wish to abdicate. It also seems that there was an intention to announce the emperor's abdication at the time of the verdicts on General Tōjō and the other war criminal suspects. MacArthur, however, thinking that the emperor could be instrumental in the occupation, opposed the idea, and it was again withdrawn. In Hirohito's message quoted above, Prime Minister Yoshida's name was mentioned. It may perhaps have been through Yoshida that MacArthur persuaded the emperor to abandon the idea. Thus, the Japanese people were unaware, but the decision that "the Emperor will not abdicate" was being dealt with secretly at the highest state policy-making level.[16]

With his continued reign now assured, the Shōwa Emperor resumed his imperial tours in 1949, and they continued until August 1954. Over eight years, they totaled 165 days, covering 33,000 kilometers throughout Japan, with the exception of Okinawa.

As for the third occasion on which the emperor's abdication was under consideration, important new historical material has been provided by the discovery of the unpublished diary of the Privy Seal Kido Kōichi in 1987. The diary revealed that at the time of the signing of the San Francisco Peace Treaty in September 1951, the emperor had resolved to take responsibility for the war and abdicate. Allow me to introduce a key portion of an entry that Kido made in his diary on October 17.

Kido Kōichi, a class A war criminal, was serving time in Sugamo prison in 1951, but through Matsudaira Yasumasa, the grand master of ceremonies of the Imperial Household Agency, he recommended that the emperor should abdicate.

> No matter how one looks at it, His Majesty bears responsibility for losing the war. Therefore, once you have thoroughly carried out the terms of the Potsdam Proclamation—in other words, when a peace

treaty has been signed—I think it is most proper for you to take responsibility and abdicate for the sake of your imperial ancestors and for the nation. . . . [I]f you do not do this, then the end result will be that only the Imperial family will not have taken responsibility and an unclear mood will remain which, I fear, might leave an eternal scar.

In reply, Emperor Hirohito entrusted the following message to Matsudaira Yasumasa, which may be read in Kido's diary entry of November 28, 1951. Upon learning of Matsudaira's answer concerning the emperor's abdication, Kido wrote, "His Majesty himself wishes to abdicate. Both Tajima, the grand steward of the Imperial Household Agency, and Matsudaira, the grand master of ceremonies, are also of the same opinion; but I am very concerned that Prime Minister Yoshida alone takes an attitude of extreme indifference to this problem."

Perhaps Prime Minister Yoshida feared that political confusion would result from the emperor's abdication. Ultimately, Kido seems to have changed his mind, deciding to keep this matter top secret until the peace treaty went into effect in April 1952 and Japan became independent. Even after the San Francisco peace treaty, however, a statement of imperial abdication was never forthcoming.

Kido wrote the following entry in his diary of April 4, 1952: "Prime Minister Yoshida was finally persuaded on the problem of the emperor's abdication and is now considering asking His Majesty to express his will on an occasion such as the anniversary of independence. But I understand that they are finding it very difficult to write a draft announcement because the state is somehow premised on the reign of His Majesty."

According to this diary entry, although Prime Minister Yoshida seems to have finally approved an expression of the emperor's will, it was extremely difficult to compose a draft statement as long as the state took the emperor's reign as its premise. Emperor Hirohito summoned the Grand Steward of the Imperial Household Tajima and made him take down the key points of a statement that he was going to read at the peace treaty ceremony on May 3. The expression "I deeply apologize to the nation for my responsibility for the defeat" appears in a few places, but these were ultimately deleted because one of his advisers opposed it, saying, "Why now is it necessary for His Majesty to apologize in such strong terms?"

At the time this draft was made Kido supposedly commented: "His Majesty should take responsibility for the war and at least formally express an apology. His true feelings should be recorded for history. Although constitutionally he cannot abdicate, it is necessary to establish the principle. Otherwise, it will cause trouble in the future that while having lost the war, the emperor took no measure whatsoever to correct his faults and ended up having no war responsibility." But at the ceremony commemorating the anniversary of the signing of the peace treaty, which took place before the Imperial Palace, Emperor Hirohito actually read out the following obscure composition, containing antiquated forms of expression: "At this time, reflecting on the past, judging from public opinion, and pondering deeply, I decided to bear the heavy burden, despite my inadequacies, and am now constantly troubled as to whether I am equal to the task."

This statement probably made it impossible for anyone to understand the implications of what the emperor was trying to say. The emperor's "deep ponderings" were, in any case, drowned out by the joyful cheers of those gathered before the Imperial Palace to celebrate the restoration of independence. Thus a stop was put to the problem of the emperor's abdication, which had been discussed for about seven years, ever since the defeat.[17]

But the fact that Emperor Hirohito lost his chance to abdicate became a burden to the imperial household until his death in January 1989. Not only did the world, and the peoples of Asia in particular, continue to view distrustfully the postwar emperor system, but critical sentiment toward the monarchy had settled deeply among the Japanese people as well.

The Third Alternative

Were there during the occupation period only the alternatives of either abolishing or preserving the monarchy? In my view, the recent publication of new materials and progress in scholarship suggest that there might have been a third alternative: the option of distinguishing the person from the institution—while Hirohito abdicated, the throne itself would be retained as a political institution.

If one views the matter initially from the U.S. side, we find that it has been coded in document SWNCC 55 of March 13, 1945 ("Politico-

Military Problems in the Far East; Treatment of the Emperor of Japan"):

> 1. After the unconditional surrender or collapse of Japan, military government will be faced with two distinct problems, namely, the treatment to be accorded the person of the Emperor . . . and the attitude to be taken toward the institution of the Emperor.

Following the defeat of Japan six months later, on September 14, 1945, Captain Robert L. Dennison wrote the following in a memorandum:

> . . . A clear distinction should be drawn between retention of the Emperor institution and retention of Emperor Hirohito. In the absence of Hirohito it is to be assumed that he would be succeeded as Emperor by his eldest son, the Crown Prince, now twelve years of age. In such an eventuality a regency could be established.

It is also well known that Nambara Shigeru, president of Tokyo University, and Sasaki Sōichi, a constitutional scholar and Kyoto University professor, both stated in the House of Peers in December 1946 that the emperor should assume moral responsibility and stand down. Neither of them were advocates of abolishing the monarchy, but rather both believed that its foundations would be strengthened by the emperor's abdication. In an essay appearing in the journal *Shinchō* in June 1946, the well-known poet Miyoshi Tatsuji wrote:

> As the Head of State, His Majesty must take the primary responsibility for this defeat. . . . His Majesty is responsible for permitting the rampant behavior of the military cliques and for many years he was also extremely negligent in the performance of his duties. . . . Today conscientious people without exception deplore the nation's moral bankruptcy. . . . However, the best way to save the situation is for the highest responsible person who allowed it to happen to clearly take responsibility upon himself and set a good example, as a person, thereby encouraging the public. This is also the most effective way. . . . It is best for Your Majesty to abdicate just as quickly as circumstances permit.

In this way, Miyoshi insisted on Emperor Hirohito's abdication, saying that (a) he bore responsibility for the defeat, (b) he permitted the unrestrained violence of the military, and (c) that unless he abdicated, the very morals of the Japanese nation would collapse. In addition to Miyoshi, old Liberals such as Abe Yoshishige, former Education Minister and President of the Peers School, writer Yamamoto Yūzō, and critic Matsumoto Shigeharu all distinguished the emperor from the imperial institution, arguing that the morals of Japan could be saved by Emperor Hirohito's abdication. Consequently, if at that time Liberals, Communists, and Socialists had united in proposing this third option, and shown flexibility in dealing with the problem, they could well have changed public opinion. The course of political developments might then have been different. The "Shōwa" era would not have dragged on for sixty-four years; and prewar and postwar differences and discontinuities would have become clearer. The historical consciousness of the Japanese would have been transformed; and postwar democracy would also have had a different development. Abroad, the process of settling accounts with the past vis-à-vis the countries of Asia could have been effected far more decisively.

Ultimately, however, the political calculations of Japanese and American officials meant that this third option could not be realized (see appendix 2). At the time both MacArthur and the Japanese government judged that the abdication of the emperor would most probably lead to Emperor Hirohito's immediate arrest, trial, and punishment. They chose, therefore, the path of preserving a symbol monarchy, and through constitutional revision Hirohito was able to continue his reign.

Going Beyond the Framework of "the Symbol"

The U.S.-Soviet confrontation intensified throughout 1947 and 1948. In China, Mao's Communist revolution grew in power as it moved from the villages to the cities, bringing the collapse of Chiang Kai-shek's Guomindang regime ever closer. Against this cold war background, the U.S. government switched from a policy of demilitarization and democratization of its former enemy to economic reconstruction in order to build up Japan as a bulwark of anticommunism.

As if to cope with this shift in policy, the American Council on Japan (ACJ) was established in June 1948 at the Harvard Club in New York City. This was the Japan lobby centered on *Newsweek* magazine's foreign affairs chief Harry Kern, its Tokyo bureau head Compton Pakenham, the lawyer James Kauffman, and others. Former ambassadors to Japan Joseph Grew and William Castle were chosen to be its honorary chairmen. They offered the Truman administration their written opinions on how to correct the "excesses" in MacArthur's occupation reforms, and they recommended such policies as the relaxation of zaibatsu dissolution, the establishment of a 150,000-man national police force, the relaxation of the economic purge, and the establishment of a fixed yen–dollar exchange rate. Almost all of these ACJ recommendations were adopted in NSC 13/2, which incorporated the reverse course in U.S. occupation policy. Moreover, the ACJ went beyond MacArthur's GHQ and aimed at direct contact with the emperor's innermost circle to reconstruct Japanese–U.S. relations.[18]

The Shōwa Emperor and his entourage of advisers seem to have perceived this shift in American policy through their own private intelligence network. The emperor was convinced that postwar Japan's diplomatic and military relations would have to be constructed on the basis of the Japanese–U.S. relationship. During the Socialist party cabinet of Katayama Tetsu in September 1947, the emperor's English-language interpreter (Terasaki Hidenari) visited W. J. Sebald, the State Department's counselor of mission to GHQ, and told him that the emperor wished to see the United States prolong its military occupation of the Ryūkyū Islands. This fact was first brought to light in 1979 by Professor Shindō Eiichi.[19] It is astonishing that the symbol emperor, who originally had been deprived of all "powers related to government" in the constitution, took such a critically significant action. Interestingly, this information is corroborated by the diary of Grand Chamberlain Irie Sukemasa, published in 1990. In reporting these facts, the *Okinawa Times* and the *Ryūkyū shimpō* went so far as to conduct a fierce anti-emperor campaign under the headline: "Emperor Hirohito Sold Okinawa to the United States."[20]

When the Korean War broke out in June 1950, the emperor sent a message of gratitude for the U.S. Army's participation in the war; and in January 1951, when John Foster Dulles visited Japan as Secretary of State Dean Acheson's consultant on the peace treaty, the emperor met him personally and gave his consent for American forces to be stationed in Japan as a temporary measure until Japan had its own defense capability.

Encouraged by the shift in American occupation policy, the Shōwa Emperor had therefore secretly begun to involve himself in politics. He summoned Prime Minister Ashida to the Palace and repeatedly made political statements, such as "I think Japan should ultimately align with the United States; it is difficult to cooperate with the Soviet Union"; and "I think it is necessary to take action against the Communist party."[21] In October 1948 the entire Ashida cabinet resigned as a result of the Shōwa Denkō scandal and was replaced by the second Yoshida cabinet. Yoshida too made frequent secret representations to the throne, reporting on domestic political trends.

These facts imply that not only was the Shōwa Emperor unable to comply with the requirements of his position as a symbol monarch; he also had great difficulty overcoming his previous style of operation under the old constitution.

Constitutional Revision and Movements
to Make the Emperor a Head of State

On April 28, 1952, the peace treaty went into effect, ending the American occupation of Japan. SCAP (or GHQ) was abolished, and Japan finally regained its sovereignty seven years after the end of the war. But the Japanese–U.S. Security Treaty, which went into effect simultaneously with the peace treaty, meant "peace with bases," or the continued presence of U.S. forces on Japanese soil. What is more, Okinawa continued under direct U.S. military control, and a network of bases was spread throughout the island. The progressive camp within Japan, centered on the Socialist party, criticized this as "semi-independence" and confronted the Yoshida cabinet, opposing the Security Treaty and the U.S. bases, and advocating a policy of unarmed neutrality.

Meanwhile, conservative forces began to divide into pro- and anti-Yoshida groups. Yoshida chose to maintain the Japanese–U.S. Security Treaty as the basis of Japan's security while reducing military costs as far as possible and pouring all energy into economic growth. But this "Yoshida line" not only aggravated relations with the Soviet Union and China but also greatly narrowed Japan's military and diplomatic options. The anti-Yoshida faction, centered on Hatoyama Ichirō and Kishi Nobusuke, resisted Yoshida's policy of subordination to the United States and advocated a foreign policy of autonomy, the restoration of diplomatic relations with the Soviet Union, and the revision of the constitution. This conflict between Yoshida and Hatoyama continued from 1952 to 1954, until Hatoyama formed the Japan Democratic party on November 24, 1954, with himself as president and Kishi as chief secretary.

The Japan Democratic party aimed to unite politically those forces seeking constitutional revision, arguing that the constitution had been unjustly foisted upon Japan by the power of the occupation forces and that an autonomous constitution should be enacted by Japanese hands. Their aim was not only to revise article 9 but to change to an autonomous defense based on remilitarization, under an emperor whose status was transformed from "symbol" to "head of state." Of course, making the emperor the head of state did not mean that they wanted to return to the prewar system of imperial sovereignty. That sort of restorationist reform was no longer possible. The ideas of the constitutional revisionists gradually changed with the times, but, generally speaking, their aims were first to increase the authority of the emperor as "the spiritual foundation of the Japanese nation." Second, they wanted to give the emperor added authority to grant pardons and ratify treaties, which are important customary powers of monarchs. Third, they wanted to give the emperor the power to declare war and peace, proclaim states of emergency, promulgate emergency orders, and suspend the Diet.[22]

In December 1954 the Japan Democratic party, acting jointly with the left and right wings of the Socialist party, tabled a motion of no confidence in the Yoshida cabinet, forcing it to resign en masse. After seven years in power, the Yoshida regime had finally fallen to be replaced by the Hatoyama cabinet. In seeking to implement constitutional revision, Hatoyama devoted all his energies to establishing a system of small electoral districts.

Chapter IX, article 96, of the present constitution stipulates that revisions require a vote of two-thirds or more of all the members of both houses of the Diet. Hatoyama's attempts at revision ended in failure, however, because of fierce public opposition and also resistance from within the conservative camp itself. The Socialist party, which had long been split between left- and right-wing groups, feared that the government had still not abandoned its intention to revise the constitution. When the Socialists achieved party unification in October 1955, the conservatives responded by seeking to strengthen their own unity. In November the Liberal and Democratic parties formed a coalition and established the Liberal-Democratic party (LDP) with Hatoyama Ichirō as its first president. This marked the start of the era of two-party politics, or the "1955 system."

In the House of Councillors election of July 1956, the third Hatoyama cabinet gambled on making constitutional revision the main issue. The election resulted, however, in sixty-one seats for the LDP versus forty-nine for the Socialists, five for the Ryokufūkai, two for the Communists, and ten independent seats. The progressives had secured over one-third of the seats in the Upper House, frustrating the intentions of the Hatoyama faction. If the LDP had obtained more than two-thirds of the seats at the time, articles 1 and 9—the two distinguishing features of the Constitution of Japan—would have been revised and the speed of Japan's expansion of military power, as well as the campaign to make the emperor a head of state, would surely have grown. But in 1956, with memories of the war still vivid in people's minds, Japanese voters delivered a firm "no" answer to the Hatoyama cabinet. This marked a turning point in postwar politics, after which conservative governments were no longer able openly to advocate constitutional revision. The emperor's local tours, discussed earlier, had already ended in 1954, and press coverage of the emperor steadily declined.

The "Mitchii Boom" and Campaigns against the Government

It was not until 1958 that the Japanese media began once again to give large-scale news coverage to the imperial house. On November 27 of that year, the engagement was announced of Crown Prince Akihito to Shōda Michiko, the oldest daughter of the president of the Nisshin Flour Milling Company. It was the first time that a commoner had married into the imperial family, and newspapers and television sensationalized the "love that bloomed at Karuizawa," creating in the process the "Mitchii [Michiko] boom."

In the background, orchestrating this engagement, were Koizumi Shinzō, the former president of Keiō Gijuku University, who was in charge of Crown Prince Akihito's education, and Usami Takeshi, grand steward of the Imperial Household. These men thought it necessary to reestablish the monarchy on a broader social foundation by changing it from a closed, rigidly traditional institution to one that was open to the people. But Yoshida Shigeru, whom Koizumi consulted on this matter, expressed his opposition to the fact that the prospective princess was a commoner. In Yoshida's opinion, it was the duty of the Imperial Household of Japan to always maintain tradition. When Grand Steward Usami went to seek the consent of the emperor and empress, Hirohito is said to have stated his opposition by saying, "Don't you think it will be too difficult for someone who knows absolutely nothing about the customs of the palace?"[23] Michiko was, furthermore, a graduate of the Sacred Heart University and came from a Catholic family. It therefore seems likely that the emperor was concerned not only that the candidate for princess was a commoner but also that, given her religious background, she was unfamiliar with court rituals based on Shinto tradition. But with support from Koizumi and others, and the determination of Crown Prince Akihito, the matter was settled.

The marriage of the crown prince and Michiko took place on April 10, 1959. Following the ceremony, a commemorative parade took the couple from the Imperial Palace to the crown prince's temporary palace, with an estimated 540,000 well-wishers crowding the route. Television stations mobilized all their resources, deploying 108 cameras and 1,200 news gatherers to cover the event. Japanese television broadcasting had started in 1953, but many families bought television sets in order to watch the marriage parade. On the day, television viewers averaged an unprecedented ten hours and thirty-five minutes in front of their TV screens.

Watching this royal fever, political scientist Matsushita Keiichi wrote an article in the April 1959 issue of *Chūō kōron* in which he stated that the "Mitchii boom" was undermining the divine image of the imperial family and creating a new image of the emperor that matched the spirit of the new constitution. He went on to note that the social foundation of the monarchy had changed from the old to the new middle class. The imperial house was now no longer an object of awe—it had become "a sacred family of stars beloved by the masses." In short, a transition had been effected from the prewar absolute emperor system to a mass monarchy, and thus one may say that the intentions of Koizumi and others had succeeded. High economic growth had already got under way in 1955, and the traditional agrarian community was disintegrating. In the cities the white-collar phenomenon of giving priority to family and private life, or "my-home-ism," had emerged, centered on the office worker. As article 24 of the Constitution of Japan had stipulated that "Marriage shall be based only on the mutual consent of both sexes," the marriage of the crown prince appealed to the younger generation's understanding of the new constitution. Briefly stated, the "Mitchii boom" was also a social phenomenon reflecting the change in the Japanese people's sense of values that accompanied high economic growth (see fig. 2).

The Campaign against Revision of the Police Law

There was another side, however, to the "Mitchii boom." Starting in 1958, the Kishi cabinet (1957–60), successor to the Hatoyama regime, began negotiating with the U.S. government to revise the Japanese–U.S. Security Treaty based on its desire to develop a more autonomous diplomacy with the United States. In October 1958, in preparation for an anticipated intensification of popular demonstrations, the Kishi cabinet submitted a "Bill on Revision of the Law Concerning the Conduct of Policemen in the Performance of Their Duties." Kishi later said that he "was determined to revise the treaty in spite of opposition . . . and thought that a revision of the Police Officers Law was absolutely essential in order to maintain public order."[24]

The bill greatly restricted the freedom of assembly, demonstration, and free speech by empowering police officers to question people, to conduct body searches, and to enter private land and buildings such as union offices, meetings, and lodgings. In reply, sixty-five organizations, including the Socialist party and the labor federation Sōhyō, formed the People's Council to Prevent Revision of the Police Law and staged nationwide, unified demonstrations on five occasions in October and November. Weekly magazines and newspapers wrote about the revival of police "arrogance" and the "police law that even interferes with dating." Given the growing popularity around that time of the ideals of "my-home-ism," which respected privacy and gave priority to happiness within the family, these slogans were all the more effectively spread, helping to enhance popular opposition to the revision of the Police Duties Law. Indeed, in time this campaign gradually combined with the movement to overthrow the Kishi cabinet and oppose the revision of the Security Treaty.

In these circumstances, the government concluded that passage of the Police Duties Bill was almost impossible during that session of the Diet. On the night of November 4 it forced through a thirty-day extension of the

Figure 2. Popular Feeling toward the Showa Emperor (by age)

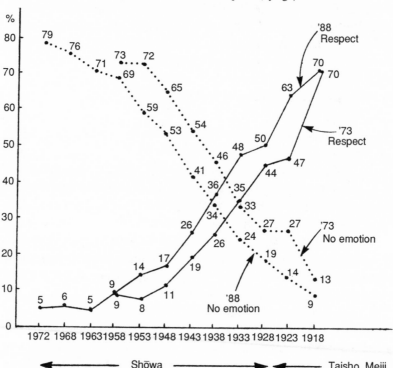

Source: NHK seron chōsabu hen, *Gendai Nihonjin no ishiki kōzō, dai sanban* (Tokyo: Nippon Hōsō shuppan kyokai, 1991).

Diet in spite of resistance from the opposition parties. The next morning the Kishi cabinet came under fire from all the newspapers. That day, four million labor union members belonging to Sōhyō and other federations that had participated in the People's Council went on strike solely on the basis of their opposition to the revision of the Police Law. This was the largest mass mobilization of the 1950s. Clearly, the movement against the Police Law had given rise to a new state of affairs.

The heightening of opposition movements intensified the LDP's internal conflicts. The LDP's antimainstream factions criticized the mainstream, in which Kishi and others were the driving force, and called for a conference of the leaders of the Socialist party and the LDP. To calm the opposition campaign and maintain the Kishi cabinet, the mainstream factions were forced to shelve the police revision bill, and after ten days of meetings between leaders of the Socialist party and the LDP, the Bill on Revision of the Police Officers' Performance of Duties Law was finally withdrawn. Five days later, the engagement of the crown prince was announced. The "Mitchii boom" had helped to deflect the nation's attention from politics, and was also effective in temporarily postponing the merger of the anti–Police Law movement with the campaign against revision of the Security Treaty.

The Campaign against Revision of the Security Treaty

In January 1960 Prime Minister Kishi visited Washington and on the 20th of that month signed a new security treaty with President Eisenhower. The old treaty of 1951 had given the United States the unrestricted right to station its military forces on Japanese territory, but had carried no obligation of prior consultation with the Japanese government concerning the dispatch of those forces. It also failed to specify the length of time the treaty would remain in effect. The object of the revision was therefore to correct these defects and make it more equitable.

The Diet that reconvened on January 30 was called the "Security Treaty Diet" (Ampo kokkai) as its main task was the ratification of the new treaty. When it was presented to the Diet, the government and opposition parties engaged in fierce controversy over the area of the Far East that should be defended under the treaty, as well as the article on "prior consultation" with the Japanese government at times when the United States exercised its military power. According to the new security treaty, if the United States opened hostilities with another country in the Far East and that country attacked U.S. bases in Japan, the Japanese Self-Defense Forces would inevitably be forced to act jointly with U.S. forces in Japan. The opposition pursued the Kishi government over this, charging that if the new Security Treaty were concluded, there would be a danger that Japan might be drawn into a war against its will.

Meanwhile, outside the Diet, the campaign against treaty revision had been renewed by the People's Council to Prevent Security Treaty Revision, an extension of the People's Council to Prevent Revision of the Police Law. This organization was formed in March 1959 by 134 organizations, including the Socialist party, Sōhyō, and Gensuikyō (Japan Council against Atomic and Hydrogen Bombs). Even university students joined in the antitreaty struggle while they themselves were divided into opposing pro- and anti-JCP organizations.

On April 19, 1960, a campaign erupted to overthrow the Syngman Rhee dictatorship in South Korea. On April 26, Rhee finally resigned, and in May fled into exile in Hawaii. The fact that student demonstrations had succeeded in overthrowing the thirteen-year-long Syngman Rhee dictatorship spurred on the antitreaty forces in Japan. On May 5, Soviet leader Nikita Khrushchev announced that an American U–2 plane had been shot down while infringing on Soviet air space on a spying mission. This incident helped many Japanese to realize the danger of becoming involved in a war as a result of the U.S.–Soviet confrontation, and led to a significant growth in the antitreaty forces.

But the Kishi cabinet refused to listen to public opinion, pushing to complete the ratification of the treaty before President Eisenhower's visit to Japan, which was expected on June 19. On May 19 the Kishi cabinet and the Liberal Democratic party brought five hundred police officers into the House of Representatives and unilaterally forced a vote on the treaty ratification bill. This forced ballot shocked the entire nation. Thereafter, until the treaty was automatically ratified on June 19, a month of violent turmoil began, spurred by an unprecedented mass movement. Day after day, waves of demonstrations took place outside the Diet building and chants of "Prevent the Security Treaty" and "Overthrow Kishi" echoed through the Diet. On June 4 and 15 the national railway system was paralyzed by union strikes in which nearly six million workers participated.

It was under these circumstances that President Eisenhower's press secretary James Hagerty visited Japan on June 10. The day he arrived, about ten thousand labor unionists and students belonging to the Zengakuren's antimainstream (pro-JCP) faction rushed out to Haneda Airport where they surrounded the official car carrying Haggerty and Ambassador Douglas MacArthur III. Screaming "Stop Ike's visit!" they proceeded to mob the car. About an hour and a half later both men had to be rescued by a U.S. military helicopter.

On June 15, approximately 5.8 million people participated in a second national mass demonstration against revision of the treaty, during which right-wing thugs suddenly attacked a demonstration of the "new theater people's association" and housewives gathered outside the Diet, injuring over sixty of them. That night students of the anti-JCP

Zengakuren mainstream faction attempted to force their way into the Diet building. In the ensuing clash with fully armed riot police, a female Tokyo University student was killed. Fearing that this June 15 struggle would affect the whole country, Prime Minister Kishi consulted with Akagi Munenori, minister of the Defense Agency. Akagi later bore witness that he refused Kishi's request for troops by saying "The demonstrations are confined to Tokyo right now, but if the Self-Defense Forces are called in and it results in deaths, the disturbances will spread like a revolution though the entire country. If that happens, we won't be able to control it."[25]

Why, then, did Prime Minister Kishi even consider such forceful measures as dispatching the Self-Defense Forces? Kishi was planning to ask Emperor Hirohito to welcome President Eisenhower in person at Haneda Airport. The emperor apparently also indicated his firm resolve to go by saying, "It is my duty to welcome the President at Haneda no matter what dangers might arise."[26] If the first ever American president to visit Japan rode together with the emperor in an open car from Haneda Airport to the Imperial Palace, it would certainly have invited a rapturous welcome from the people, and might even have discouraged the antitreaty forces. But the director of the National Police Agency, Kashiwamura, notified Kishi that he had no confidence in his ability to protect the route from Haneda to the Imperial Palace. With Director General Akagi also opposed to calling out the Self-Defense Forces on the day of Eisenhower's visit, Kishi was forced to call off the visit entirely at a cabinet meeting on June 16.

At noon on June 19, while 330,000 people surrounded the Diet building, the new security treaty automatically went into efect without a vote by the House of Councillors. Following this, Prime Minister Kishi announced his resignation, and on July 15 the Kishi cabinet resigned en masse. Thus "it ended without either the Emperor card or the Self-Defense card being played. . . . The 1960 antitreaty struggle marked a major turning point in the operation of conservative politics and, along with it, the position of the emperor within the structure of political rule."[27]

11

THE ENTERPRISE STATE AND THE EMPEROR SYSTEM

The Income Doubling Plan

AFTER KISHI had been driven from power, the next cabinet was formed by the Finance Ministry bureaucrat Ikeda Hayato, adopting a conciliatory stance with his motto "tolerance and patience." The anti-treaty movement, which lasted over a year and had been the largest of the postwar period, had taught that the hard-line posture of the Kishi cabinet would no longer work politically. In the summer of 1959, a solution to the Miike strike, which had started with notifications of mass dismissals at the Mitsui Coal Mines, became the Ikeda cabinet's first priority. The Japanese economy, then in the midst of high economic growth, was proceeding to shift from coal to oil in an "energy revolution." Small- and medium-scale collieries were being forced to close down one after another, and even large mining firms were being forced to reorganize themselves, dismissing workers en masse and introducing new technology.

When the Mitsui Mining Company posted notices for the dismissal of 1,278 miners, including union activists, at its Miike mines (Japan's largest, with about fifteen thousand employees), it precipitated a violent confrontation with the Miike miners union. In January 1960 the management locked out the miners, and their union responded by calling an indefinite strike. The Miike union received support from Tanrō, the national organization of miners, and from Sōhyō, while Mitsui received financial backing from business and financial magnates throughout the country. The strike, which was at the time dubbed "the confrontation of organized capital and organized labor," moved toward a climax in July, after the settlement of the antitreaty struggle. On July 19 the company secured a court order to make provisional disposition barring workers from entering in the vicinity of the coal hopper. Ten thousand armed policemen and twenty thousand armed pickets confronted one another, creating an explosive situation. To avoid a bloodbath, the union accepted the mediation plan of the Central Workers Committee and acknowledged the fact of the firings. The strike had ended in the defeat of labor.

However, the antitreaty struggle and the Miike strike had deeply shocked both the government and leaders of business and finance and spurred the LDP to change its political course. Originally selected by Yoshida Shigeru and the nation's top businessmen, Ikeda Hayato was the faithful successor to the Yoshida line. Unlike Hatoyama and his successor Kishi, both of whom were Yoshida's political enemies, Ikeda chose to base his policy on Japan's relationship with the United States, giving priority to economic growth while pursuing limited rearmament. He avoided confrontations over divisive issues like strengthening policy on public order and constitutional revision, seeking instead to govern by mutual consent. In running for president of the LDP, Ikeda is said to have spoken confidently of how, "with income doubling, I am going to brighten up public sentiment, which has become darkened by the security treaty disturbances. This is a change of pace and also a genuine reform."[1]

In December 1960 the Ikeda cabinet decided on a plan that promised to double the national income in ten years. The Japanese economy had continued to develop steadily since the "Jimmu boom" of 1955–57, and a 1956 Economic White Paper declared that Japan was "no longer in the postwar era." In 1959 a second sustained boom, the so-called "Iwato boom," far exceeded the Jimmu boom and continued until the end of 1961. The long-term economic plan to double the national income had already begun the previous year under the Kishi cabinet, but it could not be realized until the antitreaty struggle and the Miike strike had ended.

Under the Ikeda cabinet, the speed of Japan's economic growth far exceeded the prime minister's expectations. Ikeda seems to have allowed for a nominal growth rate of 7.2 percent initially and 9 percent at the highest, but Japan registered a real rate of growth of 9.6 percent between 1960 and 1965.[2] In 1964, after Ikeda's death, Satō Eisaku took the helm of state affairs, and the high growth rate continued. Real growth between 1965 and 1970 reached 11.6 percent. Thus from 1955 until the first oil crisis of 1973, Japan's nominal growth rate had been 15 percent compared to a rate of 6 to 9 percent for the other advanced industrialized countries, while maintaining a real rate of growth of 10 percent. As a result, the Japanese economy had expanded 5.8 times in eighteen years. In 1968 Japan's GNP surpassed that of West Germany, making it the second largest in the capitalist world.

The Formation of the Enterprise State

Japan's enterprise state had assumed an unusual form: it was neither a military nor a welfare state, but a state system centered on large enterprises. The 1960s saw the creation of "Japanese-style management," based on the three pillars of lifetime employment, seniority wages, and enterprise unionism; and in large firms, a system of labor control was established. Together with these developments, government and large enterprises completed a political and social system that could control the nation without having to rely on the traditional, authoritarian formula of imperial rule.

In July 1964 the LDP's Constitutional Research Group, which had spent seven years investigating a plan for revision of the constitution, presented to the Ikeda cabinet a report favoring constitutional revision. Ikeda, however, took exception to it, saying that "Now is not the time for constitutional revision. As long as an absolute majority of the public is against it, I will not consider revising the constitution."[3] Ikeda feared that if he presented a revision of the constitution to the people, they would be likely to attack it again and provoke a second antitreaty struggle. Rather than have that happen, he therefore put the emphasis on his own political goals, which were to avoid confrontation and induce the people to concern themselves with economic growth. Prime Minister Ikeda's policy worked well, bringing two large victories in the general elections of November 1960 and November 1963, but what I should particularly like to note here is that in the early 1960s, Japan achieved full employment for the first time since the Meiji Restoration of 1868. Having accomplished that change, movements of social rebellion became noticeable in Japan from the late 1960s.

Miyazawa Kiichi, the powerful political oligarch of the Ikeda faction, once said this in an interview:

In the age of Keynes it didn't seem necessary to consider how human beings might change their nature when full employment was realized. By the same token, when the income doubling plan succeeded, and we achieved full employment, things that nobody ever imagined, like the anti-establishment movements and the troubles in the universities, erupted. In his later years, Mr. Ikeda also noticed these changes. . . . Toward the end of his term as prime minister, he began to talk about a round-table conference on character-development. That was because he constantly observed the changes occurring around him concerning the family, human feelings, and so forth, as a result of his own income doubling plan.[4]

High economic growth destroyed the rural village communities that had been the social foundation of the prewar emperor system and drove farm households to the verge of dissolution. The percentage of the agricultural population within the total employed population declined dramatically: from 45.2 percent in 1950 to 30.0 percent in 1960, and from 17.9 percent in 1970 to 9.7 percent in 1980. In the big cities, where the families of white-collar workers and young laborers from the countryside had increased, a mass society emerged. This meant that on one side a new middle-class sense of anti-authoritarian values and egoism ("me-ism") was developed, while at the same time many of the traditional values of the old middle class remained. One could say that a dual structure, as it were, of modern and premodern values had taken root in Japanese society.

Figure 3 shows the results of public opinion surveys of the Showa Emperor between 1973 and 1988. In the generation born between 1933 and 1938, "respect" and "indifference" intersect one another. In other words, in the 1988 survey, about 70 percent of the older generation (aged sixty and above) answered that they "feel respect" for the emperor. In contrast, about 70 percent of the younger generation (aged thirty and below) answered that they "do not feel anything" toward the emperor. This tendency was a common phenomenon even in the 1960s. "The feelings of the Japanese toward the Showa Emperor depend on when they were born. In other words, it is clearly determined by what sort of education their generation received regarding the emperor."[5]

The Meiji Centennial and Emperor Ideology

At a news conference held soon after the formation of his cabinet, Satō Eisaku, who came to power in November 1964, stated that "the spirit of the new constitution is becoming an integral part of the nation. I think it would be better for us, myself included, to read the constitution once again." This unexpected statement, coming from a man with an image as a hard-line conservative, is said to have made his elder brother, Kishi, furious. But the smooth management of politics was a priority for Sato, and he could not help being prudent on the issue of constitutional revision. Indeed, the prime minister who maintained power for eight years from 1964 to 1972—the longest continuous tenure of the postwar period—was consistently negative toward constitutional revision.[6]

As seen in figure 2, news reports on the emperor steadily declined from 1962 to 1967, then increased slightly in 1968, the year of the Meiji centennial celebrations. The Satō cabinet, after two years of preparations, marked the anniversary by sponsoring tree-planting events, the construction of parks, the preservation and exaltation of history, and the promotion of international understanding by sending young people abroad on sea voyages. At the main ceremony held on October 23 in the Budōkan [Martial Arts Hall] in Tokyo, the Showa Emperor and Empress, Prime Minister Satō, the diplomatic corps, and nine hundred youth representatives paid homage to the success of Japan's modernization since the start of the Meiji era.

The government had established a Meiji Centennial Preparatory Council to plan the celebrations, appointing all twenty ministers of the Sato cabinet, twenty-five group representatives, such as the president of Keidanren and the chairman of the National Governors Association, and forty-two men of "learning and experience." Notable among the council members was Yasuoka Masahiro, an ultranationalist of prewar fame appointed to the centennial publicity committee. A vehement emperor worshiper, he maintained that the success of the Meiji Restoration lay with the greatness of the Meiji Emperor; that thesis became the guiding theme of the centennial celebrations.[7]

The process of preparing for the Meiji Centennial stirred up the right wing, who had previously maintained a low profile, and spurred their activities on behalf of constitutional revision. From August 9 to 14, 1967, for example, the rightist Kodama Yoshio convened a lecture series for young students by Lake Motosu at the base of Mount Fuji. There he is reported to have negated the Constitution of Japan, calling it a "constitution of occupation," and delivered a speech in which he declared that, "The present constitution is only recognized as the basic law of the occupation. Even considered from a purely legal standpoint, the Meiji Constitution should be a living thing." "We should quickly revise the constitution so that we can possess nuclear [weapons]."[8]

There were, of course, social forces in Japan that responded to this sort of agitation; but the imperial view of the past, and right-wing ideology of the Yasuoka and Kodama variety, could no longer attract the Japanese people. The Satō government therefore aimed at the ideological mobilization of the nation by holding aloft a modernization that brought "a century of growth and prosperity." At the time, there was a dispute among Japanese historians over whether it was this modernization theory or the emperor ideology that was at the heart of the Meiji Centennial. Many of the participants saw emperor ideology as the focus, but that judgment was incorrect.[9] Rather, the main current was modernization theory, the emperor ideology being merely its supplement.

For example, reading publications like the *Nikkeiren Times* and the "Manager" (*Keieisha*) from around that time, one notices that the managers of large-scale enterprises did not have a clear vision of the state. Managing directors of Nikkeiren, such as Maeda Hajime, declared that the Japanese economy had entered an age of full internationalization and labor shortages, while lamenting the fact that office and factory workers were completely immersed in "my-home-ism." In their view, the main reason why wage earners had become "petty economic animals" was that politicians were unable to articulate national objectives like the "rich country, strong military" (*fukoku kyōhei*) sentiment of the Meiji era. Accordingly, by deploying the logic of "the company exists, therefore you [employees] exist," they came up with the slogan "Love the home, love the company, and love the country," equivalent to the notion that the fate of the enterprise was the fate of the community. Nagano Shigeo, president of Fuji Steel, and Maeda Hajime frequently said that "if the company collapses, managers and workers alike will perish together with it." However, even though loving the home and loving the company could be forced on workers by company indoctrination, it was difficult to make employees associate their corporate patriotism with love of the country. For this reason, Maeda introduced the idea of the centrality of the emperor as a distinctive trait of the Japanese, and tried to find an ideal image of the state. At the

Figure 3. Number of News Reports on the Imperial Household and the Emperor Printed Annually in the *Asahi Shimbun*

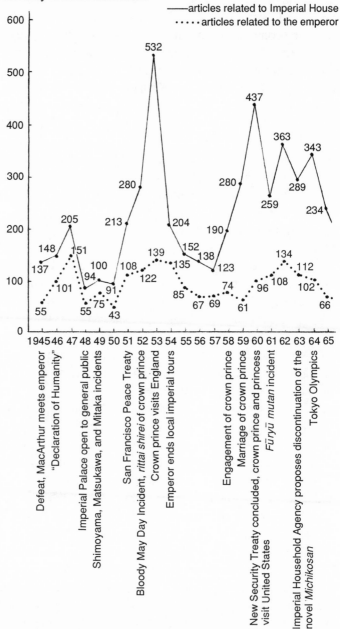

Source: Momna Naoki, "Tennō shikyo hōdō no shisō—minshū ni totte sengo no tennōsei to wan nan datta no ka," in Iwanami Shinsho, henshūbu, *Shōwa no shūen* (Tokyo, Iwanami Shinsho, 1990), pp. 114–15.

Notes: News reports (unbroken and dotted lines) cover only from August to December 1945; News reports for 1988 cover only from January to August 1988 prior to the emperor's critical illness in September.

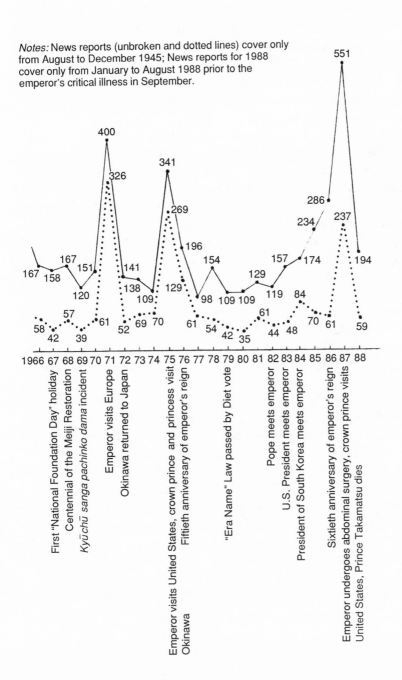

seventeenth general meeting of Nikkeiren in April 1964, Maeda declared: "We are not Americans and cannot completely become Europeans. We are forever Japanese. Although our four islands are small, it is our land. Here lives the Japanese race, unmixed with alien races, seeking the foundation of its national sentiment in the emperor as the symbol of the state. This is an absolutely unique national and racial characteristic, not to be seen anywhere else in the world; and that characteristic should be maintained forever."

At the time, Maeda's statement was noted for its unusual honesty in expressing the true feelings of Japan's business and financial leaders; but it was too anachronistic to become the mainstream view of the business world. A round-table discussion in *Nikkeiren Times* on New Year's day 1968, chaired by Maeda, completely ignored his previous statement but reached a consensus on the need for creating a national image to which Japan should aspire.The participants laid out a variety of menus—defense state, peace state, moral state, welfare state, and so forth—but could not reach a decision as to how best to present its image, and instead ended up talking nostalgically of the Meiji state in the age of *fukoku kyōhei.*

Thus the Meiji Centennial, despite all the propaganda it generated, failed to yield the expected results. In the end, it left behind only historical works sponsored by local governments and an abundance of memorial trees.

Interestingly, the next peak period of news items concerning the emperor was in 1971, when he and the empress toured seven European countries. Despite the many warm official welcomes Emperor Hirohito received during the tour, in Britain, West Germany, and the Netherlands he encountered noisy demonstrations of students and ordinary citizens reminding him of his war responsibility with shouts of "Hiro-Hitler" and "Go Home Murderer." The European tour was a disappointment for the emperor and the Japanese government, and, what is more, accidentally revealed the "scarred symbol emperor system" discussed in chapter 10.

The Emperor's American Visit

In October 1975, the emperor and empress paid their first visit to the United States and met President Gerald Ford. Plans for the emperor's trip had begun in 1973 under the Tanaka cabinet, but the visit was postponed due to the opposition of Director of the Imperial Household Agency Usami and others. President Richard Nixon, then in the throes of the Watergate scandal, wanted Hirohito to visit the United States, but the Vietnam War had still not ended, economic frictions were worsening, and Japanese–U.S. relations were not in a satisfactory state.

At home, an incident had occurred in which Masuhara Keikichi, director general of the Defense Agency, resigned after speaking to reporters about what the emperor had said during an informal report to the throne. In May 1975, when Masuhara had visited the palace to report on the situation in neighboring countries and the condition of Japan's Self-Defense Forces, the emperor is reported to have said: "Why is the press writing that our Self-Defense Force will be increased markedly with the fourth Defense Build-up Plan, when the number of Self-Defense Force units is actually smaller than the military forces of neighboring countries? ... The problem of defense is very difficult but it is important to defend the country. I want you to work hard to incorporate the good practices and not follow the bad practices of the former imperial military."[10]

Opposition parties regarded Masuhara's public quotation of the emperor's words, at a time when the Fourth Defense Plan was being discussed in the Diet, as equivalent to a political use of the emperor, and demanded that Prime Minister Tanaka dismiss him. In addition, the nation was astonished that the emperor had spoken in this way. I understand that the emperor sighed upon receiving reports of the Masuhara incident, and said "There's no way for me but to become a papier-mâché doll or something."[11]

In view of the above circumstances, the 1973 plan for the emperor's trip to the United States was postponed. Later, after the downfall of President Nixon, Director of the Imperial Household Agency Usami spoke boastfully about his foresight, saying, "It would have been an incalculable loss of prestige if [the emperor] had shaken that scandal-stained hand at that time."[12]

In November 1974, President Ford, who had succeeded Nixon, became the first American president to visit Japan while still in office. In return, Emperor Hirohito visited the United States the following year. There the emperor and empress were welcomed, and it seems that this was an easier and more enjoyable trip than their stressful European tour. On their way home they stopped at Disneyland. The Japanese press reported that the cheerful-looking emperor "smiled like an innocent child" as he stood next to the empress, who was embracing an American child. After the emperor's return to Japan, Grand Chamberlain Irie Sukemasa recorded in his diary (regarding the unexpected success of his trip to the United States) that "I encouraged him by saying that the trip's success was indeed due to Your Majesty's virtue. He was so happy that tears came to his eyes."[13]

However, in an interview at the Imperial Palace with fifty Japanese journalists on October 31, 1975, the emperor was asked a question about war responsibility and the dropping of the nuclear bombs. His reply provoked the anger of the Japanese nation as well as the citizens of Hiroshima.

> Journalist: "Your Majesty, at your White House banquet you said 'I deeply deplore that unfortunate war.' Does Your Majesty feel responsibility for the war itself [i.e., not just for the defeat], including the opening of hostilities? Also, what does Your Majesty think about so-called war responsibility?"
>
> His Majesty: "I can't answer that sort of question because I haven't thoroughly studied the literature in this field, and so don't really understand the implications of those words." "I feel it is very regrettable that nuclear bombs were dropped, and I feel sorry for the citizens of Hiroshima. But it couldn't be helped because it happened in wartime."[14]

One poet who heard this statement used an old military song to query how those who had died on land and sea during the war felt about "the implications of those words," while another, Ibaraki Noriko, said "It was the most absurd black humor in thirty years."

Era Name Legislation and Grass-Roots Conservatism

The fiftieth jubilee of the Shōwa Emperor's reign was celebrated at the Tokyo Budōkan in November 1976. About 7,500 people attended, including the emperor and empress, the crown prince and princess and other members of the imperial family, Prime Minister Miki, the Speakers of the House of Representatives and the House of Councillors, the chief justice of the Supreme Court, and representatives of the diplomatic corps. During the ceremony, the prime minister wished the emperor a long life and prayed for the prosperity of Japan. That year, however, the emperor became seventy-six year old, and the Japanese government began to prepare for the legalization of the system of era names. Should the emperor die, the system of naming eras would end, and the "unbroken line of succession" would be destroyed. The government therefore rushed to legalize the system of naming era names to ensure a smooth succession to the throne, and from around 1977 the religious sect "House of Growth" (Seichō no Ie) and the Association of Shinto Shrines (Jinja Honchō) also started a campaign to legalize the system of one era name for each emperor.

The leaders of this campaign argued that "Our main goal, and the most important issue in the campaign, is to strengthen the ties between the emperor and the nation, further enhancing the emperor's authority." They stressed that the use of era names, though it worked indirectly, make the people continually conscious of the emperor's existence, and was extremely effective in unifying national consciousness.[15] In conducting their campaign, the activists organized a national "caravan," applying pressure in prefectural assemblies to secure the passage of era-name resolutions. Those who responded were mainly local assemblymen and women of the LDP and the Democratic-Socialist party, as well as local people of influence. By December 1978, a large number of conservative prefectures, such as Kumamoto, Miyazaki, Ehime, and Ōita, had passed resolutions calling for the promotion of era-name legislation. It was the first time such a situation had existed since the war, and it gave the impression of strong grass-roots conservatism. The strategy of going "from the local areas to the entire country" had proved successful: social groups imbued with prewar values rapidly came to the fore.

In June 1978, 411 members of the upper and lower houses of the Diet joined together to form the "Diet Members League for the Promotion of Era Name Legislation." Ishida Kazuto, a former chief justice of the Supreme Court, was chosen to be its chairman, and in October, twenty thousand people gathered at the Budōkan in a political rally in support of the era-name bill. The LDP's Executive Board chairman, Nakasone Yasuhiro, attended, and a message from Prime Minister Fukuda Takeo was read out.

The Kōmeitō (Clean Government party) and the Minshatō (Democratic Socialist party) also supported era-name legislation, and public opinion at the time was similarly supportive of the bill: 77.9 percent "approved of retaining the era name"; 7.2 percent disapproved; and 14.9 percent were either indifferent or did not know. But to the question "Do you approve of using the era name system exclusively?" 26.0 percent answered "yes" in 1975 while only 9.9 percent answered "yes" in 1977. As to whether both the Japanese system and the Western calendar should be used, 61.0 percent agreed in 1975, and 54.4 percent in 1977. A survey in July 1978 revealed that 15.1 percent thought that era-name legislation should be enacted while 64.5 percent agreed with the statement that "We should use the era name but not go so far as to legislate for it."[16]

Those opposing the bill included the Socialist and Communist parties, Christian organizations and various citizens groups. In their view, the people should be free to choose which calendar to use, and as imperial era names were recognized only in Japan, making their use compulsory by law contravened freedom of expression and religion. Other influential voices argued that such legislation would distort Japanese historical consciousness and international awareness. And there were people like the playwright Kinoshita Junji, author of *Yūzuru* (Twilight crane), who said at a meeting of the Japan Pen Club that "When I read a book I change the era name to the Western calendar with a blue pencil."

Nevertheless, in the LDP presidential election of November 1978, Ōhira Masayoshi, a Christian, defeated Fukuda Takeo. Ōhira maintained his promise to Fukuda, and in June 1979, carried the era-name bill through the Diet, where it was promulgated and went into effect on June 11. Thus, when Emperor Hirohito died on January 7, 1989, the "Shōwa" era automatically ended, and a new era, "Heisei," began. Had it not been for this legislation, a smooth change of era-name would probably have been impossible. The enactment of the era-name system became a major springboard for enhancing the authority of the emperor.

Suzuki's Textbook Problem and the Rise of the Nakasone Cabinet

Prime Minister Ōhira died suddenly in June 1980 and was succeeded by Suzuki Zenkō. It was an unusual choice, leaving foreign journalists asking "Zenkō who?" Indeed, Suzuki accomplished little and retired after two years and four months in office. During this time only one issue had achieved much prominence: the textbook problem.

In 1982 an international incident had been precipitated by the Ministry of Education, which, in authorizing school textbooks, had made authors use the word "advance" instead of "invasion" to describe prewar Japanese militarism in China and Korea. The Chinese government had issued a statement in July condemning the Japanese government for this action, and the following month, the government of South Korea also protested the description of Japanese colonial rule in Japanese textbooks, demanding that it be corrected. In August, the government agreed to rectify the matter, and in September, Prime Minister Suzuki had to promise Zhao Ziyang, China's prime minister who was visiting Japan at that time, that changes would be made.

But this was not the sort of problem that could be disposed of simply by changing "advance" back to "invasion." For the problem is connected with Professor Ienaga Saburō's lawsuit against the textbook authorization system which is still a matter of great concern to many Japanese people. It is also pregnant with issues pertaining to basic political philosophy and Japanese foreign policy: the handling of the emperor's war responsibility, the war responsibility of the Japanese people, the way in which Japan should deal hereafter with the rest of the world and, not least, the countries of Asia.

Yasuhiro Nakasone was a strongly individualistic politician, long known as a proponent of constitutional revision. But he was also a politician with a reputation for malleability, known since his youth as the "weather vane." Sharply observing the shifting sands in international and domestic affairs, and sometimes changing his policy direction accordingly, he was able to maintain power for five years, from November 1982 until November 1987. Having skillfully ridden out the two oil crises of 1973 and 1979, by the mid-1980s the Japanese economy had come to occupy an unshakeable position as a world economic power, with its shares of both the world's GNP and the world's exports exceeding 10 percent. In per capita GNP, it stood second in the world, having surpassed West Germany. Japanese journalists had started to use the term "Japan, the international state"; and with this enormously enlarged economy behind him, the new prime minister acted confidently from the very start.

In November 1983 Nakasone met President Ronald Reagan in Washington and declared that Japan shared a common destiny with the United States in the Pacific, saying, "The Japanese archipelago is an enormous unsinkable aircraft carrier pointed at the Soviet Union." On his return to Japan, Nakasone asked the Diet for a "full settlement of accounts with postwar politics to challenge former taboos." His political strategy was designed to have Japan play an international role commensurate with its status as a major economic power, and to shift Japan's conservative politics away from the model of the 1960s and 1970s when it concentrated on economic growth, while leaving defense to the Pax Americana.

The Nakasone cabinet stressed administrative reform, privatized the national railways and Nippon Telephone and Telegraph Corporation, reduced social spending on education and welfare, and tried as much as possible to restrain the growth of state expenditure. Internationally, Nakasone's politics were a response to the fashion for "small government" advocated by Reaganomics in the United States and Thatcherism in Great Britain.

There was no other prime minister who used the word "state" as much as Nakasone.[17] At a Liberal Democratic party seminar in the resort town of Karuizawa in the summer of 1985, Prime Minister Nakasone appealed to party members to revitalize the power of the state:

> What surprises me most when I go to foreign countries is that in their eyes Japan appears, more than we can ever imagine, to be a very powerful country. . . . Japan must advance rapidly as an international state, and from this standpoint it is extremely important to reevaluate Japanese "identity.". . . When one is defeated in war . . . a tendency develops to look down on oneself; everywhere in Japan today there is a *mea culpa* tendency to say Japan is wrong whenever something happens. . . . I am against that way of thinking. In Japan in particular, the state is not contractual, but has been generated over a long period of time as a natural community, and we are therefore still a state whether we win or lose. Since glory and shame alike belong to the people, it is our duty as a state and as a people to advance, seeking glory and abandoning shame.[18]

In addition, Nakasone declared, "If there is no place to express gratitude toward those who have died for their country, then who will offer their lives for the state?" Not surprisingly, on August 15 of that year he became the first prime minister of the postwar period to worship publicly at the Yasukuni Shrine.

Before the war, Yasukuni played an important role in the support of emperor worship and militarism. With the souls of 2.4 million war dead from Meiji to the Pacific War enshrined within it, it was a special shrine under the supervision of the Army and Navy ministries. In the postwar period, thanks to the U.S. occupation's "Shinto Directive" of December 15, 1945, separating religion from the state, the Shrine was forced to end its official connection with the state and the following year was redefined as an independent "religious juridical person" certified by the governor of Tokyo. But from 1969 on, right-wing LDP Diet members, members of the Bereaved Society of Japan, and the Association of Shinto Shrines began to press for the nationalization of Yasukuni Shrine. Successive LDP governments tried repeatedly to pass a Yasukuni Shrine bill, but on each occasion opposition from the nongovernment parties, Christian organizations, and citizens groups forced them to abandon the effort. The official visit to the Shrine by Prime Minister Nakasone and eighteen cabinet ministers was therefore intended to be a substitute for the failed legislation. Moreover, in October 1978 fourteen war criminals were secretly enshrined there, including Tōjō Hideki and other Class A criminals convicted of crimes against humanity.

In addition to protests against these actions from many quarters, Nakasone's official patronage of Yasukuni had widespread repercussions abroad. In South Korea and Singapore the press gave the story full coverage, and as the message reached the public, there were protests in different Asian countries. Interestingly, on September 19, 1985, when about one thousand Chinese university students gathered at Tiananmen Square to commemorate the fifty-fourth anniversary of the 1931 Manchurian Incident, the demonstrators shouted "Down with Nakasone!" and "Down with Japanese militarism!"[19]

The Textbook Problem and Racist Statements

In April 1986 the ceremony honoring the sixtieth anniversary of Hirohito's reign was held at the Ryōgoku Kokugikan, famous for its sumo wrestling. Although the fiftieth jubilee of the Shōwa Emperor's

reign was celebrated on November 10, the same day as his enthronement in 1928, Nakasone had moved it ahead by over six months to
April 29, the day of the emperor's birthday. The prime minister's
political strategy was to get elected for a third term by celebrating the
sixtieth anniversary in April, playing the leading role in hosting the
Tokyo Summit, scheduled for May, and, if all went well, win a third
term with a big victory in the election of the House of Councillors in
June.

On July 6, two months after the conclusion of the seven-nation
Tokyo Summit, the cabinet opted for holding twin elections on the
same day for representatives to the upper and lower houses of the Diet.
Just as Nakasone had intended, the LDP was victorious and, at a
stroke, increased the total number of its seats in the House of Representatives from 250 to 304. Nakasone was reelected for a third time as
president of the LDP, and in July his third cabinet was inaugurated.
Nakasone promptly coined the new term "1986 system," saying he
would "stretch out a hand to the left wing." This meant that the "1986
system" had started to replace the "1955 system" by bringing even
supporters of the progressive camp into the conservative fold. Never
before had the president of the Liberal Democratic party said such a
thing; it was indeed the height of the Nakasone era.

However, Nakasone and four cabinet ministers decided, after the
bitter criticism they received from China the previous year, to delay an
official visit to Yasukuni Shrine on August 15, the fortieth anniversary
of the ending of the war. Having weighed in the balance "Japanese
identity" and the "international state," Nakasone had come down on
the side of the "international state."[20]

But stretching out a hand to the left wing soon provoked an attack
from his own right. On July 31, a group of ultranationalist LDP Diet
men, alarmed by Nakasone's diplomacy of "submission to foreign
pressure" on issues like textbook revision and the Yasukuni Shrine
problem, formed the "Association of Those Concerned with Fundamental Problems of the State," and in September, Education Minister
Fujio Masayuki spoke at the Japan Press Club and criticized Prime
Minister Nakasone for not having worshiped publicly at the Yasukuni
Shrine. He also touched upon the textbook issue, saying: "World history is the history of war and the history of belligerence. Therefore we
want them [i.e., writers of textbooks] to correct the mistaken view of

history in which only Japan committed aggression."

On August 15, Fujio worshiped at the Yasukuni Shrine in his official capacity as minister of education and told journalists that "Some say the collective enshrinement of Class A war criminals is the problem, but I have a different point of view. I do not recognize the Tokyo Trials as legitimate." And he did not stop there. In an interview in the October issue of *Bungei shunjū* entitled "The Bombastic Minister Howls Loudly," Fujio said the Korean government shared responsibility for Japan's annexation of its own country. The next day, September 6, the press played up the story, reporting "Once Again Education Minister Fujio Makes Controversial Statement." South Korea's minister to Japan visited the Foreign Ministry and protested that "if the news reports are true, this is the gravest incident since the normalization of relations between Japan and the Republic of Korea." He demanded that the Japanese government take appropriate measures to deal with the matter. Chinese government circles also expressed their displeasure. On September 8, the South Korean government proposed a delay in the scheduled talks between the foreign ministers of Japan and South Korea. Seeing these developments, Nakasone summoned Fujio to his official residence that same day and fired him.

But just as the Fujio problem seemed to have been settled, Nakasone himself made an appalling gaffe. After stating that Japan had become an information intensive society, he went on to remark that "Japan is a society with a high level of formal schooling, and is becoming a considerably 'intelligent' society, far more so that a country like the United States. In the United States, where there are a considerable number of [literally, such types as] Blacks, Puerto Ricans and Mexicans, it [the intelligence level of society] is, on average, still very low."

The American media immediately seized upon these racist remarks and scathingly criticized them. From early in the morning, the Japanese Consulate General in New York was flooded with protest calls. The chairman of the Congressional black caucus told journalists he would propose that Congress pass a resolution seeking a public apology from Japan's Prime Minister. On September 27, Nakasone apologized to Andrew Young, the visiting mayor of Atlanta, and also sent a message of apology to the American people. On the surface at least, the storm had died down.[21]

The textbook problem, the Fujio statements, and Nakasone's racist remarks showed how deeply rooted was the self-centered racial consciousness of the Japanese people. Japanese politicians and economic leaders had displayed "arrogance through success" throughout the 1970s, but the nationalistic tide in Japanese society began to break noticeably from the time of the Nakasone cabinet.

A good example of this new nationalism was the ceremony, mentioned earlier, commemorating the emperor's sixtieth year on the throne. The Showa Emperor, who had reached his eighty-fifth birthday, became the longest living monarch in Japanese history. The March 1985 issue of *Bungei shunjū* published a three-person symposium on "The Age of the Great Emperor Hirohito" in which former Tokyo University President and Member of the House of Councillors Hayashi Kentarō participated with critic Yamamoto Shichihei and Sophia University Professor Watanabe Shōichi. Here, Mr. Watanabe stated that the sixtieth year of Showa was equivalent to England's Victorian age: "In the Victorian era, when the Queen celebrated the fiftieth year of her reign, they called it the 'golden jubilee'; but when she reached her sixtieth year, the English coined a new word and celebrated her 'diamond jubilee.' In Japan too we have just about reached the diamond jubilee. I think we are very fortunate to have such a head of state in our country."

Words such as "the great Emperor Hirohito" and "golden jubilee" were never used at the time of the fiftieth anniversary celebration, but over the next decade the rhetoric of journalism changed greatly. Moreover, prefectural assemblies around the country passed resolutions one after another requesting that celebrations be held under the auspices of the prefecture to "Honor His Majesty the Emperor's Sixtieth Year of Reign." As with the movement for the promotion of era-name legislation, so this time also grass-roots conservatism displayed its power. In the national ceremonies, Prime Minister Nakasone served as chairman of the Ceremonies Committee and delivered a message of congratulations.

Power and Authority

Just as he overused the word "state," probably no other politician used the word "emperor" as much as Prime Minister Nakasone, and his clear awareness of the relationship between power and authority accounts for this. Speaking as president of the LDP in his last summer seminar at Karuizawa, Nakasone said that the emperor was a symbol of racial unity backed by a tradition of nearly two thousand years, going on to add:

> As prime minister I often meet prime ministers and foreign heads of state. No one knows better than I how fortunate Japan is to have such a dual structure of worldly power [on the one hand] and authority in national unity [on the other]. Superior persons might not always become prime minister.... However, the existence of the emperor transcends all that, and for this reason he is like a sun shining brilliantly in the universe.[22]

Even as he stepped down as prime minister, he stated:

> The emperors of Japan were, from the very beginning, people of peace and culture. According to mythology, the arms-bearing emperors were only those from Emperor Jinmu to Emperor Keikō; the others who bore arms were the Meiji Emperor and his successors. Statues of all other emperors carry the wooden mace of peace.... The fact that, after the war, the emperor of Japan abandoned power and abandoned the properties of the Imperial Household therefore simply meant that he returned to the condition existing before Meiji. In short, the postwar emperor is the symbol of the Oriental way of thinking that having nothing makes one inexhaustible. For that reason he is once again advancing with the people.... There is a worldly, secular prime minister, but above him is the emperor: a transcendent being who has a symbolic universal meaning. We must not forget that it is this dual structure that maintains the external authority and the domestic unity of Japan, as well as the functions of the state.[23]

Nakasone frequently stated that Japan's task for the twenty-first century was to foster healthy patriotism while bringing about harmony between Japan's cultural identity and internationalism. To this end, he always situated the emperor at the center of his concept of "Japanese cultural identity." As I noted in my essay on "The Origins of the 'Symbol' and Its Future" (see appendix 1), no power can control or unify a nation without strong authority. Successive conservative party governments have compensated for the weakness of their own power by drawing upon the authority of the emperor. And no one has been more aware of the idea than Prime Minister Nakasone himself.

Nakasone established a close personal relationship with President Reagan (they were known as "Ron and Yasu") and on the international stage played a prominent role unlike any Japanese prime minister before him. For that reason, the Japanese people appreciated Nakasone and gave him strong support, while also expressing their concern with his controversial statements and actions. But in June 1988 the "Recruit (influence peddling) scandal" was exposed. This involved the transfer of unlisted stock belonging to the Recruit Company, an information conglomerate, to politicians, bureaucrats, and business leaders. When it became clear that Nakasone himself had taken part in the scandal, he was forced to leave the Liberal Democratic party, which he did not rejoin until 1991.

The Death of Emperor Hirohito

On September 8, 1988, the mass media reported that Emperor Hirohito had vomited blood and was gravely ill. For the next 111 days until his death on January 7, 1989, the entire Japanese archipelago sank into a strange mood. Every day the television reported on his vital signs: his temperature, pulse and the amount of blood he had lost. Starting on September 22, the Imperial Household Agency established twelve registry areas nationwide where citizens could sign their names in "get well" registers, and local governments soon followed with their own registries. The total number of signatures reached two million in one week, and by early November the number was reported to have reached six million.[24] One after another, in cities, towns, and villages throughout the country, scheduled marriage ceremonies, sports meets, and autumn festivals were canceled. Department stores, banks, and supermarkets hung their flags at half mast and stopped selling celebratory goods such as red bean rice. Television stations stopped showing "inappropriate" commercials. "Registry book" (*kichō*) and "self-restraint" (*jishuku*) became household words.

Many were astonished at the extent of this emperor fever. Why did it spread so widely throughout all of Japan? The causes were generally thought to be the strength of traditional feelings of emperor worship, the characteristic conformist behavior of the Japanese, and the mobilization of the people by the mass media. Watanabe Osamu, however, stressed that the phenomenon should be seen in the light of "the enterprise society and the LDP," and the strength of their control.[25]

Watanabe noted that the mood of "self-restraint" was started by companies such as department stores, banks, supermarkets and large enterprises. Old established stores like Mitsui and Takashimaya, which were purveyors to the Imperial Household Agency, stopped their baseball victory anniversary sales and various other events, including even the sale of Christmas trees. Following their example, other department stores joined in practicing "self-restraint." A psychology of mass conformism emerged, one of "They're doing it over there, so we'll do it too."

Watanabe says this was a form of commercial competition among firms, and had nothing to do with emperor worship. Guided by the Ministry of Finance, banks hung their flags at half-mast. Mitsubishi Electronics, an industry synonymous with modern Japan, canceled its annual autumn "Family Festival." Toshiba prohibited soccer games and "karaoke" (singing to accompanying music). Sony ordered its annual autumn recreation bus not to stop in front of the company premises, and recommended that its employees wear black neckties. More than anything else, these companies acted out of fear of right-wing attacks, rather than for the sake of the emperor.

Next, one can point to the LDP's strong regional control. On September 22, directly after the emperor fell gravely ill, LDP Headquarters issued a notice to every prefectural association "concerning registry books wishing His Majesty the Emperor a recovery," and ordered the establishment of registry booths in prefectures, cities, towns and villages. Over a number of years, local branches of the LDP had developed a machine for turning out the vote in return for government subsidies to their regions, and local government bodies and agricultural cooperatives encouraged everybody they could find to sign the registers in response to this directive. However, I understand that in some places one person signed on behalf of many others, and the six million signatures collected in this way were thus diluted.

Watanabe did not analyze the phenomena of "registers" and "self-restraint" merely from the standpoint of the emotional, mystical factor of popular emperor worship. Rather, the success of his analysis lies in having explained such phenomena in terms of the distinctive characteristics of the state and society in contemporary Japan. (Following Watanabe's viewpoint, Ōkado Masakatsu has looked at the "enterprise" and "the region," explaining the political dynamics of compulsion and reaction concerning the registers.)[26]

Furthermore, during the sixty-two years of the longest imperial reign in Japanese history, the Japanese people experienced the "upheavals of Shōwa": world depression, the "Fifteen Year War," defeat, foreign occupation, rapid economic growth, and the two oil shocks. No other generation had ever gone through such traumas while under the same emperor. We also cannot ignore the undercurrent of emotion during the final days of his reign: the unique feeling of having shared sadness and joy together with the emperor. In particular, the older generation (aged sixty years and over), whose own lives of hardship overlapped with the life of the Shōwa emperor, were affected by this sentiment.

The Symbol Emperor and High Economic Growth

On the day of the emperor's death, Prime Minister Takeshita made an "announcement concerning the Imperial House" in which he said that Japan's postwar economic prosperity was largely due to the existence of the Showa Emperor.[27] The next day an editorial in the *Mainichi shinbun* said that "When postwar Japan moved from recovery to prosperity, and everyone together strove to achieve high growth . . . was not His Majesty there, deep in our hearts, as a symbol of stability? The stability of society was indispensable for high economic growth."

Social stability is undoubtedly essential for economic growth. But can one say, as Prime Minister Takeshita did, that it was "because His Majesty was there as a symbol of Japan and a symbol of national unity"? That assertion requires serious scholarly investigation, and sure enough, the readers' column of the *Asahi shinbun* on January 12, 1989, carried a sharp criticism from one reader, Professor Nishinarita Yutaka, who wrote as follows:

> The argument that the unprecedented prosperity of the postwar Japanese economy was the result of the people's unity based on their feeling for the emperor as a symbol of national unity was noisily advocated at the time of the Shōwa Emperor's death. However, there is no argument more unscientific than this. Many scholars, deploying various

theories, have tried, from a purely economic standpoint, to explain the causes of postwar Japan's economic growth; and if non-economic factors are cited, it is usually the political-bureaucratic-financial complex, as seen in theories of "Japan, Incorporated," that is cited, rather than the symbol emperor system. It is a matter of common sense to explain the unity and cooperation of the people not at the state level, i.e., in terms of the symbol monarchy, but at the enterprise level, as shown in theories of Japanese-style labor/capital relations. . . . I deplore the national soil which enables unscientific, emotional glorification of the monarch to be promoted in the name of mourning for the death of the Shōwa Emperor.

As the professor says, the object of Japanese loyalty in the postwar period shifted from the emperor to the firm. If contemporary Japanese had continued to be selflessly devoted to their country (*messhihōkō*) as they had been before and during the war, an advanced consumer society would never have been established. Instead, the dominant values and life-style of the younger generation became purely self-serving (*mekkōhōshi*).[28] Herein lies the reason why younger Japanese were the most apathetic during the period of "self-restraint." Those who were blinded by the emperor propaganda could not adequately understand the structure of contemporary Japanese society and instead argued about "the reemergence of the ancient past" or a "return to a traditional view of the emperor." Indeed, once the mass media became preoccupied with the introduction of the consumption tax and the Recruit scandal, emperor fever instantly disappeared.

The Future of the Symbol Emperor System

Emperor Akihito's ascension to the throne was celebrated at the Imperial Palace in November 1990. A total of 2,500 people attended, including about 1,500 foreign dignitaries from 158 countries, the United Nations, and the European Community. Emperor Akihito had already assumed his imperial duties at the time of the Showa Emperor's death on January 7 of the previous year, but according to Imperial Household Law, he could not hold the enthronement ceremony until the completion of a year's mourning for his father.

One year and ten months later, on November 12, the new emperor proclaimed his accession, stating that he would "abide by the Constitution of Japan and assume the duties of the symbol of Japan and the unity of the Japanese people." At the time of his succession the previous year, he pledged to "protect the Constitution of Japan and fulfill his duties in accordance with it." Since Article 9 of the constitution stipulates that "the Emperor or the Regent as well as Ministers of State, members of the Diet, judges, and all other public officials have the obligation to respect and uphold this Constitution," his royal message was merely a statement of the obvious. The new emperor's words were favorably received by the Japanese people. There is no denying, however, that they hurt right-wing forces who were planning to revise the constitution and make the emperor the head of state.

Emperor Akihito was twelve years old at the time of Japan's defeat in the Second World War. He witnessed Japan's reemergence from postwar confusion and poverty as a peace-loving nation and must have keenly felt the value of peace. As Crown Prince, in August 1975, he had remarked: "Must we not seek more sincerely to construct a peace-loving and cultural state that has been our goal since the end of the war?" In August 1981 he also stated that "On these four days—the anniversary of the ending of the war, the days of the nuclear bombing of Hiroshima and Nagasaki, and also the day of the final battle of Okinawa—we offer silent prayers and show our gratitude for peace, and wish to continue this peace."

Under the Meiji Constitution, the Shōwa Emperor had been "head of state" and in the postwar period he became a "symbol." As I noted previously, Hirohito, who had considered abdicating on more than one occasion, lost the chance to speak publicly about his own war responsibility. For that reason, the postwar imperial institution could not help but exist as a "scarred symbolic monarchy" both at home and abroad. That fact had an incalculable negative effect on postwar Japanese history, and especially on the moral history of the Japanese, in particular, their shirking of political and moral responsibility. By contrast, Akihito was enthroned as a symbol from the very beginning. In that sense, the symbol emperor system actually started from his enthronement. But whether or not it will stabilize as a true symbol emperor system remains to be seen.

Next, I would like to mention briefly three points about the future of the symbol emperor system. First is the problem of the emperor's war responsibility. Second is the problem of whether or not the emperor system and democracy are compatible. And third is the emperor's role in international society, or (in contemporary idiom), is the emperor system compatible with internationalization?[29]

Unlike the Shōwa Emperor, Emperor Akihito bears no direct responsibility for war. At the time of his enthronement ceremony, however, he stated that "I bear in mind the benevolence of my father, the Shōwa Emperor, who, during more than sixty years of his reign, always shared both suffering and joy together with the people." Thus he implied that the sixty years of prewar and postwar Showa had continued as if nothing had happened. Not only is this contrary to the facts of history, it also contravenes the spirit of the Constitution of Japan, founded on the basis of reflection on the history of aggressive war. What the emperor really should have done was to refer the war responsibility of the Shōwa Emperor, and state clearly that he would defend the Constitution of Japan and its three fundamental features of renunciation of war, popular sovereignty, and basic human rights. Although the peoples of Asia have progressed during the forty-five years since the end of World War II, the scars of war have yet to heal. Moreover, Japan's present economic advances in Asia have provoked fears of a return of the "Greater East Asia Co-Prosperity Sphere." In the eyes of other Asian people, past and present, overlap and misgivings toward Japan are increasing. It is precisely at this time that Emperor Akihito should indicate at home and abroad that his own pacifism is genuine. It is not too late for him to do so. Hereafter, his anticipated visits to China, South Korea, Thailand, and the other countries of Asia present opportunities for him to express his sincerity regarding the pacifism of Japan. The Japanese people, too, rather than relying too heavily on the emperor to convey their intentions, must deal with the world, and especially the nations of Asia, on the basis of an accurate understanding of history.

Second, the problem of the relationship between monarchy and democracy was a theme hotly debated at home and abroad toward the end of the war; and opinions are still divided over it today. For example, China's Dr. Sun Fo argued that the emperor system was incompatible with democracy. "The Japanese empire must be overthrown," said Dr. Sun, "and a Japanese republic set up in its place. It is only by this means that real democracy can be introduced and instituted in Japan and the peace of the world safeguarded."[30]

Such views were also common among American liberals and progressive intellectuals. Even when they did not go so far as to advocate a republic, they believed that the emperor system was a major obstacle for the future of democracy in Japan. If the system was retained in postwar Japan, they felt conservative forces would surely use it to undermine the achievements of the occupation army's democratic reforms. To prevent that from happening, scholars like T. A. Bisson argued that efforts at "reform from below" by Japanese seeking to abolish the monarchy should be encouraged.

Against them, conservative Japan experts like Joseph Grew felt that if the monarchy were abolished, Japanese society would be thrown into chaos and probably destroyed. Grew argued that the imperial institution was a stabilizing mechanism in Japanese society and that even if American democracy was grafted onto Japan, it would not take root immediately.

Similar arguments continue today in Japan. Some political scientists, such as Kosaka Masatake, argue that "it is dangerous to concentrate authority and power in one person, as in a presidential system. . . . When all is said and done, it is safer for a political system to have power and authority divided." Having said that, he goes on to say that "The secret of the state lies precisely in the irrationality of monarchy."[31] On the other hand, other historians, such as Miyachi Masato, have argued that the main ideological function of the symbol monarchy has been to "wear down rather than to destroy" the people's consciousness of human rights, preventing the growth of democratic values and pacifism by the "ceaseless expansion and enlargement" of the emperor's symbolic acts.[32]

In view of the above, "constitutional monarchy" and democracy can either appear to coexist harmoniously, or contradict one another. But in any case, what is needed now more than anything else to make democracy work in Japan is to eliminate the emperor taboo and to establish civic freedom enabling the people to speak freely about the emperor and the emperor system.

In 1988, the Christian mayor of Nagasaki, Motoshima Hitoshi, declared, in response to a question from a city assemblyman, that he thought the emperor bore responsibility for the war. Immediately Motoshima became the target of repeated threats from the right wing, and ended up being shot and seriously wounded. The suppression of freedom of speech by violence should not occur in a democratic society, and such a barbaric act should never have been permitted. The iron law and basic principle of democracy is summed up in the phrase "I may not share your opinion, but I shall defend to the death your right to say it." If the symbol emperor system cannot guarantee this democratic principle, it will lose the people's support, and they will turn their back on it.

Furthermore, the Japanese government should recognize imperial abdications and the practice of women reigning as "emperors." Article 2 of the Constitution of Japan merely states that the succession to the throne shall be dynastic and "succeeded to in accordance with the Imperial Household Law." If one looks at clause 16 of article 3, governing the regent for an emperor in the Imperial Household Law, it states that "When the Emperor has not come of age, a regent will be established." It then goes on to say that when the Emperor is spiritually or physically ill or cannot conduct national affairs due to some serious accident, an imperial household conference will establish a regency. However, there is absolutely no clause in it specifying abdication. And so, for over one hundred days starting in September 1988, when the Shōwa Emperor fell gravely ill, television and radio reported only news of his vital bodily signs, such as his temperature, pulse rate, and amount of blood loss, but said nothing about abdication. I wonder if it was necessary to report in detail on such matters which normally belong to the realm of privacy. It is indeed an inhuman institution for an emperor to be unable to step down until he dies. If this was the case of a prime minister or the chief executive officer of an enterprise, that person would have been replaced long before his death. It would be a different story if the Japanese emperor had not been guaranteed his fundamental human rights under both article 11 and article 13 of the constitution, but he had been guaranteed those rights.

Next, judging from the principle of sexual equality in the Constitution of Japan, there should be recognition of the "empress." Article 1 of the Imperial Household Law states that "The Imperial Throne shall be succeeded to by male offspring belonging to the Imperial Line" and thus only permits male emperors. Yet both the Shōwa Emperor and Emperor Akihito frequently expressed their wish to move Japan's monarchy closer to Britain's constitutional monarchy. In that case the Japanese Imperial House should have no objection to having an "empress" on the model of the British monarchy which is headed by a queen. However, putting aside the emperor who lacks powers of initiation, shouldn't the cabinet and members of the National Diet, who have the obligation to respect and uphold the constitution, as specified in article 9 of the Constitution of Japan, seriously examine having an empress in accordance with the spirit of Article 24, which specifies the essential equality of the sexes? If we really respect democracy, then we cannot call it the real thing unless we carry this out.

The final point is how to view the relationship between the emperor system and internationalization. The introduction to "The United States Initial Post-Surrender Policy for Japan, SWNCC 150/3," stated that the ultimate objective of the occupation was "to ensure that Japan will not again become a menace to the United States or to the peace and security of the world." In order to accomplish this, the main goal of the occupation had to be the destruction of Japanese militarism, which is why the initial occupation policy placed its main emphasis on demilitarization and democratic reform. Article 9 of the Japanese constitution therefore prescribed the renunciation of war in order to assuage Asian fears of the emperor system's continuation. Recently, however, not only has this original principle been forgotten, but a historical regression has occurred wherein the emperor's spirituality has started to be emphasized as a last resort in maintaining the identity of the Japanese. If one reads discussions in Asia, Europe, and the United States at the time of Japan's surrender, the belief in the emperor's divinity and the cult of emperor worship were indeed ideological dogmas that isolated the Japanese people from the rest of the world. The Japanese government should therefore appreciate this historical lesson, vigilantly defend the constitution, and never use the emperor for political purposes; and Emperor Akihito in turn should maintain a firm posture of never allowing himself to be used in this way by politicians.

Since the Gulf War of 1991, politicians and intellectuals have been using the pretext of making an international contribution to argue that Japan should revise its constitution so as to enable the Self-Defense Forces to be deployed overseas. To allay the fears of many Asian countries that Japan's military power was on the increase, the Japanese government once again drew up plans for the emperor and empress to make an Asian tour, again for political ends. But the emperor stuck to his own belief in pacifism and a position of strict defense of the constitution, and did not betray the wish for peace of the Asian peoples.

Today, twenty-seven countries in the world, with a total population of 402 million, have monarchies.They account for a mere 8 percent of the total world population of 5 billion. World history clearly shows a significant decline in the supremacy of monarchies. For Japan to place too much emphasis on Imperial House diplomacy in the current global environment would be to invite unforeseen consequences. Since the 1960s, Emperor Akihito has shown a keen interest in environmental problems.[33] As we head into the twenty-first century, the world must address seriously the problems of arms reduction, peace, human rights, and the environment. The success of the symbol emperor will depend on how he responds to these and other issues.

Appendix 1

THE ORIGINS OF THE "SYMBOL" AND ITS FUTURE:

Thoughts on the Symbol Emperor System*

FROM LATE August to December 1989 I studied at Oxford University, collecting material on subjects such as British policy toward occupied Japan and the comparison of the British and Japanese systems of monarchy. At the same time, I was privileged to observe at close range the last days of Thatcherism and the turmoil in Eastern Europe. It was indeed a "lucky" study tour. I was also able to obtain interesting information on Sir George Sansom, Britiain's greatest Japan specialist. The purpose of this short essay is to reexamine certain issues remaining from *The Japanese Monarchy*, which was published immediately prior to my departure for England. But before beginning, I would like to recount some experiences I had during my time in Britain.

September 1, 1989, about a week after I arrived, was exactly fifty years to the day from Nazi Germany's invasion of Poland. For over a week, there were special television programs and newspaper issues on the fiftieth anniversary of World War II. Looking at these forced me to think long and hard about the aggression committed by the prewar Japanese army in Southeast Asia and the many barbarous acts I saw on the television screen. In documentary-style films, the word "Jap" came out repeatedly. We were also shown magnified images of the Bataan death march and the British prisoners of war who were brutalized and reduced to skin and bones during the famous Taimen railroad construction as portrayed in the film *Bridge on the River Kwai*. Old soldiers who had been cruelly abused by the Japanese army during the

* This is a revised version of Nakamura Masanori, "Shōchō no yurai to yuku e—Igirisu de kangaeta shōchō tennōsei," *Sekai*, no. 544 (August 1990): 169–79.

war also gave graphic descriptions of their experiences in television interviews. Any British person seeing these scenes could not help but feel that the Japanese were a cruel people.

When the Showa emperor fell critically ill, the British tabloid, *The Sun*, led with a headline that read "Hell is awaiting this truly evil emperor." Journalistic sensationalism accounts for such a shocking title, although the article simply said that "a special seat in hell is being prepared for the emperor." I found this unpleasant to read, but it seems to have been well received by the British people. Visiting England helped me to understand why. For as I said earlier, it was connected with what the Japanese army did in Southeast Asia.

As I watched BBC television, I was reminded of the words of Sir George Sansom to Prime Minister Shidehara Kijūrō over forty years ago. Sansom, on a visit to Japan in January 1946 as the British Commonwealth representative to the Far Eastern Commission, said, "British opinion is still very bitter over Japanese brutality. The Japanese army's atrocities may have done more damage to Japan than the defeat in war."

The British view of Japan is linked to memories of the wartime atrocities committed by the Japanese army in the Philippines, Singapore, Thailand, Burma, and elsewhere. In Australia and New Zealand too, where a very bitter anti-emperor campaign erupted last year, the situation is basically the same. While in England, I received a lettter from an American scholar to whom I had sent my book. Even he said that "the British have not forgotten what the Japanese army did in Southeast Asia just as Americans have not forgotten Pearl Harbor." This was certainly more than I had expected. How different is the Japanese perception of history with its attitude of "let the past flow like water and be forgotten."

Such matters cannot be understood just by living in and thinking only of Japan. It is said that annually about ten million Japanese tourists have been going abroad in recent years. Most of them tour famous historic sites or bring back brand name goods such as Gucci, Louis Vuitton, or Pierre Cardin. They are not too interested in the history and culture of the countries they visit. But, on the other hand, something good must also come out of the fact that so many Japanese are going abroad every year. The number of Japanese who can understand Japan's relative position or see their country in a world perspective has increased considerably. I imagine that in perhaps another two or three decades a generation of Japanese will grow up that is completely different from the narrow-minded and insular Japanese of today. Strange words like "internationalization" (*kokusaika*) will have become obsolete by then. (After all, Europeans cannot be expected to understand immediately what we mean by this.) But enough of introductory remarks; let us proceed directly to our main topic.

More on the Origins of the "Symbol"

In *The Japanese Monarchy* I attempted to explain why the prewar absolutist monarchy lingered on in postwar Japan in the form of the symbol monarchy, by focusing on the thoughts of Joseph Grew, former U.S. ambassador to Japan. Grew was prewar America's greatest authority on Japan and the person who, even in the United States from the earliest stage of the war, advocated that the emperor system be retained in postwar Japan.

Grew set off on his mission to Japan on May 14, 1932. That same day, a correspondent from the *Herald-Examiner* who had come to meet him at Chicago station handed him the Sunday evening paper bearing the headline "Japanese Premier Slain." Thus he learned of the outbreak of the May 15, 1932 incident. He wrote in his diary that "the military are simply taking the bit in their teeth and running away with it, evidently with a fascist regime in view. But in spite of the press reports, I can't believe the Emperor is threatened, considering the supposedly universal veneration for the throne. There must be something wrong there [in that report]." We should note in this entry the early appearance of Grew's image of the emperor as the spiritual authority of the Japanese facing an evil military. Grew left Chicago for San Francisco and arrived in Yokohama via Honolulu on June 6, 1936. He went immediately to the American embasssy in Akasaka. For a period of about ten years, from that day until the start of the Japanese-U.S. War, Grew, as America's ambassador to Japan, left his legacy in numerous ways in the management of Japanese-U.S. relations. I will not relate the details of that period here, but in my book I have clarified the following three points:

—Discovery of Grew's ghost writer (Paul Linebarger, Jr.) who helped him write *Report from Tokyo.*

—Confirmation of the names of the moderate faction—Makino Nobuaki, Yoshida Shigeru, Shigemitsu Mamoru, and others— which Grew concealed in *Ten Years in Japan.*

—Genesis of the word "symbol" in article 1, clause 1 of the Constitution of Japan.

The origins of the word "symbol," to which I devoted the most work, drew various responses from readers. Three points summarize the derivation of "symbol." First, there were two paths on the American side: (1) Joseph Grew—Bonner Fellers—MacArthur; and (2) Kades, Hussey, Rowell, Poole, and the other constitutional drafters in the Government Section of GHQ. The important point is that these two groups had nothing to do with one another and were completely separated. Upon confirming that MacArthur had used the expression "He [the emperor] is the symbol which united all the Japanese; destroy him and the nation disintegrates," in his famous secret telegram to Army Chief of Staff Eisenhower of January 25, 1946, I assumed that his words must have entered into article 1 of the Japanese Constitution.

But Kades, the former deputy chief of Government Section, informed me in reply to my letter requesting information that as far as he knew, MacArthur gave no instructions to use the word "symbol." I now had to consider an entirely different trail. Since Americans had no monarchy as a frame of reference, I conjectured that they would surely have sought some clues in the English theories of monarchy. I decided to look into Walter Bagehot's *The English Constitution*, the definitive theory of the English monarchy.

And there, in Bagehot's famous book, I discovered the expression "a visible symbol of unity." The First Earl of Balfour (Arthur James Balfour) adopted it and the expression eventually appeared in the 1931 Statute of Westminster.

But still I wasn't satisfied. On reaching England, the first thing I did was to investigate whether this hypothesis was correct. After arriving at Oxford, I purchased *The Oxford Illustrated History of the British Monarchy* (Oxford University Press, 1988) by professors John Cannon and Ralph Griffith. There I found that Bagehot had noted the English crown's ability to act as "a symbol of national unity" due to its religious and mystical character.[1] Bagehot also wrote that "the monarch is an indispensable social head and the head of the moral order." In addition, I noticed that in the same book, Balfour had also described the British sovereign as "the symbol of imperial unity."

But *The Oxford Illustrated History* cites no sources whatsoever, perhaps because it is a picture book intended for the general reader. Later I learned that the expression "a symbol of national unity" appears in an essay on "The Income of the Prince of Wales," which appeared in the *Economist* in volume 5 of Bagehot's collected works. Also, the expression "symbol of imperial unity" turned out to have been used by the Earl of Balfour in a letter of 1901 to King Edward VII and in a speech in Parliament in 1902.[2] In that speech, Balfour said that "the countries of the Great British Empire beyond the seas (the colonies and self-governing communities) are linked to us through the person of the Sovereign, the living symbol of Imperial unity."

Further, in 1926, the Balfour Report was submitted to Parliament. This formalized the relationship of equality between England, the mother country, and the self-governing territories and made it clear that English laws could not be forced upon them without consent. The 1931 Statute of Westminster developed this idea further.

According to the statute, "The crown is the symbol of the free association of the British federation of states. The member states are unified by their common loyalty to the crown." In short, in Britain the word "symbol" had the strong connotation of a symbol for the whole British Commonwealth of nations. In those days, British colonies and self-governing territories were strengthening their demand for national self-determination and seeking independence from the mother country. English conservative politicians, fearing the collapse of the unity of the British empire, attempted to unify the commonwealth, by situating the monarch as the "symbol of imperial unity." By contrast, in Japan the emperor was not, and could never have been, designated as the "symbol" of the former colonies such as Taiwan and Korea. For in the 1930s, under the pretext of carrying out an assimilationist policy, the Empire of Japan compelled Koreans and Taiwanese to worship at Shinto shrines, eliminated the Korean language from the school curriculum, and forced Koreans to study Japanese. Then, in the early 1940s, Japan began to develop a colonial policy which deprived Koreans of their identity by forcing them to take Japanese names. Consequently, the defeat of Japanese militarism in the Pacific War signified the liberation of the Korean and Taiwanese people. For them the emperor had no meaning as a symbol. The "symbol" in Japan was always just for Japanese.

In any case, we are able to confirm from the above that in England the word "symbol" was used in a genealogy that went from Bagehot to Balfour to the Statute of Westminster.

Symbol and Head of State

On November 21, 1989, British television began to broadcast live sessions of Parliament for the first time, giving me the chance to reflect on the connection between symbol and head of state. On that day, the popular newspaper, *The Daily Mirror*, went so far as to comment sarcastically that whereas the American Congress and Japanese National Diet had introduced television much earlier, the British Parliament was now at long last entering the twentieth century. Since I heard that there would be a live television broadcast of Parliament from 10 A.M., I tuned in and saw Queen Elizabeth being conducted by her royal guards from Buckingham Palace to Parliament. When she arrived, she was wearing a purple crown topped with a large, oblong sapphire beneath which glittered diamonds and rubies. The television fully conveyed the dignified mood of the occasion. Upon reaching the throne, Queen Elizabeth read aloud her speech, opening the new session of Parliament.

When she had finished speaking, the television commentator said, "Sovereignty does not reside in Parliament, but in the Queen." For a moment I couldn't believe my ears! So, when the program ended, I immediately went to the dining hall of St. Anthony's College and told two friends what I had heard. They, too, found it hard to believe that sovereignty did not lie with parliament but with the queen and insisted that the commentator had made an error. But I persisted saying "I know that sovereignty does not really lie with the queen," but in a nominal sense it does, doesn't it? And I added, "Queen Elizabeth said, 'My government will introduce . . . bills.' " Under my persistent questioning they seemed to lose confidence and suggested that I go and ask an Oxford University specialist on the matter.

Several days later I questioned a professor whom I knew and received the following answer: "The British prime minister writes the draft of the speech that Queen Elizabeth reads out at the opening of Parliament. But even if a Labor party government should be formed after the next general election, and that government presents quite contrary bills, the queen will still say 'My government will introduce.' In that sense, sovereignty does not lie with the queen. For even if we say that sovereignty resides in the queen, it is a completely nominal sovereignty, and just the same as saying 'King in Parliament.' " In short, it is entirely characteristic of the English not to state clearly whether sovereignty lies in parliament or in the queen. My doubts were somewhat dispelled.

In contrast to this English way of dealing with sovereignty, how is the relationship between the head of state and the symbol handled in the Constitution of Japan? Responding to a question in the House of Peers, during deliberations on the enactment of the constitution, State Minister Kanamori Tokujirō said that, domestically, one cannot call the emperor a head of state (this is why he is regarded as a symbol). But for external purposes he should be treated as the head of state, representing the Japanese nation.[3]

Also, in the interim report on the emperor, produced by "Committee Number One of the Constitutional Reseach Association," there are views, albeit minority opinions, that say, "The emperor is the head of state and the center of Japan's national unity"; and that "in order to clarify that the emperor represents the Japanese nation to foreign countries or that he occupies a position somewhat like a head of state, it is appropriate, while avoiding the expression 'head of state' (*genshu*), to revise the text to say 'The emperor represents Japan in a formal, ceremonial sense.' " Ultimately, however, even though the emperor is the symbol of the unity of the Japanese nation, the constitution does not consider him to be the head of state. In that sense, the Japanese emperor should be seen as having become less powerful and more restricted than the British monarch.

However, ever since the enactment of the constitution under the first Yoshida cabinet (May 22, 1946–May 20 1947), successive conservative cabinets have treated the emperor as though he is the head of state in foreign relations. As I shall explain later, the cost of doing that came due when President Roh Tae Woo of South Korea visited Japan in late May 1990. But one must say that the root cause of the vagueness in the emperor/head of state relationship is inherent in the very word "symbol."

When I investigate the meaning of "symbol," I am astonished at the variety of interpretations that different people hold. The view of SCAP's constitutional drafters was certainly clear enough. It was shown vividly in the "Explanatory Notes to Constitutional Revision" which the head of Government Section, Courtney Whitney, presented to MacArthur on February 10, 1946. As stated, "The Emperor becomes the symbol of the state instead of being the state. He remains as a focus and the center of respect around which the people's thoughts, hopes and ideals can be fused into a cohesive whole, but forever deprived of that mystic power which has been used from time immemorial by unscrupulous leaders to exploit the people to evil ends."[4] Thus SCAP designated the symbol emperor as a constitutional monarch devoid of all powers pertaining to government.

View the matter from the Japanese side, however, and the symbol means something quite different from what GHQ originally intended. The Japanese side had a distinct concept of "symbol" from the very moment the postwar constitution was enacted, and this different perception continues to exert influence to this day. The representative examples are Tsuda Zōkichi's understanding of the imperial house as "the center of national unity" and Watsuji Tetsuro's view that "From the very beginning, the emperor has symbolized the unity of the groups [making up Japan]." Here the emperor is presented as the Japanese people's identity and the center of their adoration.[5]

Recently I noticed the following entry of October 18, 1945 in the diary of Tsugita Daizaburō, the chief cabinet secretary in the Shidehara cabinet who worked with Shidehara Kijūrō right after the war to maintain the emperor system. "Ishiguro Tadaatsu came over and said that he wanted me to read an indispensable book which bore on the problem of constitutional revision, that is, the theory of Satomi Kishio. So I asked him to go to Minister Matsumoto and tell him about it." (October 18, 1950) Matsumoto, needless to say, was Matsumoto Jōji, home minister in the Shidehara cabinet, responsible for constitutional revision.

Who, then, was Satomi Kishio? Apparently, he was the first person in Japan to define the emperor as a symbol, according to a letter I received from a reader in Yokohama. Satomi, born in Tokyo in 1897, graduated from the philosophy department of Waseda University and went on to become a prolific writer on the national polity. In 1941 he was lecturing on the constitution at Ritsumekan University. Upon examining his *Tennō no kagakuteki kenkyū* (Scientific study of the emperor), published in 1932, I found in chapter 4 a separate section on "The Emperor as a Symbol." There, Satomi defined the emperor as "the highest symbol in Japanese society and state." Now I have not read Satomi's *Kokutai kenporon* (On the national policy and the constitution), which Ishiguro called an "indispensable text" at the time of constitutional revision; but I did discover in Satomi's other works, such as *Kokutai kenpō kōgi* (Lectures on the national polity and the constitution) and *Bansei ikke no tennō* (The emperor in a line unbroken for ages eternal), that he emphasizes how, ever since antiquity, the symbolic nature of the emperor has been contained in his religious and traditional authority. And in his 1962 study, *Nihon koku no kenpō* (The constitution of Japan), Satomi also stated that "The Constitution of Japan did not establish the symbol emperor as a new category but stipulated that he already existed as a symbol. That is to say, it formally codified what had been, up to that time, an unwritten category."

Thus we see that although they used the same word, "symbol," its meaning was completely different in the American and Japanese contexts. A distinct Japanese concept of the symbol existed from the very beginning of the enactment of the Japanese Constitution and it constantly undermined the interpretation given by GHQ, which is probably also the standard interpretation of Japanese constitutional scholars. Moreover, as seen in Tsugita's diary entry, Japanese statesmen had an understanding of the constitution which regarded Satomi's theory of the national polity as an indispensable text. Conflicts over these different concepts of the symbol are, in reality, deeply connected with arguments among historians and legal scholars over how they understand the essence of the emperor system.

Authority and Power

The Japanese medievalist Amano Yoshihiko said in a discussion with historian Yamaguchi Masao that "Up to now there seem to be two very distinct lines of interpretation concerning the emperor." One line is the power-wielding emperor—Temmu, Go-Daigo, Meiji—represented by the historians Hiraizumi Kiyoshi and Muramatsu Tsuyoshi. The other is the ceremonial emperor divorced from political power, a view espoused by Yasuda Yojūrō and Ishii Ryōsuke.[6] The former view sees the emperor as a power holder; the latter sees him as neither having nor exercising power. Setting himself against these two positions, historian Araki Moriaki argues that, for methodological purposes, the dichotomy of power holders and ceremonial figureheads is unrealistic and that it is better to see the two as a single set.[7] In connection with the critic Kan Takayuki's statement that "The symbol emperor is the highest form of the emperor system," I too once said that the true nature of the monarchy is most clearly expressed in the ancient and modern emperor systems which succeeded in unifying power and authority. I called this the manifest form of the emperor system. How one views the present symbol emperor system depends entirely on which of these three positions one takes. This is a point of vital importance in determining the consequences of emperor theory. For example, former Prime Minister Nakasone Yasuhiro once remarked:

> I think that the fundamental nature of the Japanese monarchy, from ancient times right down to the present day, is exactly like today's symbol emperor entity. The emperors were maintained for over two thousand years of history because they had no political power, were never drawn into political disputes and power struggles, and stood above all the contending forces. . . . In short, this is the symbol emperor: an emperor who has no real power but exists as a spiritual centripetal force. (*Sande Mainichi*, June 24, 1973)

If one adopts such a perspective, then the prewar, arms-bearing emperors under the Meiji Constitution become either exceptions or mistakes in the history of the imperial system, and the symbol emperor system is a return to the original form, or monarchy as it should be.[8] But how can the essence of the imperial system possibly be understood in such a way? Perhaps the key to solving this problem lies in clarifying the relationship between authority and power.

No power can control or unify a nation without authority. Power always requires authority in order to secure its own legitimacy to control the nation. In the Bakumatsu Restoration period. (1853–68), the antibakufu forces sought the authority of the emperor in place of the Tokugawa shogun. The Meiji state, by creating the constitution of the Empire of Japan and the Imperial Rescript on Education, heightened the power and authority of the Meiji emperor, thereby legitimating his control of the people. In pre-1945 Japan this empowerment of the emperor was carried to a fanatical extreme and, in the end, the "Empire of Japan" destroyed itself.

The postwar Constitution of Japan, formulated in the light of this history, took the form of a symbol emperor system. But because the imperial system was deliberately retained and the emperor's existence was recognized right from the start of the postwar period, his political manipulation by others was unavoidable. Of course, the Constitution places restraints on the form of his manipulation: the emperor cannot be utilized as he was in prewar and wartime Japan. Nevertheless, successive conservative cabinets have been compensating for the weakness of their own ideological control by borrowing the authority of the Shōwa Emperor. This manipulation of the emperor is the fate of power that lacks authority: it is also the treachery of politics. Dichotomous theories which separate authority and power cannot properly understand the constant urge of this power and so downplay its importance.

The reality of postwar history is that it has departed from the articles on the emperor as stipulated in the constitution and furthered the process of increasing the uses of the symbol emperor. Traditional authority is not something that can be easily created. It would be a different story if the holders of power in Japan could create an authority which compensated for the emperor. But if that is impossible, then the exploitation of authority by power will probably never cease.

The Enthronement Ceremony and Japan after the Great Food Offering

The visit to Japan of South Korean President Roh Tae Woo in late May 1990 evoked concern as to where the symbol emperor system was heading. The newspapers and television focused their attention mainly on Emperor Akihito's "message," but that alone is insufficient. We should situate Roh's visit in the larger context of the November enthronement ceremony and the *daijōsai*. Last year, the leading representatives from 164 nations gathered in Tokyo for Emperor Hirohito's funeral. But in South Korea, Australia, the Netherlands, Britain, and other countries, criticism arose over whether or not to participate because of his war responsibility. In England, Queen Elizabeth abandoned the idea of attending herself, and her husband, the Duke of Edinburgh, went in her place. After returning home, the Duke felt he had to justify himself to the nation by saying, "I did not bow before the coffin of the Showa Emperor but merely nodded slightly." (Incidentally, after returning to Japan, I saw a television program entitled "The Upheavals of Shōwa," and there the Duke of Edinburgh bowed.)

Certainly the Shōwa Emperor did not bear sole responsibility for the war, but by no means was he innocent of war responsiblity. If this fact were ignored, the same problem was likely to be rekindled at the time of the enthronement and the *daijōsai*. As November approached, for example, there was a possibility that voices of opposition to the president's visit would arise in South Korea; and the same sort of opposition was brewing in other countries. Therefore, the Japanese government had to have this problem of the Shōwa Emperor's war responsibility settled before November to assume that the international event would go smoothly. That is why Emperor Akihito made an unexpectedly liberal statement and Prime Minister Kaifu issued an apology. At that time, the Japanese government tried hard to weaken the contents of Akihito's statement by saying that there are some things the symbol emperor can and cannot do. But citizens of South Korea replied in a television interview that "since the emperor is the Japanese head of state, we want a proper apology from him." Earlier, when I said that the long outstanding cost would finally come due at the time of President Roh's visit, this is exactly what I meant. (And, as I predicted, President Roh did not attend the new emperor's enthronement ceremony but, instead, sent his prime minister, as did China.)

In any case, in exchange for this apology, the Japanese government needed to receive from the Korean authorities words to the effect that the problem of the emperor's apology was settled forever and would never arise again. In a press conference on May 26, 1990, Prime Minister Kaifu stated his impression that, sure enough, "the matters of the past have all been settled." He also agreed with the suggestion put to him that "when the president of South Korea visits Japan in the future, could we think there will be less possibility of a repeat of past problems?"

For President Roh as well, this visit to Japan had to be successful. Had he failed, it would have had quite an impact on his ability to maintain his own regime. I understand that 70 percent of public opinion in South Korea was dissatisfied with the emperor's address, but that 60 percent regarded the president's visit as a success. Considering that President Roh's address to the Diet was well received, this would seem to be a correct assessment. His visit also made it easier for the Japanese side to conduct the enthronement ceremony.

In the 1990s, while the turbulence in eastern Europe and the Soviet Union continue, regionalism and nationalism will be rising up on a global scale. The signs are appearing already: European Community union in January 1993, the unification of East and West Germany in 1990, the independence demands of the three Baltic republics, and the Tibetan independence movement. But at the same time, since this is the age of "borderless economies," the traffic in money, goods, information, and people across international borders will probably continue to intensify beyond the current level. The conflict and competition between nationalism and internationalism will probably advance at a speed greater than anyone can even imagine. The great problem will be how to situate the symbol emperor system in international society before this age arrives.

First, the weight of the Japanese emperor in international society will diminish as Japan confronts the challenges of a new age of globalism. In Europe, too, the importance of the British monarchy will inevitably decline as Britain enters deeper into European union. Among the English there are apparently those who would like to see Queen Elizabeth as the sovereign of a United States of Europe. The chances of that ever happening must be next to zero. Looking at the world as a whole, the monarchical states, with a combined population of about 402 million, account for a mere 8 percent of the world's total population of about 5 billion. Thus the trend of world history vividly indicates that the significance of monarchies is gradually declining.

Nevertheless, after the enthronement ceremony, the Japanese government and the Liberal Democratic party will without doubt use the emperor as the nucleus of Japanese nationalism and try to develop imperial diplomacy. Emperor Akihito and the empress will probably visit China and South Korea in the near future, a dangerous gamble indeed.[9]

For "the unfortunate past" in Japan's relations with those two countries cannot be settled simply by the leaders holding talks over a period of several days. At a palace banquet on May 24, 1991, President Roh pointed out that "The truth of history can neither be erased nor forgotten," stating further that "Our two countries must wash away the mistakes of the past on the basis of a true historical understanding and open up a new era of friendship and cooperation." But so many problems remain to be resolved before the two nations can have "a true historical understanding." Of course there must be an improvement in historical education, but the various accumulated problems of the "unfortunate past" must also be solved, one by one.

That means, for example, such matters as improving the legal position of Koreans from the north and south living in Japan, and eliminating problems of discrimination in their employment. It means aid for the Korean victims of the atomic bombs, and repatriation and aid for the Korean workers who were forced to go to Sakhalin Island. Without concrete efforts on these issues, promoting imperial diplomacy by itself will only produce negative results. This is not something limited just to Japanese-Korean relations. How will Japan try to deal hereafter with China and the nations of Southeast Asia that suffered during Japan's war of aggression? After the enthronement ceremony these questions will again be asked by nations all over the world.

Appendix 2

THE THIRD WAY, OR THE PATH NOT TAKEN

AS WE HAVE SEEN, the symbol monarchy was a product of Japanese and American bilateral cooperation. In the United States, however, the active parties were the federal government and SCAP but not the American people, whereas in Japan, the emperor, his close advisers, and the Japanese government all played a part, as did the Japanese people. Evaluations of the decision to maintain the emperor system will differ depending on how much importance one assigns to this fact. However, even though 80 to 90 percent of the Japanese people supported the emperor system at the time, I think we should reexamine whether preserving it was the only feasible policy.

Up to now preserving or abolishing the monarchy seem to have been the only two options open to postsurrender Japan; but I have become increasingly convinced that there was a third alternative: to differentiate the emperor from the institution of the throne and have Emperor Hirohito abdicate, leaving behind the emperor system as a political institution. This position was debated within SWNCC, while (as we have seen) in Japan it coincided with the views of people like Nambara Shigeru, the president of Tokyo University, who argued that the emperor should face his moral responsibility and abdicate. The development of postwar Japan would surely have been quite different had this third path been taken.[1]

The idea also existed within SWNCC and even within court circles, of getting Hirohito to stand down in favor of his son, the crown prince, and was shared in nonofficial society by Nambara Shigeru, mentioned previously, and other old liberals such as Abe Yoshihisa, Yamamoto Yūzō, and Matsumoto Shigeharu. Here, however, I would like to focus only on the activities of the opposition Socialist and Communist parties.

Insofar as is known from contemporary public opinion surveys, letters sent to MacArthur, and the results of the first postwar general election, the overwhelming majority of the Japanese people wanted the emperor system maintained. But popular feelings toward the emperor can by no means be accurately measured on the basis of statistics alone. Immediately after the defeat, the priority of the mass of Japanese was to secure food, clothing, and shelter rather than "preserving the national polity." The true feelings of people at that time were captured in slogans like "Food before the constitution" and "Food before the national polity." The highly touted "preservation of the national policy" was a secondary concern for people who were trying to find food and shelter. Indeed, if anything, the "national polity" was an object of resentment and criticism.

At the May Day "food" demonstration in the Imperial Palace plaza on May 19, 1946, Matsushima Matsutarō (a Communist party member) held aloft a placard reading, "My belly's filled with food, why don't you people starve to death!"

He was charged with the crime of *lèse majestè* but later acquitted. Although such acts were few in number, they were widespread. For example, according to "Matters Concerning Acts of *Lèse Majestè* and the Spreading of Rumors," sent by the police chief of Shiga Prefecture to the Home Ministry in September 1945, a situation had been reached wherein "The distrust and antipathy of the common people toward the military and politicians is intensifying, and above all, they are showing a tendency to be disrespectful toward the emperor in their speech and actions." Among the "rumors" that were being spread was that Japan would be doomed "if we don't break with the sanctity of the national polity"; that the Emperor was "confined to his bed with a nervous facial twitch"; and that he must "step down because of his war responsibility."[2] Also, according to the recollections of one Tokyo housewife, an incredible situation existed immediately after the defeat, with people living inside the most sacred parts of shrines and temples and hanging their baby's diapers out to dry in the wind.[3] Released from the wartime repression of their personal aspirations, and forced to defend their livelihoods, people adopted a very pragmatic and egoistic attitude. Life began again without any thought of the national polity. Indeed, for several years after 1945, people distanced themselves entirely from the state.

As we have seen, the poet Miyoshi Tatsuji believed that Hirohito must face up to his war responsibility and abdicate quickly as the only way to prevent Japan's total moral collapse, and many intellectuals shared his view.[4] If he had stepped down early in the occupation, leaving the throne without its occupant, then later historical development would have been considerably different, but that was not the case.

Japan's political parties, dissolved in 1940 after the establishment of the Imperial Rule Assistance Association, were reconstructed one after another. In November 1945, the Japan Socialist party and the conservative Liberal and Progressive parties were formed. The imprisoned leaders of the Communist party, Tokuda Kyūichi, Shiga Yoshio, and others were released from Fuchū Prison on October 10. Miyamoto Kenji was set free from Abashiri Prison in Hokkaido on October 19. Immediately, Tokuda, Shiga, and the others issued an "Appeal to the People," in which they stated publicly that their goal was "to overthrow the emperor system and establish a people's republic based on the popular will." On December 1 at their party convention in Tokyo, they formally decided to reestablish the Japan Communist party and begin their activities as a legal political organization.

Reconstruction of the Japanese state and economy were urgent tasks for all the political parties. In particular, the central issue for politicians deciding the future direction of Japanese politics was what sort of attitude they should take toward the emperor system. Accordingly, each party drafted a plan for constitutional revision and hurriedly prepared for the first postwar general election. In November 1945 the Communist party became the first organization to issue a statement on "The Outline of a New Constitution." Article 1, stating that "Sovereignty resides in the people," clarified the principle of popular sovereignty as opposed to imperial sovereignty. In January 1946, the Liberal party issued its "Summary of a Revised Constitution," stating that "The holder of sovereign power is the Japanese state" and "The Emperor is the superintendent of the powers of sovereignty." In February the Progressive party issued a similar document, more conservative than the Liberal party draft in that it recognized the emperor's right to issue emergency imperial decrees based on the principle of monarchical sovereignty. That same month the Socialist party also issued its own "Draft of a New Constitution," stating that "Sovereignty resides in the state (the community of the nation including the emperor)."

The Socialists divided the powers of government between the Diet and the emperor, stating that "The emperor system [*tennōsei*] will be maintained." This was an eclectic draft, representing neither popular nor monarchical sovereignty. The undercurrent of conflict between the left and right wings of the party that had existed since prewar days meant that they were only able to produce a compromise between their two factions at the time of drafting a revised constitution. This division later became a factor preventing the formation of a united front with the Communist party, an outcome anticipated as early as November 7, 1945, by *Akahata* (Red flag) the newspaper, the organ of the Japan Communist party.[5] "If the gentlemen of the Socialist party are unable to agree on overthrowing the emperor system, they will have to endure the criticism that they themselves refused to participate in the democratic revolution and sided with the emperor as a reactionary force."

The leadership of the Communist party at that time were all acting in accordance with the May 1932 "Theses," dedicated to the overthrow of the emperor system. They were also still bound in part by the prewar theory of social fascism which regarded the Social Democrats as the main enemy of the Communists. Yet this did not mean that the Communist party of Japan was united in its opinions. In May 1945 Nozaka Sanzō, who was in Yan'an, China, looked toward a postwar Japan and differentiated the emperor system as a political institution from the emperor who played a semi-religious role among the people. He declared that even after the war, "Our demands cannot be realized against the wishes of the vast majority of our people. If the overwhelming majority of Japanese fervently demand the retention of the emperor, we must accede to this." [6] In addition, Nozaka stated that:

> There is no part of the general program of our Liberation League that demands the overthrow of the emperor or the imperial house. The reason for this is that the Liberation League is an organization which mobilizes the broad masses to meet the urgent goals of the Japanese people: to oppose the war, overthrow the military and build a democratic Japan. There are those in the League who will not give up their worship of the emperor even though they oppose war and the military; naturally, we must win these people as well. The masses will flock to our cause if we refrain from calling for the overthrow of the emperor. But if we commit ourselves to his downfall, we risk becoming isolated from the people and will not win popular support. That is why the problem of the emperor is not addressed in the platform of the Liberation League.[7]

After the war ended some party theoreticians such as Toda Shintarō and Nakanishi Kō were "opposed to the Communist party's support for the overthrow of the emperor system and their making it a slogan for the mass movement and even a condition for a united front." On January 15, 1946, Nozaka returned from China. At a welcoming party at the Communist party headquarters he stressed the need for "a Communist party beloved by the masses" and a "very broad-based democratic front." Responding to this, the Marxist theoretician of the "Labor-Farmer faction," Yamakawa Hitoshi, similarly advocated a "democratic popular front," uniting all factions, while within the Japan Socialist party a mood supportive of a broad left-wing alliance began to show itself. On January 26, 1946, about thirty thousand people gathered in Hibiya Park for a "National Rally to Welcome Nozaka Sanzō." Leading members of the Communist party as well as theorists and others associated with the Socialist party, such as Yamakawa Hitoshi, Arahata Kanson, Mizutani Chōzaburo, Katayama Tetsu, and Katō Kanjū, participated and passionately appealed for the formation of a democratic united front. Even the conservative politician Ozaki Yukio sent a message saying he "gladly approved" of a popular front.

When Nozaka came to the podium, he thanked the people for their good wishes, called for the Shidehara cabinet to step down, and stressed the great significance of forming a democratic united front.[8] The first thing Nozaka emphasized was that true democracy would be achieved only by the establishment of a people's government controlled by workers and peasants. Second, as the realization of this democracy was being delayed by divisions and splits among the democratic forces, their unity was a matter of urgent necessity. Third, the conditions for the formation of such a united front had now matured, and with the general election just ahead it was necessary to cooperate fully with the Socialist party and develop a joint campaign. Fourth, a democratic united front would be consistent with the trend in the rest of the world.

Nozaka did not mention the emperor problem even once in his speech, for he was probably opposed to including abolition as an aim of the democratic front. Instead, he appealed for "food for the starving masses," and "economic democracy which will shift wealth out of the hands of the few—in other words, the use of state power to transfer capital and land for the purpose of reconstructing the national territory and stabilizing the people's lives." This was a wise and realistic appeal. The *Asahi*, *Mainichi*, and *Yomiuri* newspapers all welcomed Nozaka's proposal, and Matsumoto Shigeharu, president of the Minpō, even put his signature to an editorial wishing for the success of the democratic front.

The call for a democratic popular front began to spread to local areas, and in Kyoto the "Kyoto Council of the Democratic Front" was formed with twenty-six groups participating, including the Socialist and Communist parties. It produced a campaign plan based on five slogans: "secure stability for the people's lives, remove all elements of feudalism, put political sovereignty in the hands of the people, thoroughly pursue the search for those who bear war responsibility, search for hidden documents."[9]

However, the Socialist party leaders decided not to cooperate in joint campaigns with the communists and confined themselves to participating as individuals in the "Democratic Popular League" proposed by Yamakawa. In addition to its anti-communism, which long antedated the war, the Socialist party was at that time drafting a new constitution whose nature was totally incompatible with the Communist party draft constitution. Thus, rather than joining forces with the Communist party in the approaching general election, their priority was to expand their own forces.

The general election of April 1946 resulted in an overwhelming victory for the conservatives, with the Liberal party winning 141 seats, the Progressive party 94, the Socialists 93, the Cooperative party 14, and the Communist party 5. The Communists' main slogans had been abolish the emperor system, establish a people's republican government, stabilize the people's lives and raise their standard of living, and immediately form a popular front. The only successful communist candidates were Nozaka Sanzō (Tokyo), Tokuda Kyūichi (Tokyo), Shiga Yoshio (Osaka), Ezawa Toshiko (Hokkaido), and Takakura Teru (Nagano Prefecture). The Liberal party had secured its large number of seats by focusing on "anticommunism" and "protect the emperor system," the reverse of the Communist party slogans.

Hidaka Rokurō, who stated that he "agreed with nearly all" of Nozaka Sanzō's views on the emperor issue, later wrote, "In the April 1946 general election, the Communist Party should have campaigned on the slogan of rooting out all remnants of Japanese militarism rather than of overthrowing the emperor system.[10]

Clearly, the party's central leadership did not adopt Nozaka's view; instead they took the abolition of the emperor system as their highest strategic task. The priorities of the people, however, lay elsewhere. They were more concerned with seeking food, clothing and shelter than the abolition of the emperor system. If, while calling for Emperor Hirohito to accept his war guilt and abdicate, the Communists had adopted a more flexible stance, leaving the issue of the emperor system's future to the judgment of the people, the outcome might have been quite different. Indeed, exercising the "third option" was by no means unrealistic, as the experience of Italy shows.[11]

On September 8, 1943, after Italian King Victor Emanuel III and the government of Marshal Badoglio surrendered unconditionally to the Allies, the problem of the monarch's abdication rapidly came to the fore. The famous philosopher Benedetto Croce and Carlo Sforza, the former foreign minister and moderate liberal living in exile in the United States, demanded that Victor Emanuel III, who had helped bring Mussolini to power, abdicate; but they did not insist on the immediate abolition of the monarchy.

Upon returning to his country after eighteen years of exile in Moscow, the Italian Communist party leader Palmiro Togliatti identified three aspects of the problem of the monarch's abdication. First, without total liberation from Germany, it would be impossible to resolve finally the issue of Italy's future political form, that is to say, the maintenance or abolition of the monarchy. Second, there were forces who wished in their hearts to retain the monarchy while strongly insisting on the abdication of the monarch. Considering this, care would have to be taken not to conflate the problem of an individual monarch's abdication with the issue of the future political form of the state. Finally, Togliatti argued that the choice of the political structure of Italy would have to be decided in a constituent assembly after Italy's liberation.

On September 9, the day after Italy's surrender, the Committee of National Liberation (CLN), a united front organization composed of six antifascist parties, was formed in Rome. Of these, the Christian-Democratic party, Communist party, and Socialist party were mass organizations with a combined membership of over 4 million, while the remaining three—the Action party, Liberal party, and Workers

Democratic party—had memberships numbering in the thousands. The CLN nevertheless adopted egalitarian organizational principles, with a unanimous vote being required to approve action. Ideologically, it contained a wide variety of groups ranging from moderates who supported the monarchy to left-wingers who favored a republican form of government. This organization conducted its affairs democratically on the basis of unanimous voting. The process whereby these united parties forced the monarch and the Badoglio government into a corner contrasts vividly with what occurred in Japan.

From September 1943 to March 1944, with resistance from the king and the Badoglio government on one side and conflicts within CLN on the other, the problem of the king's abdication reached a dead end. Against this background, Churchill and Roosevelt vied over bringing postwar Italy into their respective spheres of influence. Roosevelt supported the immediate resignation of the king whereas Churchill wished to see him remain on the throne. This Anglo-American rift provoked much strife in Italian politics, with the Socialist party threatening to withdraw from the CLN over the issue of the monarchy. The question was now how to extricate Italy from this impasse and overcome domestic conflicts while still maintaining Italy's national autonomy? The deadlock was broken by someone no one had expected.

On March 27, 1944, Togliatti landed at Naples after an eighteen-year absence. A few days after his return, he delivered a famous speech to a party conference in Naples in which he pointed out that the Italian state faced a crisis of existence. To achieve the task of liberating the nation in a short period of time, the unity of the most diverse groups had to be realized. To that end he proposed the famous "Salerno switch," declaring himself ready to join the government and cooperate with the king and Badoglio. Behind this startling new direction lay the Soviet Union's decision to recognize the Badoglio government.

Togliatti knew through his long experience in the Comintern how many sacrifices had to be made in order to construct a socialist state. As long as his own country was occupied by foreign armies, revolution was out of the question. Togliatti saw that to liberate Italy from two decades of fascism and to achieve a socialist revolution, Italy had to pass through several interim stages. Consequently, his "Salerno switch" was brought about as part of his democratic revolutionary strategy, or the "Italian path" to socialism, which Toyoshimo Naruhiko describes as follows: "Togliatti's strategy was one of 'progressive democracy': in short, until Italy reached the stage of socialism, he envisioned a long period of transitional democracy; socialism was only to be implemented when democracy had reached its highest point of development. Thus, his was a strategy of 'revolution as process' in contrast to the Russian style of 'revolution as rupture.' "

Because of this vision, Togliatti could consent without hesitation to the compromise policy, carefully worked out by Croce and De Nicolla, a leader of the Naples group who had once served as head of the lower house of the Italian parliament. Their plan was to withdraw the king from public life immediately after the liberation of Rome and transfer his authority to his son, Crown Prince Umberto. Togliatti thus agreed to postpone until the end of the war a final resolution of the problem of the political form of the state.[12] For him, the behavior of the monarch was not essential; the urgent task was rather to form a national united front government in order to fight the German Nazis. This was to be accomplished by a government in which all the anti-fascist and democratic parties participated.

Although within CLN the Socialist party and the more radical Action party were strongly opposed to Togliatti's "compromise," they had no alternative solution of their own. In the end, Togliatti was able to persuade the executive committee of CLN to approve the new policy.

In June and August 1944 Rome and Florence were liberated from the Nazis, and by April 1945 all of northern Italy had been set free. The king was supposed to have abdicated, as promised, at the time of Rome's liberation, but conservative factions maneuvered to prolong his reign. On June 2, 1946, two years after the liberation of Rome, Italy held its first postwar general election and referendum on the monarchy. The antimonarchist forces supporting a republic won by a margin of two million votes; Umberto II and his family went into exile in Switzerland. However, his father, Victor Emanuel III, judging that his continued reign would exert a bad influence on the national referendum, had abdicated suddenly in early May 1946, leaving Umberto II to preside from exile over the demise of the monarchy. Thus Italy shifted from a monarchy to a republic; and in the parliamentary elections held at the same time, the Christian Democrats won 35 percent of the vote, the Socialists 20.7 percent, and the Communists 19 percent. All told, in just two years and three months after the "Salerno switch," the three leading parties managed to win 75 percent of the vote.[13]

In contrast, the road taken by Japan's reformist forces was hopelessly fainthearted, rigid, and lacking in imagination and creativity, and betrayed their ignorance of the international situation. The Socialist party remained wedded to its prewar policy of anticommunism and rejected the formation of a democratic alliance with the Communist party.

On the other hand, the Communist party leaders, with the exception of Nozaka, were ignorant of the concept of a popular front and lacked the ability to carry it out. This may be partly, but not completely, explained by their long imprisonment. Communist antagonism toward Social Democrats, which had existed ever since the "1932 theses," carried over into the postwar period. The Communists attacked those who were opposed to abolishing the emperor system as "pseudoliberal, pseudosocialist supporters of the emperor." Their draft constitution was the first to present a workable path by calling for popular sovereignty and denying imperial sovereignty, but they lacked concrete plans and the organizational apparatus to realize their ideas, and could only resort to restating their slogan of "overthrow the emperor system."

Japan's Socialists and Communists thus lacked the practical experience and the theoretical imagination to conceptualize a "Japanese path" to socialism such as Togliatti had done in Italy. Only Nozaka Sanzō had a plan that was close to Togliatti's, but the "National Rally to Welcome Nozaka" did not become a "Salerno switch." One therefore cannot avoid saying that the postwar responsibility of the progressive political parties, centering on the Communists and Socialists, is heavy indeed.

When I stated that the symbol emperor system is the product of a joint Japanese and American effort, which included the Japanese but not the American people, I had all these thoughts in my mind. History means that the road taken was not the only one available at the time. Other roads were possible depending on how the leaders of popular movements acted. The investigation of those possibilities frees historiography from simplistic formulas and contributes to our understanding of the future paths that humanity will take.

Notes

Introduction

1. Joseph Grew, *Ten Years in Japan: A Contemporary Record Drawn from the Diaries and Private and Official Papers of Joseph C. Grew* (New York: Simon and Schuster, 1944), p. x.

2. Joseph Grew, *Zai Nichi jūnen*, (Japanese translation of *Ten Years in Japan*), trans. Ishikawa Kinichi (Tokyo: Mainichi Shinbunsha, 1948), p. 3.

Chapter 1

1. Joseph Grew, *Report from Tokyo*, p. ix. (This quotation was also used by U.S. President Ronald Reagan in his inauguration speech on January 20, 1981.)

2. Ibid., p. vii.

3. Ibid., p. 6.

4. Joseph Grew, *Ten Years in Japan*, p. 536.

5. Ibid., p. 537.

6. Ibid., p. 303.

7. Grew, *Report from Tokyo*, p. 22.

8. Ibid., p. 21.

9. Ibid., p. 44.

10. Ibid., p. 50.

11. Ibid., p. 33.

12. Ibid., pp. 9–10.

Chapter 2

1. "Radio Address by the Former American Ambassador to Japan" [transcription of Grew's radio broadcast of August 28, 1943], *Department of State Bulletin*, 1943, 9:127.

2. Ibid., p. 128.

3. Ibid.

4. Ibid.

Chapter 3

1. "War and Post-War Problems in the Far East" [transcription of Grew's "Chicago speech," December 29, 1943], *Department of State Bulletin*, 1944, 10:10–11.

2. Ibid., p. 11.

3. Ibid., p. 12.

4. Ibid., p. 13.

5. Ibid., p. 16.

6. Letter to J. R. Hildebrand, assistant editor of *National Geographic*, January 15, 1944.

7. Letter to Erle Dickover, January 29, 1944.

8. Letter to E. A. Rhoads, Toccoa, Georgia, January 25, 1944.

9. Letter to Captain M. Frehn, February 1, 1944.

10. Letter to Shane Leslie, London, March 6, 1944.

11. Letter to Captain M. Frehn, February 1, 1944.

12. Letter to former British Ambassador to Japan Sir R. H. Clive, June 28, 1944.

13. As noted in The Armaments Group Council on Foreign Relations paper, prepared by Julius W. Pratt, "The Treatment of the Japanese Emperor," April 4, 1944.

14. Ibid.

15. Ibid.

16. Sun Fo, "The Mikado Must Go," *Foreign Affairs* (October 1944): 17–25.

17. Ibid., pp. 18–19.

Chapter 5

1. Grew's diary, April 5, 1933. See John W. Dower, *Empire and Aftermath: Yoshida Shigeru and the Japanese Experience 1878–1954* (Cambridge: Harvard University Press, 1979), p. 109.

2. See Grew Foundation, eds., *Kabayama Aisuke Ō* (Tokyo: International House, 1955).

3. See Waldo H. Heinrichs, *American Ambassador* (Boston, 1965), p. 193.

4. Grew's diary, July 5, 1935.

5. An abridged English translation of this book was published in 1962 by Houghton Mifflin under the title *The Yoshida Memoirs*.

6. Yoshida Shigeru, *Kaisō jūnen*, (Tokyo: Shinchōsha, 1957–58), p. 53.

7. Andrew Roth, *Dilemma in Japan* (London: Victor Gollancz, 1946), pp. 33–34.

8. Grew's diary, April 16, 1940, as cited in Dower, *Empire and Aftermath*, p. 190.

9. Heinrichs, *American Ambassador*, p. 196.

Chapter 6

1. As Gorer had described in "The Special Case of Japan," *Public Opinion Quarterly* (Winter 1943).

2. PWC–145, April 5, 1944.

3. PWC–146, April 5, 1944.

4. Department of State, *Record of Hearings Before the Committee on Foreign Relations* (Washington, D.C: U.S. Government Printing Office, 1944), pp. 18–19.

5. See "Minutes of the Inter-Divisional Area Committee on the Far East, Meeting 169, November 26, 1944. Subject: Mr. Grew's visit to Hawaii," in NA Microfilm T 1197.

6. Iokibe Makoto, *Beikoku no Nihon senryō seisaku*, 2:106.

7. Grew, letter to Hull, December 4, 1944.

Chapter 7

1. Stimson's diary, May 8, 1945.

2. Dean Acheson, *Present At the Creation: My Years in the State Department* (New York: W. W. Norton, 1969), p. 112.

3. Joseph Grew, *Turbulent Era* (Boston: Houghton Mifflin, 1952), 2:1428–31.

4. Ibid., p. 1431.

5. See *Foreign Relations of the United States, 1945* (Washington, D.C.:Government Printing Office). 1:889–93.

6. Ibid., p. 894.

7. See Yamagiwa Akira, "The Drafting of the Potsdam Proclamation," Yokohama City University Essay Series, Faculty of Humanities, 1986.

8. Minutes of the 133d Meeting of the Secretary's Staff Committee (extract), *Foreign Relations of the United States, 1945*, The Conference of Berlin, 1:900–1.

9. Takeda Kiyoko, *Tennōkan no sōkoku* (Tokyo: Iwanami Shoten, 1978) p. 222.

10. See Grew, *Turbulent Era*, p. 1426.

Chapter 9

1. Mears, *Mirror for Americans, Japan* (Boston: Houghton Mifflin, 1948).

2. Mears, "The Japanese Emperor," *Yale Review* 33,2 (December 1943): 241.

3. Ibid., p. 243.

4. Ibid., p. 250.

5. Ibid., p. 253.

6. Ibid., p. 256.

7. Bonner F. Fellers, "Memorandum to Commander-in-Chief," October 2, 1945.

8. For a transcription of MacArthur's telegram, see *Foreign Relations of the United States*, 1946, 8:395–97.

9. Morita Hideyuki, "Amerika ni okeru seifu to minshū no tennōkan no sokoku ni tsuite" (Rival government and popular views on the emperor in America) *Rekishigaku Kenkyū*, October 1985.

10. Walter Bagehot, *The English Constitution*, 7th ed. (London: Kegan Paul, Trench, Trubner & Co., 1894), p. 45.

11. Ibid., p. 90.

12. Ibid.

13. Takayanagi Kenzō, Ōtomo Ichirō, and Tanaka Eiji, eds., *Nihonkoku kenpō seitei no katei—I. Genbun to honyaku* (Tokyo: Yūhikaku, 1987), pp. 414–16.

14. Ibid., pp. 98–100.

15. Ibid., p. 104.

16. See GHQ Government Section, *Political Reorientation of Japan*, and Takayanagi et al., *Nihonkoku kenpō seitei no katei*.

17. See Takayanagi et al., *Nihonkoku kenpō seitei no katei*, pp. 130–42.

18. Letter to the author from Charles Kades, June 1, 1989.

19. Letter to the author from Charles Kades, June 22, 1989.

20. See Kenpō seitei no keika ni kansuru shōiinkai, *Nihonkoku kenpō seitei no yurai* (Tokyo: Jiji Tsūshinsha, 1961), p. 253.

Chapter 10

1. See Hata Ikuhiko, *Shiroku, Nihon saigunbi* (Tokyo: Bungei Shūnjusha, 1976); and Tanaka Hideo, *Kenpō seitei katei oboegaki* (Tokyo: Yūhikaku, 1979).

2. Takeda Kiyoko, *Tennōkan no sokoku*, pp. 26–261; and Takahashi Hiroshi, "Kaisetsu," in Kinoshita Michio, *Sokkin nisshi, (Tokyo: Bungei Shunjūsha, 1990), pp. 336–40.*

3. Hirakawa Sukehiro, *Heiwa no umi to tatakai no umi* (Tokyo: Shinchosha, 1983).

4. "PR–34 Preliminary a. Treatment of the Institution of the Emperor," December 18, 1945. Reported by the SWNCC Subcommittee for the Far East, U.S. government, RG 53, Box 119, "PR" Documents, National Archives, Notter File.

5. Ibid.

6. Takahashi Hiroshi, "Kaisetsu," p. 338.

7. *Sokkin nisshi*, p. 89.

8. Cited in Takahashi Hiroshi, "Kaisetsu," p. 341.

9. T. A. Bisson, *Prospects for Democracy in Japan* (Macmillan, 1949), p. 23.

10. Ohara Yasuo, "Sengo o hōkōzuketa futatsu no shōsho," *Bungei shunjū*, special issue (March 1989): 708.

11. Takahashi Hiroshi, *Heika, otazune moshiagemasu* (Tokyo: Bunsho Bunko, 1988), pp. 252–53.

12. Watanabe Osamu, *Sengo seijishi no naka no tennōsei* (Tokyo: Aoki Shoten, 1990), p. 93.

13. Letter to W. E. Houstoun-Boswall, March 20, 1944.

14. Letter to Rear Admiral J. F. Shafroth, October 18, 1945.

15. Takahashi Hiroshi, *Shōchō tennō* (Tokyo: Iwanami Shoten, 1987), pp. 48–50.

16. Hata Ikuhiko, *Hirohito tennō no itsutsu no ketsudan* (Tokyo: Kodansha, 1984), pp. 209–10.

17. *Asahi shinbun*, December 5, 1987; Awaya Kentarō et al., eds., *Tokyo saiban shiryō, Kido Kōichi—Jinmon chosho* (Tokyo: Otsuki Shoten, 1987), pp. 559–60.

18. See Howard Schonberger, "The Japan Lobby in American Diplomacy, 1947–1952," *Pacific Historical Review* 46 (1977).

19. Shindō Eiichi, "Bunkatsusareta ryo," *Sekai* (April 1979).

20. *Asahi shinbun* January 11, 1989; and Irie Tamatoshi, ed., *Irie Sukemasa nikki* (Tokyo: Asahi Shinbunsha, 1991), 5:419.

21. Shindō Eiichi, ed., *Ashida Hitoshi nikki, Dai ni kan* (Tokyo: Iwanami Shoten, 1986), entry of July 22, 1947, p. 13; March 10, 1948, p. 72.

22. Watanabe Osamu, *Nihon koku kenpō "kaisei" shi* (Tokyo: Nihon Hyōronsha, 1987), p. 271.
23. Togashi Junji, *Chiyoda jō* (Tokyo: Kobunsha, 1958), p. 16.
24. Kishi Nobusuke hoka, *Kishi Nobusuke no kaisō* (Tokyo: Bungei Shunjū, 1981), p. 196.
25. See "This Is Yomiuri," May 1990.
26. Sakakibara Kamenosuke, *Tennō no nenrin* (Tokyo: Sankei Shuppan, 1981), p. 15.
27. Watanabe Osamu, *Sengo seiji shi no naka no tennōsei* (Tokyo: Aoki Shoten, 1990), p. 234.

Chapter 11

1. Itō Masaya, *Ikeda Hayato to sono jidai* (Tokyo: Asahi Bunko, 1985), p. 96.
2. Ekonomisuto Henshubu, *Shōgen: Kōdo seichōki no Nihon,* (Tokyo: Maninichi Shimbunsha, 1984), 1:26–27.
3. Igarashi Hitoshi, *Kōdo seichō to hoshu honryū seiken* in *Nihon: dōjidai shi* (Tokyo: Aoki Shoten, 1990), 4:15–16.
4. Nihon: dōjidai shi, (Tokyo: Aoki Shoten, 1990), 1:46.
5. NHK Seron Chōsa Buhen, *Gendai Nihonjin no ishiki kōzō,* dai san pan (Tokyo: Nihon Hōsō Shuppan Kyokai, 1991), pp. 103–15.
6. Watanabe Osamu, *Nihon koku kenpō "kaisei" shi,* p. 458.
7. Matsuo Shōichi, " 'Meiji hyakunensai' hihan," in Matsuo Shōichi, *Sengo Nihon fuashizumu shiron* (Tokyo: Yubiterusha, 1987), p. 27.
8. *Asahi shinbun,* evening edition, August 26, 1967.
9. "Tokushū, Meiji hyakunensai hihan: gendai fuashizumu no shisō to undō," in *Rekishigaku kenkyū* (November 1967).
10. "Hoshutō naikaku o yusaburu 'naisō' mondai no shōgeki," in *Sande Mainichi,* June 17, 1973.
11. Irie Sukemasa nikki, Dai go kan (Tokyo: Asahi Shinbunsha, 1991), p. 17.
12. *Shūkan bunshun,* May 26, 1978.
13. Iwata Hideo, "Irie Sukemasa nikki ga egaku Shōwa tennō no sugao," *Gekkan Asahi* (August 1991): 37.
14. Heika, otazune moshiagemasu, pp. 226, 227.
15. Yokota Kōichi, *Kenpō to tennōsai* (Tokyo: Iwanami Shoten, 1990), p. 111.
16. See table 18 in "Gengō hōseika to wareware no rekishigaku," *Rekishigaku kenkyū* (April 1979): 15.
17. Watanabe Osamu, "Gendai Nihon kokka no tokushu na kōzō," in Tokyo Daigaku shakai kagaku kenkyūjo hen, *Gendai Nihon shakai,* (Tokyo: Tokyo Daigaku Shuppankai, 1991), 1:206.
18. *Jiyū minshū,* September 1985.
19. *Asahi shinbun,* September 19, 1985.
20. Maki Tarō, *Nakasone seiken, 1806 nichi, gekan* (Tokyo: Gyoken Shuppankyoku, 1988), p. 210.
21. Ibid., pp. 217–23, 252–55.

22. Nakasone Yasuhiro, "Minshūshugi to kokkashugi no chōwa o," *Gekkan jimintō* (October 1987): 51.

23. "Sori kantei o saru ni saishite," *Bungei shunjū* (December 1987): 105.

24. *Yomiuri shinbun*, November 10, 1988.

25. Watanabe Osamu, "Gendai Nihon shakai no kōzō to tennōsei—'jishuku' to 'kichō' no shakaigaku," *Sengo seijishi no naka no tennōsei* (Tokyo: Aoki Shoten, 1990), pp. 28, 46.

26. Ōkado Masakatsu, "Gendai Nihon no shakai kōzō to 'kichō, jishuku,' " in *Mado*, 6 (December 1990).

27. *Yomiuri shinbun, yukan,* January 7, 1989.

28. Hidaka Rokurō, *Sengo shisō o kangaeru* (Tokyo: Iwanami Shoten, 1980), pp. 75–92.

29. See Nakamura Masanori, " 'Shōchō tennōsei' no kako to shōrai o kangaeru," *Ekonomisuto* May 9, 1989.

30. See *Contemporary China, A Reference Digest* 3,12 November 1, 1943.

31. Kosaka Masatake, "Tennō, sono muyō no taiyō," *Bungei shunjū*, special issue (March 1989): 238.

32. Miyachi Masato, "Sengo tennōsei no tokushitsu," *Rekishi hyōron* (August 1980).

33. Sonobe Eiichi, hen, *Shintennō no jigazō, kisha kaiken no kiroku* (Tokyo: Bunshun Bunko, 1989).

Appendix 1

1. John Cannon and Ralph Griffith, *The Oxford Illustrated History of the British Monarchy* (Oxford: Oxford University Press, 1988), p. 577.

2. Kenneth Young, *Arthur James Balfour, 1848-1930* (London: G. Bell and Sons, 1963).

3. Kanamori Tokujirō's words can be found in *Nihon koku kenpō shingi yoroku* (Tokyo: Seibunsha, 1947), p. 134.

4. Takayanagi Kenzō et al., eds., *Nihon koku kenpō seitei no katei, I, genbun to honyaku* (Tokyo: Yūhikaku, 1987), p. 308.

5. See Akasaka Norio, "Tsuda Zōkichi, mata wa 1946 nen no tennō," in *Shisō no kagaku* (March 1989); also Watsuji Tetsurō, "Mata wa shōchō toshite no tennō o megutte" in *Sekai* (October, 1989); and, more recently, "Tsugita nikki" in *Sanyō shinbun*, April 25, 1990.

6. See "Rekishi no sōzōryoku" in *Shisō*, no. 731 (1985).

7. Araki Moriaki, *Tennō, Tennōsei, Hyakushō, Okinawa* (Tokyo: Yoshikawa Kokubunkan, 1989), p. 163.

8. On this point see Watanabe Osamu, *Sengo seijishi no naka no tennōsei* (Tokyo: Aoki Shoten, 1990).

9. In fall 1990 Emperor Akihito and the empress visited Thailand, Malaysia, and Indonesia.

Appendix 2

1. Zadankai "Shōchō tennōsei—kokusaiteki kōsō to nashonaru aidenteite," *Nihongaku* (November 1990), meishokankikai.

2. *Shiryō Nihon gendaishi 2 haisen chokugo no seiji to shakai (1)* (Tokyo: Ōtsuki Shoten, 1980), pp. 246–48.

3. Yasuda Tsuneo, "Shōchō tennōsei to minshū ishiki," *Rekishigaku kenkyū* (July 1991).

4. Ibid.

5. Kanda Fuhito, *Nihon no tōitsu sensen undō* (Tokyo: Aoki Shoten, 1979), p. 194.

6. Okano Susumu, "Minshūteki Nihon no kensetsu," *Nozaka Sanzō senshū, senji hen* (Tokyo, 1965).

7. Ibid.

8. *Asahi shinbun*, January 27, 1946.

9. Matsuo Takayoshi, "Haisen chokugo no Kyoto minshū sensen," *Kyoto daigaku bungakubu kenkyū kiyō* 18 (March 1978).

10. Hidaka Rokurō, *Gendai Nihon shisō taikei 1: sengo shisō no shuppatsu* (Tokyo: Chikuma Shobō, 1970), p. 32.

11. Toyoshimo Naruhiko, "Itaria senryō ni okeru kyōwasei e no michi," *Rekishigaku kenkyū* (November 1989); and Toyoshimo Naruhiko, *Itaria senryō shi josetsu* (Tokyo: Yūhikaku, 1984).

12. G. Purokatchi, *Italia jinmin no rekishi, II*, translated by Toyoshimo Naruhiko (Tokyo: Miraisha, 1984), p. 308.

13. Ibid., p. 313.

INDEX

About the Author

When Nakamura Masanori entered Hitotsubashi University in 1957, the debates on "Shōwa history" between Marxist historians and their literary critics had effectively signaled a new concern with bringing the people back into history. Applying himself with passion to the study of Japan's century of economic development since the Meiji Restoration, Nakamura matriculated from the Economics Faculty in 1966 and remained on to establish a reputation as a potent and prolific writer on modern Japanese history. His *Nihon jinushisei no kōsei to dankai* (The composition and stages of development of the Japanese landlord system) appeared in 1972, capping a decade of specialization in the agrarian history of Japan. Four years later, in 1979, he published *Rōdōsha to nōmin* (Workers and peasants), a study of the costs of Japan's modernization that combined structural analysis and people-centered history. It earned him wide critical acclaim as a scholar who could write social history for a general audience. More studies on modern Japanese social history, the state, and historiography followed, including *Kindai Nihon jinushiseishi kenkyū—shihonshugi to jinushisei* (Studies of modern Japan's landlord system), *Shōwa no kyōkō* (The Shōwa panic), and *Nihon kindai to minshū* (Japanese modernity and the people) in 1984. His two newest books, both published in 1992, are *Sengoshi to shōchō tennō* (Postwar history and the symbol emperor) and *Rekishi no kowasa to omoshirosa* (Ferment and fascination in history).

OPPOSING
VIEWPOINTS®
SERIES

Peoples on the Move:
The Immigration Crisis

Other Books of Related Interest

Opposing Viewpoints Series

America's Changing Demographics
Human Migration
Immigration Bans
Sanctuary Cities

At Issue Series

Is America a Democracy or an Oligarchy?
Open Borders
The Role of Religion in Public Policy
Wrongful Conviction and Exoneration

Current Controversies Series

The Border Wall with Mexico
Deporting Immigrants
Hate Groups
Immigration, Asylum, and Sanctuary Cities